Maoism and Grassroots Religion

Maoism and Grassroots Religion

The Communist Revolution and the Reinvention of Religious Life in China

XIAOXUAN WANG

OXFORD

UNIVERSITY PRESS

OXFORD
UNIVERSITY PRESS

Oxford University Press is a department of the University of Oxford. It furthers
the University's objective of excellence in research, scholarship, and education
by publishing worldwide. Oxford is a registered trade mark of Oxford University
Press in the UK and certain other countries.

Published in the United States of America by Oxford University Press
198 Madison Avenue, New York, NY 10016, United States of America.

Library of Congress Cataloging-in-Publication Data
Names: Wang, Xiaoxuan, author.
Title: Maoism and grassroots religion : the communist revolution and the reinvention
of religious life in China / Xiaoxuan Wang.
Description: New York : Oxford University Press, 2020. | Includes bibliographical references and index.
Identifiers: LCCN 2019040365 (print) | LCCN 2019040366 (ebook) | ISBN 9780190069384 |
ISBN 9780190069407 (epub)
Subjects: LCSH: China—Religious life and customs—History—20th century. |
Communism—China—History—20th century.
Classification: LCC BL1803 .W364 2020 (print) | LCC BL1803 (ebook) | DDC 200.951/0904—dc23 LC
record available at https://lccn.loc.gov/2019040365
LC ebook record available at https://lccn.loc.gov/2019040366

1 3 5 7 9 8 6 4 2

Printed by Sheridan Books, Inc., United States of America

To Xuan and to my parents, Lu Chunzhu and Wang Jianyong

Contents

List of Maps, Figures, and Photos

Maps

Figures

Photos

Acknowledgments

Growing up in a place full of temples, churches, shrines, and rituals, I have always been curious about the past of Chinese religions. This long-standing curiosity, plus the realization that there were very few studies of religion under Mao, prompted me to write a history of local religious life during the Mao years. It has been more than four decades since the ending of the Cultural Revolution and almost a decade since I began research for this book. Understanding Maoism and its legacies on contemporary Chinese society and politics seems ever more important with passing time.

I have accumulated numerous intellectual and personal debt to many people while working on this book. I thank Michael Szonyi, my adviser at Harvard, for allowing me to choose religion under Mao as the theme of my dissertation even though neither of us were sure if this topic was doable given the difficulty of gaining access to materials. Michael's critical insights have helped me shape my ideas into their current form in the book. From research to writing to other aspects of creating this book, Robert Weller has been a main source of help. I thank his straightforward and useful suggestions. His thoughtful comments and his broad perspective on Chinese religions constantly impress and never fail to inspire me.

I thank the Max Planck Institute (MPI) for the Study of Religious and Ethnic Diversity, where I finished this book, and I especially thank Director Peter van der Veer for his interest in and support of my project all along. MPI has the best work environment that I could ever imagine. Not every research institute has a proper kitchen and a garden! As one of the few historians in the institute, I learned a great deal from my anthropologist colleagues. I miss countless chats with colleagues and friends: Irfan Ahmad, Suddheesh Bhasi, Chen Yan, Chen Yining, Chiu Tzu-lung, Diao Ying, Fabian Graham, He Xiao, Jin-Heon Jung, Kang Jie, Maya Kaiser, Patrice Ladwig, Samuel Lengen, Liu Jifeng, Ma Zhen, Mai Thi Thanh Nga, Tam Ngo, Paul Sorrentino, Shaheed Tayob, Sajida Tursun, Leilah Vevaina, Ngoc Thi Vuong, Yu Jingyang, Zhu Jili, and others.

Special thanks to Maya for meticulous and superb editing and truly insightful comments. I feel really lucky to have had her help.

Some colleagues have read parts of the early versions of the manuscript and provided invaluable comments. They include Peter Bol, Jeremy Brown, Henrietta Harrison, Matthew Johnson, and Paul Katz. I am indebted to them all.

I feel lucky to be publishing with Oxford University Press. It has been a wonderful experience working with Cynthia Read, the editor of my book, and her assistant, Salma Ismaiel.

I am fortunate to have received the aid of numerous individuals who greatly facilitated the task of collecting data and field researches. Above all, I want to thank the staff at the local state archives in Longquan, Pingyang, Rui'an, Taishun, Wencheng, Wenling, Wenzhou, Xinchang and Yueqing, Rui'an City Library, Wenzhou Municipal Library, and Zhejiang Provincial Library for helping me find documents. Special thanks go to Wu Zhenqiang of Zhejiang University. Among my many interviewees and local guides, I especially thank Chen Meiling, Dai Xuefu, Ding Bingkuan, Ding Yuzhen, Pan Yiheng, Shi Liaozheng, Wu Zhenwei, Xia Mingxin, Ying Weixian, the late Zhang Junsun, Zhang Shisong, Zhou Zexian and Zhu Chenlan. My friends Zhou Gang and Qin Yong helped arrange my visits to local temples, archives, and the Rui'an Religious Affairs Bureau. Wu Tianyue and Zhang Jieke not only shared their own researches but also made copies of historical records of local churches in Rui'an and the Wenzhou region available to me. Pan Junliang of the University of Paris VII shared with me documents on southern Zhejiang that he had collected. My relatives provided invaluable support during my fieldwork in Rui'an and Hangzhou. I thank my brother Xuan, cousin Zhe, in-laws Haifeng and Dong, uncle Mingxiong, aunt Caicha, and aunt Chunhua.

My parents, Wang Jianyong and Lu Chuzhu, were always supportive of me pursuing my own interest, though they do not necessarily understand the nature of my researches. They were born around the founding of the PRC and have lived through many major political movements since 1949. Naturally, when I grew up, many dinner table talks were about PRC history, especially my parents' and their peers' experiences during the Mao years. They may not have realized it yet, but I increasingly see in them the "why" for becoming a historian. This book is for them.

Finally, my wife Xuan Gui has been by my side for every up and down of the entire journey. Xuan read early versions of the book, helped polish my writing, and shared her thoughts with me. Her love, patience, and unwavering faith in me kept me going. Without her, this book would not have been possible. This book is dedicated to her.

Translations, Characters, and Abbreviations

This book uses pinyin for transliterations unless the Chinese terms already have a commonly known spelling (e.g., Chiang Kai-shek, Y. T. Wu).

Names of authors are listed in either the Chinese (surname followed by given name) or Western order (surname followed by given name), mostly depending on the order of the names appearing in the publications.

Chinese characters are used in the term list and bibliography. This book only uses traditional characters.

Frequently used abbreviations:

CCP: Chinese Communist Party

CIM: China Inland Mission

CJIC: China Jesus Independent Church

EPA: Elderly People Association

KMT: Kuomintang, the Chinese Nationalist Party

PRC: People's Republic of China

Introduction

Legacies of Revolution

On April 28, 2014, before dawn, hundreds of armed police descended on the vicinity of Sanjiang Protestant Church in Yongjia, which sits across Ou River from downtown Wenzhou. The police cut off cell phone signals and dispersed a small number of Protestants who had stayed to defend the church, which the government had declared an "unlawful building." By evening, heavy bulldozers had completely leveled the church, which had taken ten years to build. As global media watched the standoff unfold on site, the demolition put an end to a month-long vigil at Sanjiang Church, which at its height allegedly included as many as several thousand Protestant protesters from the Wenzhou region and beyond. The demolition was followed by a province-wide "Three Rectifications and One Demolition" (*sangai yichai*) campaign that partly targeted unlawful religious buildings and symbols in Zhejiang.[1] By July 2015, the campaign is said to have removed crosses from more than 1,700 church roofs.

In late 2015, with cross removal winding down in Zhejiang, many Christians expressed fear and worry as well as anger, as they saw the shadow of the Cultural Revolution in the sweeping demolition of crosses. "They want to remove every trace," said a woman living near Sanjiang Church. "During the Cultural Revolution, they burned Bibles, but they didn't remove the crosses," she added.[2] A Ms. Huang in neighboring Taizhou region told reporters, when describing the demolition: "Some wore police uniforms, with helmets and shields, some were plainclothes police and some wore red armbands—just like the Red Guards during the Cultural Revolution."[3]

In a widely circulated letter to clergy and members of the Wenzhou diocese, the bishop appointed by the Vatican, Zhu Weifang, said he was stunned and confused. "I thought that now that more than three decades have passed since our country's reform and opening, such a Cultural-Revolution-style movement should not

---

[1] "Three Rectifications" refers to the rectifications of old residential neighborhoods, old factories, and urban villages. "One Demolition" refers to the demolition of unlawful buildings.

[2] "China's Christians Remain Strong Despite Worst Persecution since the Cultural Revolution," *The Guardian*, July 15, 2014.

[3] "China Removes Crosses from Two More Churches in Crackdown," *New York Times*, July 28, 2014.

Maoism and Grassroots Religion. Xiaoxuan Wang, Oxford University Press (2020). © Oxford University Press.
DOI: 10.1093/oso/9780190069384.001.0001

have happened, given that we have once more embraced the world. It seemed impossible. Yet this campaign, which is a deep wound to us Christians, did happen and is getting worse!"[4] Curiously, some others saw hope. Wenzhou Christians had endured the government's experiment "to eliminate religion" in the late 1950s and the ordeals of the Cultural Revolution (among other campaigns of the Mao years) and welcomed an unprecedented renewal in the church. The cross-removal campaign, they believed, would invite another Christian renaissance because "the more severe the persecution, the more the church thrives" (*yue bipo yue fuxing*).[5]

These pervasive references to the Cultural Revolution are symptomatic of the enduring legacy of Maoism in China's religious consciousness, a legacy that has taken on a life of its own. People like Zhu, belonging to a cohort who weathered the political storms of the revolutionary years, are disappearing one by one, and with them the living memory of those years. Yet their narratives of religious persecution under Mao have been passed on to members of younger generations, who made up the bulk of protesters at Sanjiang Church. The trope of religious persecution under Mao has conjured up, and may continue to conjure up, emotional reactions and could at times become a rallying cry and a call to action for Christians.

The broad question addressed in this book is as follows: How has Maoism transformed religion in China? If, as the events in Sanjiang indicate, the shadow of revolution still looms large in Chinese religious life, how has Maoism affected the ways that Chinese religions organize, operate, and interact with the state?

To answer this question, the book begins by tracing the history of encounters between Communist forces and followers of various religious traditions in Rui'an County, Wenzhou, before 1949. It looks at how religious communities in Rui'an have engaged with the Communist revolution since 1949 and how the legacy of Maoism has continued to shape the religious landscape in the post-Mao era. In so doing, the case study sheds light on, more generally, the making of religious modernity and rural organizations in the People's Republic of China (PRC).

Maoism and the Contemporary Landscape of Chinese Religion

In the decades following the Communist revolution, outside observers were often pessimistic about the future of Chinese religions, citing the Mao regime's

---

[4] A copy of the letter can be found here: http://wzchurch.blogspot.de/2016/04/blog-post_6.html (accessed on May 4, 2018).

[5] "Shizijia zhi zhan: weishenme Wenzhou shengchan jiaotang 'dingzihu'" (The fight for the cross: Why are Wenzhou churches fertile ground for "nail households?"), *Duanchuanmei* (The Initium), September 1, 2015. "Nail household" is a term that analogizes households refusing to be eminent domained to nails resisting being pulled out.

harsh rhetoric and anti-religion campaigns. A survey of Christianity and other religions in China, published in 1969, described it as "a nation state, with one fourth the earth's population, in which religion as an effective force seems to be all but nullified."[6] Holmes Welch, who authored a number of seminal works on religion under Mao, saw what he believed to be unmistakable signs of the demise of Buddhism in China.[7] For Welch, the rise of Maoism marked an unprecedented break with tradition that effectively eliminated Buddhism from everyday life. In a similar vein, C. K. Yang's monumental study of Chinese religions projected that Communism as a secular ideology would replace the theistic faiths that were in decline, in keeping with the trend toward secularization that he observed in the Republican era.[8]

Given that the Mao years (1949–1978) saw what may have been the worst religious repression in Chinese history, and considering that foreign researchers lacked access to the country during the same period, the pessimistic tone of their writing is not that surprising. It is curious, however, that to this day the Mao years remain the least studied period in the history of religion in modern China. The study of modern Chinese religion has burgeoned in the period since the end of Mao's rule, yet most studies focus on the pre-1949 and post-1978 eras. A landmark study of religious history in modern China, *The Religious Question in Modern China*, mentions the Cultural Revolution only in passing, leaving out almost any mention of popular religion under Mao.[9] Very little has been written about certain facets of religious life from 1949 to 1978, such as any interactions concerning religion that occurred between local officials belonging to different levels of government, between officials and locals, or between religious and non-religious people.

Despite the lack of research in this field, we are now starting to develop a clearer picture of religious life under Maoism thanks to local experiences that are coming to light from different regions, religious traditions, and ethnicities. The narratives of those who lived through the period from 1949 to 1978 also show that the effects of Maoism on local traditions are often pervasive, complex, and multivalent. Stephen Jones's research in Hebei Province, in northern China, illustrates the survival of village rituals and ritual music associations through an era of repeated political intrusions.[10] In fact, some village ritual associations were

---

[6] Richard C. Bush, *Religion in Communist China* (Nashville, TN: Abingdon Press, 1970), 10.

[7] Holmes Welch, *Buddhism under Mao* (Cambridge, MA: Harvard University Press, 1972).

[8] See C. K. Yang, "Religion and the Traditional Moral Order," in *Religion in Chinese Society: A Study of Contemporary Functions of Religion and Some of Their Historical Factors* (Berkeley: University of California Press, 1961), 278–293.

[9] Vincent Goossaert and David A. Palmer, *The Religious Question in Modern China* (Chicago: University of Chicago Press, 2011).

[10] Stephen Jones, *Plucking the Winds: Lives of Village Musicians in Old and New China* (Leiden: CHIME Foundation, 2004) and "Revival in Crisis: Amateur Ritual Association in Hebei," in *Religion in Contemporary China: Revitalization and Innovation*, ed. Adam Chau (New York: Routledge, 2011), 154–181.

able to carry on their practices unobtrusively to such an extent that Jones asserts that "the restoration of ritual associations around 1980 was no reinvention, no piecing together of cultural fragments" but an "authentic transition."[11] By contrast, other ritual traditions were much more affected by Maoist movements. As Henrietta Harrison found in Catholic communities in southern Taiyuan, Shanxi in northern China, the crackdown and propaganda since the Socialist Education Movement in the early 1960s sparked massive resistance among Catholic villagers, deploying miracles as a rallying point. In the end, local authorities effectively curbed the public practices of Catholicism, though this had the paradoxical effect of reinforcing Catholic identity, laying the foundations for a religious revival in the reform period.[12]

In a similar vein, Paul Mariani's research on Catholic communities in cosmopolitan Shanghai shows that Catholic leaders in the early 1950s resisted the Communist Party's assault on religion, refusing to renounce the Pope and the Church in Rome; yet the Chinese Communist Party (CCP) eventually succeeded in dividing the Catholic community.[13] In south and southeast China, Protestants seemed to be more successful in resisting and surviving the penetration of the state using a wide range of tactics. In eastern and northern Fujian the revival of Protestantism might even have started toward the end of the Cultural Revolution, as research by both Chen-Yang Kao and Melissa Inouye suggests.[14]

In ethnic minority regions, where the politics of religion is closely associated with the politics of ethnicity, issues of religious repression and revival have often had a dramatic character. In Hui Muslim communities of Yunnan, in southwestern China, state violence against Islam led to a religious uprising at the height of the Cultural Revolution which contributed to a resurgence in local Islamic identity.[15] In the 1969 "Nyemo incident" in Tibet, during the early stages of the Cultural Revolution, villagers angered by government policies in the frenzy of local factional fights were mobilized by religion.[16] These case

---

[11] Ibid., 168.

[12] Henrietta Harrison, *The Missionary's Curse and Other Tales from a Chinese Catholic Village* (Berkeley: University of California Press, 2013), Chapter 6.

[13] Paul P. Mariani, *Church Militant: Bishop Kung and Catholic Resistance in Communist Shanghai* (Cambridge, MA: Harvard University Press, 2011).

[14] Chen-yang Kao, "The Cultural Revolution and the Emergence of Pentecostal-style Protestantism in China," *Journal of Contemporary Religion* 24, no. 2 (2009): 171–188; Joseph Tse-Hei Lee, "Politics of Faith: Christian Activism and the Maoist State in Chaozhou, Guangdong Province," *The China Review* 9, no. 2 (2009): 17–39; and Melissa Wei-Tsing Inouye, *China and the True Jesus: Charisma and Organization in a Chinese Christian Church* (Oxford: Oxford University Press, 2019), Chapter 7.

[15] Xian Wang, "Islamic Religiosity, Revolution, and State Violence in Southwest China: The 1975 Shadian Massacre" (MA thesis, University of British Columbia, 2013).

[16] Melvyn C. Goldstein, Ben Jiao, and Tanzen Lhundrup, *On the Cultural Revolution in Tibet: The Nyemo Incident of 1969* (Berkeley: University of California Press, 2009).

studies and numerous others show the powerful role of religion in local politics throughout China's ethnic minority regions during the Mao years.

Departing from the pessimism of earlier accounts, recent studies of religion in China see the CCP's efforts to remodel society as being far less successful than was once believed. New research argues that traditional cosmologies have, in many ways, continued to guide people's thoughts and behaviors, in spite of the preponderance of Maoist ideology.[17] The most violent attacks on religion were often short-lived and occurred within the context of local affairs, allowing for the survival of ritual traditions, in fragments or as a whole. These findings are underscored by a broad analytical shift in the study of religious life in China from religion and politics on a national scale to local, often unexpected, outcomes and to non-elite actors at the grassroots level. Improved access to state archives and a boom in the study of oral history have allowed researchers to go from studying the decline of Chinese religions to examining their survival,[18] predicated on multiple tactics including resistance, negotiation, and compliance in a wide range of forms.

This shift in emphasis raises new questions. While earlier studies tended to assume that all religious activities had diminished, regardless of their nature, it is now clear from recent studies on the ground that efforts to suppress or advance religion did not simply result in a linear decline. Instead, the development of religious life within China varied at different times, places, and for different traditions. As is shown by Thomas DuBois,[19] there was variation even among different groups from the same religious tradition, as in the Hebei villages where intra-village sects survived better than trans-local ones. The diverse outcomes of Maoist suppression demand further comparison and analysis. How is it possible that modes of action and organization, theological ideas, local history, and the politics of religion played out with so many variations, even within the same regions, in the fate of different religious groups during the Mao era?

During the campaigns against religion, the Communist government developed a distinct rhetoric with which to describe the major religious traditions, creating attributes for each based in Communist theory. The territorial temple activities, Buddhism, Daoism, and Islam were all tied to the theory of feudalism. Christian churches, both Catholic and Protestant, were associated with the concept of imperialism, an association that lent a powerful stigma to Christianity

---

[17] Steve A. Smith, "Local Cadres Confront the Supernatural: The Politics of Holy Water (*Shenshui*) in the PRC, 1949–1966," *The China Quarterly* 188 (2006): 999–1022 and "Talking Toads and Chinless Ghosts: The Politics of 'Superstitious' Rumors in the People's Republic of China, 1961–1965," *American Historical Review* 111, no. 2 (2006): 405–427.

[18] Also explaining the survival of religion under Mao, Fenggang Yang uses market analysis, though his interest is more theoretical than empirical. See Fenggang Yang, *Religion in China—Survival and Revival under Communist Rule* (Oxford; New York: Oxford University Press), 2012.

[19] Thomas David Dubois, *The Sacred Village: Social Change and Religious Life in Rural North China* (Honolulu: University of Hawai'i Press, 2005), 147–149, 166–173.

throughout China from 1949 onward. Salvationist traditions bore the harsh epithet of *fandong huidaomen* (meaning "reactionary societies, teachings, and sects"). These labels to a large extent guided government policy toward the different religious traditions. In other words, the Communist revolution presented different challenges to each, but to what extent did these account for the differences in how religious organizations and traditions navigated the tumultuous political history of the Mao era?

By exploring the multiplicity of experiences among different religious groups, this book addresses the overall evolution of the local religious landscape, as it was transformed by the changing balance of religious and political power. This study does not treat religion as a closed-off system that can be easily separated from local political and economic life; nor does it see the relations between religious traditions as a zero-sum game, as some scholars in mainland China have suggested.[20] The present study begins from the perspective that changes in religious life are inextricably linked with the religious ecology of local society. Changes in one area may reshape the entire religious landscape.

The differences in local experiences open up the possibility of exploring religious reinvention during the revolutionary years, something which has rarely been associated with that period. Until now, most research on the revolutionary era has tended to view it as one of disruption and loss. Helen Siu, for instance, suggested the Mao era as a period which saw the fragmentation of a more coherent and authentic pre-1949 tradition, arguing that the resurgence of rituals in the reform era was less a revival of "tradition" than it was a case of "cultural fragments recycled under new circumstances."[21] The "recycling" metaphor reveals the mechanism of religious revival and is well received, yet few scholars have explicitly questioned the implications of this metaphor.

Tradition is, as Adam Chau argues, "a complex, dynamic, ever-changing cluster of institutions, practitioners and consumers, knowledge and practices fully amenable to innovations, inventions and reinventions."[22] Once we see tradition as a "process that involves continual re-creation,"[23] it is entirely possible

---

[20] For a survey of discussions of "religious ecology" in Chinese academia, see Philip Clart, "'Religious Ecology' as a New Model for the Study of Religious Diversity in China," in *Religious Diversity in Chinese Thought*, eds. Perry Schmidt-Leukel and Joachim Gentz (New York: Palgrave Macmillan, 2013), 187–199.

[21] Helen F. Siu, "Recycling Rituals: Politics and Popular Culture in Contemporary Rural China," in *Unofficial China: Popular Culture and Thought in the People's Republic*, eds. Perry Link, Richard Madsen and Paul Pickowicz (Boulder: Westview Press, 1989), 134; See also Helen F. Siu, "Recycling Tradition: Culture, History, and Political Economy in the Chrysanthemum Festivals of South China," *Comparative Studies in Society and History* 32, no. 4 (1990): 765–794.

[22] Adam Yuet Chau, *Miraculous Response: Doing Popular Religion in Contemporary China* (Stanford: Stanford University Press, 2008), 6.

[23] Richard Handler and Jocelyn Linnekin, "Tradition, Genuine or Spurious," *The Journal of American Folklore* 97, no. 385 (1984): 287.

that Maoist rule could have simultaneously suppressed religion and sparked religious reinvention. In other words, fragmentation and reinvention could go hand in hand. State violence may be detrimental to orders and institutions, while efforts to avoid it often require inventive measures, and may lead to new orders and institutions being developed. In its efforts to repress religious life, the state unintentionally incited religious fervor, contributing to the diffusion of religious ideas throughout China. As religious practitioners found ways of coping with repressive policies, the state itself became a resource for cultural appropriation: its discourses, symbols, and institutions.

As this book demonstrates, the Mao era is extraordinary but not exceptional. Violent state campaigns against religions have led to religious reinvention and even expansion. The struggle to resist and survive fueled reinvention, sowing the seeds for further transformation and even growth. The Mao era is no less important than any other period of Chinese history in the making of modern religious traditions in China. Not only did the revolutionary years see many fundamental transformations in religious life, they also set the conditions for more critical religious innovations in the post-Mao era.[24] In keeping with this, we must renew our understanding of the continuities and discontinuities in the years from 1949 to 1978.

Land Revolution, Religious Property, and the Reinvention of Rural Organizations

This book pays close attention to what I term "property issues" to highlight revolutionary experiences at the local level and their consequences for rural religious organizations. "Property issues" refer specifically to land and property owned by religious groups, including religious buildings, the land they occupy, and religious artifacts such as incense burners and statues of divinities.

Property issues, in particular issues surrounding land, are at the root of so many religious issues during and after Mao's revolution and something that returns again and again. In the Sanjiang incident a more fundamental issue is in fact land. Since the Communist revolution took land away and established the state as the largest and sole landowner,[25] insecure property rights have been a

---

[24] Qigong, for instance, is a good example. As David Palmer demonstrates, the state's co-optation of Qigong in the 1950s socially and institutionally paved way for the emergence of Qigong fever in the 1980s when Chinese searched for individual empowerment and subjectivity. See David A. Palmer, *Qigong Fever: Body, Science, and Utopia in China* (New York: Columbia University Press), 2007, Chapter 1.

[25] Though the nationalization of land was formally written into the Constitution only in 1982, land has been the de facto property of the state ever since private land ownership was effectively abolished by land reform and collectivization.

huge problem to local communities. When the government tightened regulation of land use amidst rapid commercialization and urbanization that made land an increasingly precious resource, local communities have to constantly engage and sometimes clash with the authorities on the land issue.

Researchers have tended to focus on the economic and political aspects of land reform in the PRC, looking at issues such as the process of implementing land reform at the local level, especially the confiscation and redistribution of land; the economic effects of land reform, especially on agricultural production; and the politics of mass mobilization and state building.[26] Recently, interest has shifted to the cultural factors and consequences of land reform.[27]

The present study highlights the social aspects of land revolution in the PRC, extending an area of inquiry that has been well studied for the Republican era but not so far for the Mao and post-Mao eras. Land was crucial to the formation, continuation, and growth of religious activities and communities in traditional Chinese religions. It was vital to constructing a permanent ritual space, as well as to finance daily temple affairs and ritual processions. Land marked the territoriality of religious communities and the sovereignty of local deities, and in this close association with the locality, it became an anchor of society in villages and city neighborhoods. Religious organizations in imperial China were major land and real estate owners, and often had many villagers working for them or farming their landholdings. In the imperial era, religious property was sometimes a target of state attacks because of state fears that temples might become too powerful.

From the late nineteenth century onward, there were frequent confiscations of religious properties, showing the enactment of secularism in the creation of modern China. A significant number of studies have examined the encroachment on religious sites in the late Qing and Republican periods, as well as the local unrest which this generated. They have also considered the local politics of religious space, as well as the broad consequences of anti-superstition campaigns on local sociopolitical structure, revealing the crucial importance of property issues in the fate of religion in modern China.[28]

---

[26] Victor Lippit, *Land Reform and Economic Development in China* (White Plains, NY: International Arts and Sciences Press, 1974); Vivienne Shue, *Peasant China in Transition: The Dynamics of Development Toward Socialism, 1949–1956* (Berkeley: University of California Press, 1980); Julia C. Strauss, "Paternalist Terror: The Campaign to Suppress Counterrevolutionaries and Regime Consolidation in the People's Republic of China, 1950–1953," *Comparative Studies in Society and History* 44 (2002): 80–105.

[27] Philip C. C. Huang, "Rural Class Struggle in the Chinese Revolution," *Modern China* 21, no. 1 (January 1995): 105–143 and Brian James DeMare, *Mao's Cultural Army Drama Troupes in China's Rural Revolution* (Cambridge, UK: Cambridge University Press), 2015.

[28] Prasenjit Duara, "Knowledge and Power in the Discourse of Modernity: The Campaigns against Popular Religion in Early 20th Century China," *Journal of Asian Studies* 50, no.1 (1991): 75; *Rescuing History from the Nation: Questioning Narratives of Modern China* (Chicago: University of Chicago

While there are some sharp discontinuities between the Nationalist and Communist governments' policies on religious issues, as far as religious property was concerned, the Communist government was, in many ways, the "inheritor of the Nanjing Nationalist architecture of religious policies."[29] As one example, the confiscation of land and other religious property during land reform and other post-1949 political campaigns can be seen as a continuation of Republican policies on religion. Yet crucially, CCP policies toward religion were guided by international communism as well as by Chinese politics. China's Communist revolution in 1949 inaugurated a comprehensive secularization project that operated on social, political, and economic structures to transform rather than directly target religious life. This holistic approach was far more devastating to religion than the secularizing engineering of the Republican regime. Despite religion not being a priority of land reform, religious properties were affected on an unprecedented scale. The subsequent nationalization of land ultimately made religion's traditional dependence on land ownership unsustainable.

Given the challenge posed by the political and ideological environment under Mao, how much scope was left for local religious communities to manage property issues? To what extent were resistance, negotiation, and manipulation possible? When it came to the competition for religious space, local realities and politics were highly significant, as is clear from histories of the Republican era. With the extension of state power into local society and unprecedented levels of bureaucratization, what room for maneuver still existed for local actors in the Mao era?

One of the goals of land reform was to destroy the economic underpinnings of the old society, including religious property. By undermining the economic foundations of religious institutions, however, land revolution had another, more drastic effect: it deterritorialized religious groups on a scale never before seen in Chinese history. Most religious institutions were expelled from their traditional ritual sites, or saw their access restricted. How have religious communities coped with massive deterritorialization? As this book shows, the process of reterritorialization, which occurred in multiple forms and different paces across different traditions in both Mao and post-Mao years, not only allowed some religious practices and institutions to survive the day, but also essentially facilitated the reinvention of rural religious organizations. This book therefore argues that

Press, 1995), Chapter 3; Rebecca Nedostup, *Superstitious Regimes: Religion and the Politics of Chinese Modernity* (Cambridge, MA: Harvard University Asian Center, 2010); Shuk-wah Poon, *Negotiating Religion in Modern China: State and Common People in Guangzhou, 1900–1937* (Hong Kong: The Chinese University Press, 2011); Paul R. Katz, *Religion in China and Its Modern Fate* (Waltham, MA: Brandeis University Press, 2014), Chapter 1, 17–68.

[29] Rebecca Nedostup, "Superstitious Regimes," 286.

Maoist policies on religious property were a catalyst for the institutional rein-vigoration of religious organizations, which was an important and unintended consequence of Maoism.

Understanding Religious Governance in the People's Republic of China

In order to document the experiences of local religious communities under Mao, this book comprehensively revisits the Maoist governance of religion. The big question that this book sets out to answer is as follows: Why did Mao's approach to religion have such catastrophic consequences for religion in China, while on the other hand failing to achieve its policy goals in the long run? The atheistic, nationalistic ideas of Chinese Communism certainly lent an iconoclastic tone to the CCP's Mao-era policies toward religion. Yet since it was founded, the party's approach to religion has been much more pragmatic than its overt ideology might suggest.

Before 1949, the party's tough stance on religion often yielded to practical concerns. Its strategy toward local communal religious organizations focused on propaganda and education, especially on the occasion of temple fairs, which the party strove to transform into a site for Communist propaganda. During this period the CCP targeted so-called religious superstition professionals (*zongjiao mixin zhiyezhe*) such as mediums, and forced them to give up their practices. In its northern revolutionary bases, the Communist Party is known to have destroyed temples and imposed taxes on "superstition goods" (*mixinpin*) such as candles and paper money, which also occurred in Nationalist-controlled ter-ritories. Yet party officials had deliberately prevented such actions from turning to excess, fearing that attacks on temple activities might affect support for the party.[30] Salvationist traditions were considered the biggest political threat. The party wanted to disband their organizations and terminate all salvationist activ-ities. They were ruled illegal in revolutionary bases. But it was not unusual that the Communist forces found an ally in some salvationist groups.[31]

This pragmatism manifested even more prominently in the Communist Party's pre-1949 stance on Christianity. Up until the late 1930s, as the party soft-ened its tone on Western countries, authorities in Communist-controlled areas

---

[30] Wang Meng, "20 shiji san sishi niandai Jizhong genjudi miaohui yanjiu" (A study of temple fairs in the central Hebei revolutionary base in the 1930s and 1940s) (Hebei Normal University, MA thesis, 2011).

[31] Zhu Xinming, "Kangri genjudi zhili huidaomen yanjiu" (A study of control of reactionary soci-eties, teachings, and sects in revolutionary bases) (Shanghai Normal University, MA thesis, 2006), Chapters 2–3.

had allowed Western missions to operate, own land, and open schools and other enterprises. After the Civil War broke out, the Communist Party's stance shifted drastically, a change which can be largely attributed to America's support for the Nationalist government, such that Christianity (associated with American and other foreign presences) was perceived as a political threat. Christian missionaries, churches, and church land in Communist-run areas once again became subject to land reform and struggle meetings.[32]

The Communist Party's relations with local religious groups changed profoundly when it achieved national rule in 1949. The party put forth pro-atheist, anti-religious propaganda via newspapers, exhibitions, drama performances, and other means. There were brief campaigns against some religious organizations, especially salvationist groups and the Catholic church. Yet a certain level of pragmatism continued to guide policy, as evidenced by its United Front strategy in religious work. Religious policies formulated in the spirit of the United Front would suppress "counterrevolutionary activities in the disguise of religion" (*pizhe zongjiao waiyi de fangemin huodong*) while protecting religious freedom as stipulated in the Common Programme (*gongtong gangling*), later enshrined in the 1954 Constitution of the People's Republic.[33] Even during the Cultural Revolution, the government never formally abolished the distinction between "counterrevolutionary" religion, and beliefs or activities protected by religious freedom. The central government had never launched a national campaign against "superstition"—a conceptualization of religious practices which is at the root of the Republican architecture of religious policy. In fact, throughout the Mao era, the Communist government never formulated a clear definition of what "superstition" (as opposed to "religion") might mean.

The Communist government's guidelines on religion seem to signal a more balanced, pragmatic approach than we might presume from the one-sided religious suppression that resulted. How can we make sense of the discrepancy between reality and political rhetoric? The answer, I believe, lies in the nature and rhythm of the Chinese Communist revolution and the local dynamics.

To understand the impact of Maoism on religious life, one must follow the "ecological approach" recently proposed by Vincent Gooassert and David Palmer, i.e., looking at the state's political and economic agenda as well as its religious

---

[32] Tao Feiya. "Christianity and the Communist Revolution," in *Handbook of Christianity in China*, Volume 2: *1800–Present*, ed. R. G. Tiedemann (Leiden: Brill, 2010), 708–716.

[33] "Zhonggong zhongyang guanyu Han minzu zhong Fojiao wenti de zhishi" (The Party Central Committee's instruction on the issue of Buddhism among Han people) and "Zhonggong zhongyang guanyu chuli Tianzhujiao wenti de zhishi" (The Party Central Committee's instruction on the issue of Catholic Church). See Zhonggong zhongyang tongyi zhanxian gongzuo zu, ed., *Tongzhan zhengce wenjian huibian (disijuan)* (Collections of the united front policies, Volume 4) (Zhonggong zhongyang tongyi zhanxian gongzuo zu, 1958), 140–149.

policies per se.[34] The Communist Party's ambition, led by Mao, was to enact total revolution in the Marxist-Leninist tradition, uprooting the structure of China's economic institutions, its political system, and society as a whole, in order to replace them with new ones. The revolution prioritized those agendas that involved (re)distributing or amassing the material, human, or cultural resources which were required for revolution, destroying resources that it did not want, and channeling residents into social units created or sponsored by the government in order to make them comply with the everyday rhythm of socialism. Thus in many cases, instead of directly attacking religion, revolutionaries destroyed the very sociopolitical and economic order on which traditional religious life was based. In other words, the Communist Party's policies and actions toward religion were highly contingent on its political and economic agenda. In order to implement this agenda, the Communist government employed a critical instrument: mass campaigns. These included the land reform, the Great Leap Forward, and the Cultural Revolution. What happened to religious communities under Maoism, I argue, has to be understood primarily through this revolutionary temporality.

Using Archival Sources of the PRC

One of the biggest challenges in doing research on religious life under Mao is the lack of data and the inaccessibility of the data that exist. Early observers could only rely on newspaper reports and journal articles published by the Chinese government, refugees' accounts, and sometimes materials written by visitors to China. This has continued to be a challenge (though less so today), as religion remains a sensitive issue in government archives. In this regard I benefited from being a native of Rui'an and a speaker of the Wenzhou dialect, which people in China often joke is one of the most difficult dialects in the country, allowing me to gain better access to local state archives and to conduct oral history research with villagers in Rui'an.

The details described in this book concerning local religious life under Mao are mainly drawn from county-level archives in southern Zhejiang, in particular the archives of Rui'an City. The documents I collected from local state archives include statements and directives of religious policy at different levels,

---

[34] Vincent Goossaert and David A. Palmer, "*The Religious Question in Modern China*," 6–13. Adam Chau has suggested the importance of looking beyond religious policies. My focus in this book is how priority agendas of Maoism have actually affected local religious life. See Adam Y. Chau, "Chinese Socialism and the Household Idiom of Religious Engagement," in *Atheist Secularism and Its Discontents: A Comparative Study of Religion and Communism in Eurasia*, eds. Tam T. T. Ngo and Justine B. Quijada (New York: Palgrave Macmillan, 2015), 225–243.

reports on the implementation of religious policies, registers of religious organizations, religious surveys, and investigative reports of religious and other social activities.

The use of government archives also poses a challenge to researchers in the study of religion under Mao. In its efforts to control every aspect of social life, the Communist government was obsessively concerned with collecting bits and pieces of information regarding the daily life and thoughts of ordinary people. This quest left behind a voluminous record of opinions and remarks related to religion, as well as records of religious behaviors. No government in Chinese history had ever before created such a detailed body of records on the social life of ordinary people.

Yet, while they provide a valuable resource for historians, state archives require extra caution and efforts to decode. They are steeped in the political discourse of the Communist Party, presenting information through the lens of Maoist ideology. Moreover, the information contained in religious surveys or the records of religious organizations was often collected in a coercive political environment. It is difficult to judge the accuracy and authenticity of information reported to the government, insofar as it was shaped by political conditions at the time. And state archives of the Mao years have other limitations as well: they rarely mention the conditions of domestic worship; nor do they describe the transmission of religious knowledge or its evolution, as official investigations rarely recorded this level of detail.

To overcome some of these issues, I employed cross-referencing to check the consistency of official archives, comparing the records of different government sources. More importantly, I gathered oral history accounts through interviews and conversations with local religious practitioners and institutions, allowing me to compare these accounts with official records. In order to draw comparisons and situate Wenzhou in broader contexts, I have also extensively referenced the religion section of new local gazetteers (*xinfangzhi*) in Zhejiang and in other provinces in both northern and southern China.[35] The book as a whole aims to present a comprehensive picture of religious life under Maoism by bringing to light the ways in which officials perceived religious practices and beliefs, as well as how religious and non-religious villagers made sense of their own life experiences.

In the summers of 2006 and 2011–2013, I traveled to religious sites across all of Rui'an City to interview villagers and rural officials. My oral history interviews were mainly conducted in the towns of Xincheng and Dingtian, Xincheng District; Luofeng, Tangxia District; Mayu, Mayu District; and Anyang, the

---

[35] Different from traditional gazetteers, new local gazetteers predominantly cover the history of the People's Republic.

county seat.[36] Fortunately, I was able to locate and meet some of the people who had directly participated in or witnessed the events that appeared in archival sources. Their accounts lend depth to some of the events that I have documented here. As one example, the demolition of Rock Head Palace (*yantou gong*) in Mayu after the central government's call to eliminate superstition in 1983 was a high-profile case exalted by the county government as a model action, leading the countywide anti-superstition campaign. Yet my interviews show that the real events were much more ambiguous than the official story of the government's iron fist smashing "feudal superstition." Before the demolition, people were able to move statues of divinities and other facilities to another temple in the same village, and this other temple, it seems, was deliberately left intact. Rock Head Palace was eventually rebuilt and reopened in this new location.

State archival sources have other limitations. The tumultuous years of the Cultural Revolution between late 1966 and 1978 have left very few records in state archives, as the paralyzed local government was unable to collect or archive information for quite some time. This book's case studies of religious life during the Cultural Revolution have had to rely on the historical accounts of local communities. Religious followers in Rui'an and Wenzhou have produced many personal witness accounts, memoirs, and histories of religious institutions. These accounts do pose some problems of interpretation, like oral history accounts: for instance, religious testimony may be shaped by Christian speech practices, sharing life experiences as a means of preaching the Gospel. Suffering, persecution, and solidarity among religious followers may be overemphasized. Nevertheless, these accounts provide valuable information that might otherwise disappear, and I rely on them to the greatest extent possible.

The case studies in the book focus on "communal religious traditions," Protestant churches, salvationist groups, and, to a lesser extent, the Catholic church. Readers may notice that lineage organization per se is not a focus of this book. This is for two reasons: Since the land reform period, archives show that disputes over corporate lineage property have been less prominent than issues involving other religious traditions. Furthermore, lineage is a complex, multivalent phenomenon beyond its ritual dimensions.

Daoism is not treated as a separate category in the book. State archives lack records of Daoist activities. Rui'an City Archives, for instance, do not have a registry of Daoists or Daoist temples. The problem is not that Rui'an did not have Daoist activities. Many villages have a tradition of residential Daoism and families with generations of Daoists.[37] The lack of records specifically identifying

---

[36] Most names of interviewees in this book have been changed in order to protect their identity.

[37] Chen Wenzheng, a prominent leader of the southern Zhejiang communist guerrillas, was himself a residential Daoist and came from a Daoist family in the Lower Village of Xincheng District, Rui'an.

Daoism is most likely because Daoist activities were so closely intertwined with territorial cults and village life, such that local governments in the Mao era treated them indiscriminately as "superstition," together with territorial cults. Readers should consider Daoism as part of what I broadly term "communal religious tradition."

"Communal religion" or "communal religious traditions," as described in this book, mainly refer to traditions of territorial temples, Buddhist monasteries, and Daoist temples. Territorial temples refer to village temples dedicated to the worship of local deities. The communist government adopted different policy schemes on territorial temples and Buddhist monasteries and Daoist temples, with the former as sites of "superstition" and the last two as legal religious venues. Most Buddhist monasteries and Daoist temples, however, traditionally were village temples. People built those monasteries in their villages, and funded and regulated them. In the Wenzhou region, for centuries, many Buddhist monasteries and Daoist temples stood side by side with territorial temples in what we may call a "village religious compound," which remains true in many villages even today. Their proximity means an overlap in their leadership and especially their patronage. I therefore use "communal religion" as a common term for territorial temples, Buddhist monasteries, and Daoist temples because of their affinity as village religious institutions.

Why Wenzhou?

This book is mainly set in the region of Wenzhou, in Zhejiang Province. It is beyond the scope of the present inquiry to describe the experiences of an entire country. However, the Wenzhou case can serve as an entry point to understanding the broader transformations in China as a whole, for a number of reasons. Wenzhou is one of the regions where religious and lineage activities and organizations have seen the most active revival since the 1980s. The density of religious sites here, including territorial temples, Buddhist temples, Daoist temples, and Christian churches, may be among the highest in China. An official prefecture-wide survey in 2012, for instance, indicates 8,579 territorial temples with buildings larger than 20 square meters.[38] On the eve of 1949, Wenzhou Protestants constituted 41.5 percent of the entire Protestant population of

---

[38] http://www.zjsmzw.gov.cn/Public/NewsInfo.aspx?type=4&id=5d64d052-7013-4a8e-97be-1556b1464a37, these communal temples were distributed in 5,405 administrative villages and 380 urban neighborhoods around the same period. Given its number of communal temples, it is no wonder that the first national "folk belief work" roundtable organized by the State Administration for Religious Affairs took place in Wenzhou in 2012. See: http://www.wenzhou.gov.cn/art/2015/4/7/art_1214432_1731837.html (accessed on May 4, 2018).

Zhejiang Province, which had the largest Protestant population in the country.[39] Because of this, Wenzhou bore the brunt of Maoist campaigns on religion and their legacy.

After 1949, the region was one of the key areas for "religious work" (*zongjiao gongzuo*) in the province and in the country as a whole. In 1958, the first year of the Great Leap Forward, the State Administration for Religious Affairs held an on-the-spot religious work meeting in Pingyang County, Wenzhou, which Chinese Christians have since widely interpreted as an attempt to mount a national campaign to eliminate religion. Since the 1980s, following the footsteps of the well-known Wenzhou entrepreneurs, Wenzhou Protestant churches have put down roots in various areas from Northeast to Southwest China, as well as among Wenzhou migrant communities in Europe and the Americas, creating a global network of Wenzhou Protestant Christianity. When the cross-demolition movement hit Zhejiang in 2014, attracting global attention, Wenzhou was at the center of the storm. Although Wenzhou was once rather isolated, and in spite of it being located far from Beijing, it was never far removed from Maoist politics. Notably, it became a strategic locale in the frontier areas facing Taiwan. This region is therefore a hotbed of religious activities and an ideal site to observe local responses to Maoist secular governance.

It is important to note some differences in the consequences of national political campaigns, which were contingent on the dynamics of local history and politics—two parameters that this book stresses in order to illustrate the ways that Maoism reshaped the local religious landscape. The Socialist Education Movement in the early 1960s, for instance, did not generate such drastic massive resistance among religious followers in Wenzhou as it did among Catholics in Taiyuan, Shanxi, as described in Henrietta Harrison's study. During the Cultural Revolution, militarized resistance against religious suppression and extreme state violence in Shadian, Yunnan, was also absent from Wenzhou. Nevertheless, similarities can be identified at similar times across different sites. The brief religious resurgence of the early 1960s, as I will discuss in the book, was seen and reported not only in Zhejiang, but in numerous areas across the North and South of the country. My own research in Wenzhou and other studies in northern Fujian all indicate the vitality of Protestant Christianity during the Cultural Revolution. Though this is unlikely to have been a nationwide phenomenon, it was likely true for other traditional strongholds of Protestantism across the country, as research data indicate.

---

[39] Fuk-tsang Ying, "The Regional Development of Protestant Christianity in China: 1918, 1949 and 2004," *The China Review* 9, no. 2 (Fall 2009): 80.

Organization of the Book

This book is organized chronologically and thematically to compare the paths of different religious traditions after 1949. Chapter 1 examines the changes in religious life before 1949 and the intricate relationship between religious communities and the Communist revolution, situating the developments that were to follow in a broader historical context. Salvationist groups and Christian movements, both Catholic and Protestant, arose from the turmoil of the first half of the twentieth century, but they were not filling a vacuum. Communal religious traditions endured in spite of enormous challenges from anti-superstition campaigns. When the Communist guerrillas emerged at the fringes of local society, they competed, collaborated, and clashed with salvationist groups and Christian churches. The Communist Party's relations with religious communities persisted after 1949, as Chapter 2 shows, but as their relative positions shifted, their engagement proceeded on very different terms.

Although the new regime did not wage an all-out war against religion, Chapter 2 demonstrates that land reform demolished religious life. Yet the effects varied for different religious traditions. Land reform dealt a huge blow to the established activities of territorial and Buddhist temples as they lost land, major patrons, and traditional leaders, whereas young Christian churches did not have much land to lose. The most dramatic twist was the ephemeral surge of salvationist groups during land reform, followed by their rapid downfall in the government's massive crackdown, which marked a turning point in the twentieth-century history of local religious life.

Throughout the remainder of the 1950s and 1960s, various political campaigns and collectivization initiatives continued to encroach on the traditional ritual spaces of territorial and Buddhist temples in local communities. Yet villagers fought to preserve these ritual spaces and continued to pursue worship activities to a certain degree. At times, there was even a surge in communal religious practices. Chapter 3 explains why this occurred and points to the difficulties communal religious groups faced in restoring their activities during the Mao era.

From a comparative perspective, Chapters 4 to 6 zoom in on the experience of Christians, especially Protestants, after land reform. As Chapter 4 shows, though the Catholic Church stagnated in the wake of the Legion of Mary crackdown, carrying the stigma of a "counterrevolutionary" organization, most Protestant denominations made inroads after land reform. This chapter explains why this was the case. Yet a far-reaching "great leap in religious work" in 1958, the year of the Great Leap Forward, temporarily halted the rise of Protestantism, as all churches and temples were closed. This critical moment saw all worship activities restricted to house gatherings. The end of the Great Famine ushered in a new era for Protestant communities, in spite of the political turmoil of the Cultural Revolution.

Chapter 5 maps the territorial expansion and organizational reinvention of Protestant churches during the Cultural Revolution. As Chapter 6 demonstrates, though, Protestant churches had to contend with the legacy of the Mao years, which had mixed effects on the growth of Protestantism. Crucially, the social developments that occurred under Mao facilitated the explosive growth of Protestant churches after 1978. Yet churches had to grapple with the Three-Self movement and a growing schism within the religion, both of which stemmed from the Maoist past. Chapter 7 illustrates local attempts to circumvent the issue of legality stemming from Maoist policies in the temple reclamation movement that followed the collapse of collectivization. Such efforts revitalized traditional social institutions in rural life, in particular the Elderly People Association, which then moved toward the center of village politics.

Finally, in the Conclusion, I review overall the transformation of the religious landscape in Rui'an and call for a renewed understanding of the Mao era and its legacy for the religious and social life of rural China.

1

Revolution and Religion

The Pre-1949 Encounter

The region of Wenzhou, in southeastern China, is known for its pioneering entrepreneurs as well as its vivid religious life. "China's Jerusalem," as people often call Wenzhou, has a long history of evangelistic movements that have been an active presence in Chinese Christianity. It is also famous for sending migrants throughout China and abroad: Wenzhounese communities have settled in Europe, the Americas, Africa, and elsewhere.

Until the mid-nineteenth century, however, the region's geographical isolation (see Map 1.1) made it primarily a destination for migrants seeking a safe haven. Situated on the southeast coast of Zhejiang Province, facing the East China Sea, it is divided from neighboring Fujian Province and from the rest of Zhejiang by the scenic Yandang mountain range.

Most of the events in this book unfold in Rui'an County (Map 1.2), which is located in the heart of Wenzhou. It is transected by the eastbound Feiyun River, which links eastern lowlands with vast mountainous areas in the west, and the southbound Tang canal. Smaller rivers crisscross the lowland plains in the east, carving it into closely populated patches of land. By 1949, Rui'an already had a population of 456,900, covering 1,360 square kilometers of land. That figure has now risen to about 1.19 million in population, covering 1, 271 square kilometers of land, as of the 2010 census.

Up to the mid-nineteenth century, most migrants entered by sea routes from Fujian, bringing with them gods from their ancestral homes. Adapting these gods to their new locale was an instrumental part of settling down and establishing new communities in Wenzhou. Territorial temples and ancestral halls set the rhythm of daily life in Wenzhou throughout late imperial times.[1] Historically, the most important yearly communal rituals were dragon boat racing (*hua longchuan*) and "touring the deities" (*taifo*).[2] The first is a ritual boat

[1] For religious life in Wenzhou in the late imperial and Republican eras, see Paul R. Katz, *Demon Hordes and Burning Boats: The Cult of Marshal Wen in Late Imperial Chekiang* (Albany: State University of New York Press, 1995); and Xu Hongtu and Kang Bao (Paul Katz), eds., *Pingyang Xiang, Cangnan Xiang chuantong minsu wenhua yanjiu* (Studies of traditional folk culture in Pingyang and Cangnan) (Beijing: Minzu chubanshe, 2005).

[2] Though dragon boat racing is mainly performed during the spring in the plains areas of Wenzhou, a similar ritual of Great Peace Dragon [Boat] (*taiping long*) is observed in mountainous

Maoism and Grassroots Religion. Xiaoxuan Wang, Oxford University Press (2020). © Oxford University Press.
DOI: 10.1093/oso/9780190069384.001.0001

Map 1.1. Wenzhou.

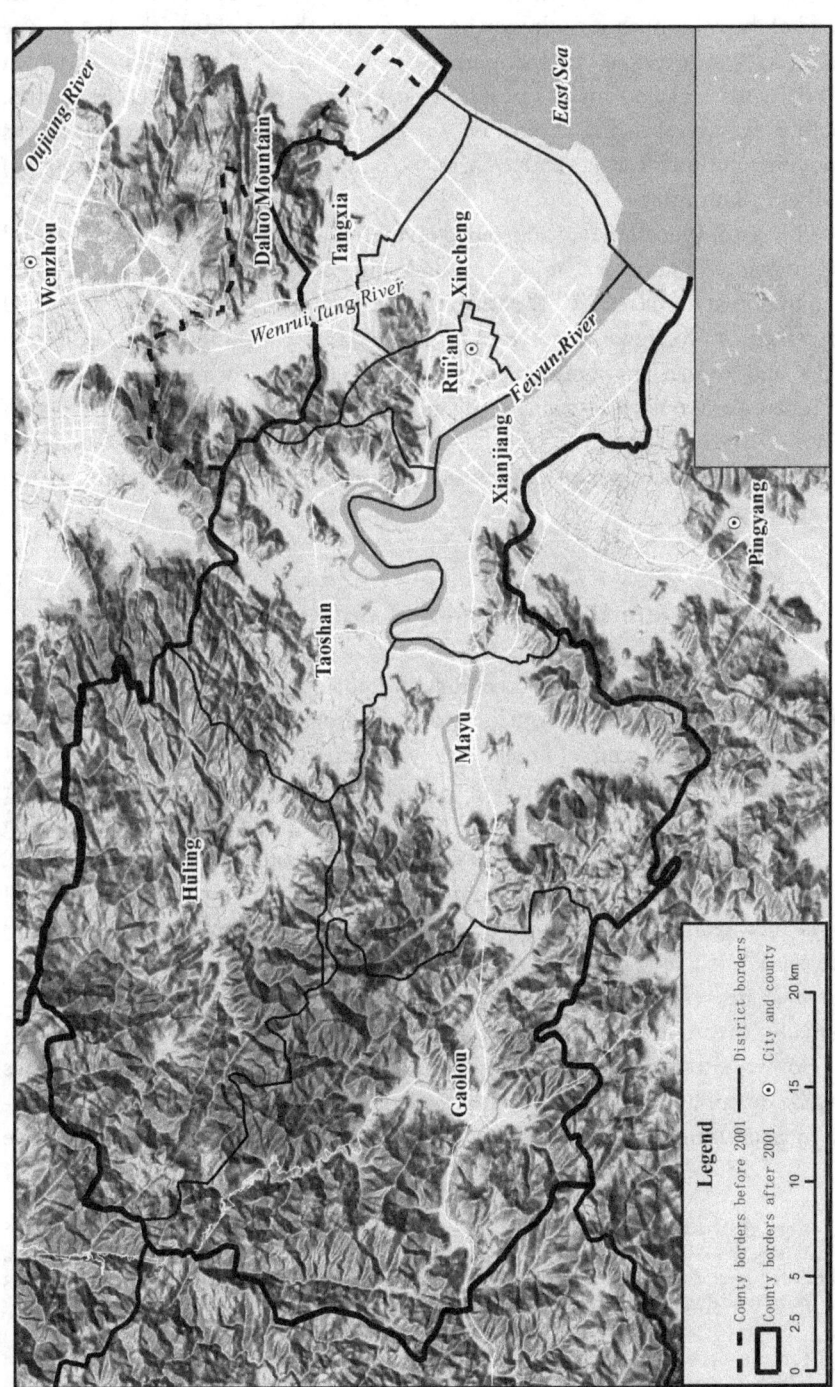

Map 1.2. Rui'an.

race between local communities, opening with a ritual procession that tours the head of the neighborhood's dragon boat to receive the blessing of the deities. The second, *taifo*, is a type of ritual parade common to southeast China in which participants make a tour of statues of local deities in their own communities. Both dragon boat racing and tours of deities were believed to prevent plagues and other natural disasters and to "bring blessings with great peace" (*bao taiping*) to the communities.

Villages in Wenzhou typically relied on their land to finance the operation and maintenance of temples, temple fairs, and ritual processions. Territorial temples and Buddhist monasteries were financed by a "common field," which was farmed or rented out for income (*miaozhong* and *sizhong*, meaning "temple common field" and "monastery common field," respectively). The common field might be purchased and owned by a single village, multiple villages, or a smaller group of people. "The head of affairs" (*shoushi*) charged with managing the common field was a rotating position, typically chosen from among the founding members and their heirs.

A Watershed Moment in Communal Religion

Throughout the late nineteenth century, religion was at the core of the political sphere and of everyday life. Both locals and the Qing government recognized deities as symbols and sources of power. Local deities were at times co-opted to secure local governance and consolidate the dominance of local elites. In 1855, for instance, the Taiping rebellion provoked a local Qu Zhenhan uprising in Yueqing County against local elites. Members of the elite invoked Lord Yang (*yangfuye*), the most prominent deity in the territorial cult of the region, as their symbol of resistance against the uprising. At their request, the Qing authorities endorsed stories of Lord Yang pacifying the Qu uprising and recognized the deity by conferring a new title on him in order to curb conflicts between local groups and to remedy governmental relations with local society.[3]

However, starting from the early twentieth century, village religious activities faced enormous challenges. In a critical change, the government shifted to classifying communal religious activities and referring to them in political discourse

---

areas, and the ritual of dragon lantern is observed in the winter. The ritual of Great Peace Dragon [Boat] is very similar to dragon boat racing in terms of ritual procedures, rituals texts, and purposes. The major difference is that the main body of the dragon boat in this ritual is made of paper. During the ritual, residents carry this type of paper dragon boat to travel through the community.

[3] Shih-Chieh Lo, "The Order of Local Things: Popular Politics and Religion in Modern Wenzhou, 1840–1940" (PhD dissertation, Brown University, 2010), Chapter 1.

as "superstition." This change affected territorial cults in particular.[4] First the Qing, then the Republican government initiated a series of anti-superstition campaigns in the name of modernization. When Western-style education and news media inculcated local students in the discourses of science, democracy, and progress, local deities such as Lord Yang and their temples in Wenzhou became the targets of encroachment and demolition. In the cities, strict prohibitions and lack of patronage ended certain annual rites and temple processions, such as the annual tour of the city god (*chenghuang*) in Rui'an's county seat.

This profound change in the relationship between the political and religious spheres shook the foundations of communal religion.[5] Local elites were split over whether to remain invested in temple activities or shift to new arenas of power, such as modern education. Nevertheless, traditional communal religion remained active, especially in villages. Rituals and processions continued, though less frequently than before. In villages, government maneuvers to curb religious practices did not gain enough support from local elites to be effective and had very little impact. They only served to "[line] policemen's pockets."[6]

From 1900 to 1937, around 40 percent of Buddhist temples and 12 percent of territorial temples listed in the city's Republican period gazetteer underwent reconstruction. Most of the reconstruction took place after 1911.[7] Because of the "temple-to-school" movement which had started in 1898 to push through religious and educational reforms,[8] a small portion of temples and ancestral halls were converted into schools or other public institutions. However, by 1937, out of a total of 609 entries in the temple (*miao*) entry of the "Religion" (*zongjiao*) section in the Rui'an Republican gazetteer, only ten territorial temples were being converted for use as schools or for other purposes (less than 2 percent).[9]

[4] Vincent Goossaert, "1898: The Beginning of the End for Chinese Religion?" *Journal of Asian Studies* 65, no. 2 (2006): 307–335.

[5] Lo, "The Order of Local Things," Chapter 5.

[6] See Paul R. Katz, *Religion in China and Its Modern Fate* (Waltham, MA: Brandeis University Press, 2014), 52–56. See also Zhang Gang, *Zhang Gang riji* (Zhang Gang's diaries) (Shanghai: Shanghai shehuikexueyuan chubanshe, 2003), 306–307 and Lo, "The Order of Local Things," Chapter 5.

[7] These numbers are based on the "Religion" section of *Minguo Rui'an Xian zhi gao*, a local gazetteer compiled in the period 1924–1948. Out of 352 Buddhist temples and Daoist pavilions in the "Buddhism" entry of the "Religion" section in the gazetteer, 143 were reconstructed between 1900 and 1937 (the year marking the beginning of the Second Sino-Japanese War), with 129 during the period 1911 (the year of Xinhai Revolution that toppled the Qing empire)–1937 and 14 during the period 1900–1910. Sixty-two out of 609 communal temples in the "temple [*miao*]" entry were reconstructed between 1900 and 1937, with 62 during the period 1911–1937 and 10 during the period 1900–1910. See Rui'an Xian xiuzhiju, *Rui'an Xian zhi gao* (Draft gazetteer of Rui'an County), daziben (big character version) (Rui'an: Rui'an Xian xiuzhiju, 1946–1948), 7–45, 58–75.

[8] For the "temple-to-school" campaign in the late Qing, see Vincent Goossaert, "1898: The Beginning of the End for Chinese Religion?" For the campaign in the early Republican period, see Prasenjit Duara, "Knowledge and Power in the Discourse of Modernity: The Campaigns against Popular Religion in Early 20th Century China," *Journal of Asian Studies* 50, no. 1 (1991): 75.

[9] Rui'an Xian xiuzhiju, *Rui'an Xian zhi gao*, daziben, 58–75.

This number likely only refers to cases of complete conversion, as it was more common for temples and schools to coexist in the same religious complex. Despite the "temple-to-school" efforts of the mid-1930s, a significant number of village temples and monasteries in Rui'an kept land holdings ranging from a few *mu* to several dozens of *mu*.[10] Most temples remained in operation as sites of communal religion.

The exact number of territorial temples and monasteries in the Wenzhou region in 1949 is unknown. A survey of the Rui'an City Government in 2010 recorded around 1,200 "unregistered" territorial temples and 153 "Daoist" temples (about 120 of which were territorial temples registered as Daoist temples).[11] It is very likely that the number of territorial temples in Rui'an in 1949 was considerably higher, at least 1,300 or more. A survey of Buddhist monasteries found at least 317 Buddhist sites remaining in 1957,[12] which suggests that active Buddhist monasteries were more numerous before 1949.[13]

Christianity Makes Inroads

While communal religious activities were waning under the influence of government campaigns, Christianity was experiencing a rapid rise. In the first half of the twentieth century, there was a steep increase in the number of churches, missionaries, and Christians in the Wenzhou region.

Some scholars trace the history of Christianity in Wenzhou back to the fourteenth century, when China was under Mongol rule.[14] Yet there are hardly any traces of Christianity in local history before the arrival of Christian missionaries in the late nineteenth century.

The 1860 Treaty of Nanking, put in place after the Qing empire's defeat in the Opium Wars, gave Western missionaries extensive rights to proselytize throughout China. This was when Catholic and Protestant missionaries (re) introduced Christianity to the Wenzhou region. Under the Treaty of Chefoo in 1876, Wenzhou became a treaty port and a stopping point for foreign ships. The China Merchants' Steam Navigation Company established a branch office there

---

[10]   Ibid., volume 9: "Religion."

[11]   These numbers do not include the number of temples/churches in Xianyan, Li'ao, and Meitou—three religiously very important towns that were incorporated into the municipal area of Wenzhou Prefecture in 2001.

[12]   These numbers perhaps only refer to those churches/temples that were still active at the time. See "Guanyu dangqian zongjiao huodong qingkuang de baogao" (Report on current religious activities), April 4, 1957, Rui'an City Archives 1-9-85: 65–68.

[13]   In 2010, the city had 228 registered Buddhist temples. This number does not include the number of temples/churches in Xianyan, Li'ao, and Meitou.

[14]   Mo Fayou, *Wenzhou Jidujiao shi* (History of Christianity in Wenzhou) (Hong Kong: Alliance Bible Seminary Press, 1998), 1–7.

in 1878 and a regular line between Wenzhou and Shanghai. In the years to follow, more shipping lines were established between Wenzhou and places such as Hong Kong, Guangzhou, Fuzhou, and Taiwan. New river lines were also created in the 1900s linking Wenzhou and its counties. These sea routes and inland river routes provided new ways of travel to, from, and within the region. The greater facility of travel would profoundly reshape local society, facilitating the dissemination of Christianity, among other changes.[15] In the last years of the Qing dynasty and throughout the Republican era, Protestantism and Catholicism firmly embedded themselves into the life of the region, becoming an integral part of Wenzhou society.[16]

Catholicism was (re)introduced to Wenzhou in the late 1860s. Among its early converts, many were former members of salvationist groups. A parish was established in 1880, which was then promoted to a diocese on the eve of 1949 in response to the expansion of the Catholic church in Wenzhou. The Methodist Church (of Great Britain) (*xundao gonghui*) was the first Protestant denomination to arrive in the area and very likely the largest one by 1949. At the eve of the Communist takeover, it had a headquarters and four pastorals consisting of twenty-one churches in all.

The second missionary group to arrive was the China Inland Mission (CIM) (*neidi hui*), an interdenominational Protestant missionary society founded by British evangelist Hudson Taylor. The China Jesus Independent Church (CJIC; *Zhongguo Yesujiao zili hui*), the Seventh-Day Adventist Church (*anxiri hui*), and the Assembly (*juhuichu*) were all latecomers. The Seventh-Day Adventist Church began its evangelical activities in Rui'an in the 1920s but did not build its first chapel in the county seat until 1930. The Seventh-Day Adventists established a church in Mayu in 1925 and then turned their focus to the Huling District in the northwestern mountains, where they established churches in Zhushan, Zhuyuan, and Dongkeng villages during the 1930s and 1940s.

The CJIC and the Assembly both grew out of the independent church movement in the early twentieth century but appeared in Rui'an during different periods. A group of former members of the Methodist Church created the first independent church in the county seat in 1914. However, the CJIC expanded

<hr/>

[15] Xiaoxuan Wang, "Yixiang, guxiang, qiaoxiang: liudong de Wenzhou shehui—yige lishi de kaocha" (Foreign land, native land, adoptive land—a fluid Wenzhou society from historical perspective), in *Jiangyi ji* (Collected writings in pursuit of learning), eds. Chen Ruihuan and Wu Tianyue (Shanghai: Fudan daxue chubanshe, 2016), 1–14; Zhang Zhicheng, ed., *Wenzhou huaqiao shi* (History of overseas Wenzhounese) (Beijing: Jinri Zhongguo chubanshe, 2009); Philip Kuhn, *Chinese among Others: Emigration in Modern Times* (Lanham, MD: Rowman & Littlefield, 2009), 335–341.

[16] Mo Fayou, *Wenzhou Jidujiao shi*; Li Shizhong, "Wanqing jiaohui shili de qieru yu difang quanli geju de yanhua" (The intrusion of Christian churches and the evolution of local power dynamics in the late Qing), *Shilin* 5 (2005): 39–47; and Lo, "The Order of Local Things," Chapter 3.

fastest in Huling in the following decades because there were no established churches to compete with there.[17] By 1949, it had established ten churches in Huling. The Shayang Church at Mayu, which was a branch of the Methodist Church, became independent in 1935.[18]

The Assembly (or Local Churches [difang jiaohui], or Little Flock [xiaoqun]) arrived in Rui'an even later. Its establishment and development occurred after the outbreak of the second Sino-Japanese War. It first set up a gathering point with little more than twenty people in the west gate of the county seat. In the 1940s, some former members of the Methodist Church and the CIM founded their own local assemblies in Xincheng and Xianjiang. To the Assembly, Huling was also a major site for evangelization; it continued to expand there, even during the civil war (1946–1949). Local assemblies were established in the villages of Jiangshan, Shangyang, and Kengkouyang in 1947. The town center of Huling and three other neighboring villages also organized local assemblies on the eve of liberation.[19]

At first, the spread of Christianity in Wenzhou met with fierce resistance. Many early converts, like former sectarians, were members of marginalized or disadvantaged social groups who sought protection in the church.[20] As they appropriated the status of church members to reassert themselves in so-cial life, non-Christian locals responded to their presence with hostility against Christianity. Christians refused to participate in traditional communal practices such as dragon boat racing, escalating the tension between Christians and non-Christians. By the turn of the twentieth century, resentment against Christians and the church, mixed with nationalist sentiments, stirred up a series of violent attacks on churches and Christians.[21]

Yet the Protestant and Catholic churches eventually found ways to reach out to non-Christian local society, through initiatives like ritual healings and exorcisms. Exorcism and ritual healing were common occurrences in evangelical work, though they were rarely recorded in the writings of foreign missionaries in Wenzhou. A native pastor, Chen Shangsheng, wrote: "The church in Rui'an has long been known for opening the door of evangelization by curing illness and

---

[17] For example, Tangxia and Xincheng are both in the plain areas, and were respectively the strongholds of the Methodist Church and the CIM. Mayu to the south of Feiyun River was the base of the Catholic Church. The CJIC had other competitors such as the Seventh-Day Adventist Church and later the Assembly.

[18] Rui'an jiaohui, Rui'an jiaohui shi (A history of Rui'an church), internal document, 1998, 6–9.

[19] Ibid., 10–11.

[20] Lo, "The Order of Local Things," Chapter 3, especially 102–135.

[21] Lo, "The Order of Local Things," Chapters 3 and 4; Li Shizhong, "Wanqing jiaohui shili de qieru yu difang quanli geju de yanhua"; Wang Lei, "Shangdi yu zuzong: Yongjia Xian Fenglinzhuang de Jidujiao, zongzu yu shequ zhengzhi (1860–1896)" (God and ancestors: Protestant churches, lin-eages, and communal politics in Fenglinzhuang, Yongjia County, 1860–1896) (MA thesis, East China Normal University, 2013).

expelling demons (*yi bing gan gui*). . . . When adherents in this county joined the Church, it was most likely (*shi you ba jiu*) because of either illness or demons."[22]

Chen was serving the Methodist Church of Tangxia town center in 1937 when the head of nearby Xiantan Township and his entire family converted to Christianity.[23] It was unusual at that time for a local official to become a Christian. Chen recorded their story of conversion: "Early this month, Shaoxian, younger brother of Du Shaofu, the [Xiantan] town head, who is nineteen, suddenly went insane, screaming and swearing aloud, crying and laughing uncontrollably. The doctors' efforts were to no avail and the deities showed no efficacy. Therefore, they came to our church. People in church willingly accepted their request and prayed all day and night. In the name of Jesus Christ, demons were repelled and the illness was cured." Shaoxian's parents and brothers, including Shaofu, who witnessed the miracle, then decided to convert to Christianity.

Christian preachers such as Pastor Chen, like Buddhist monks and Daoist priests, presented themselves as healers to attract potential converts. Pastor Lin Hongbing of CJIC explained why ritual healing was important: "Fortunately relying on the power of prayers; [people] confessed and repented; illness cured and demons expelled . . . the Holy Spirit must be operating through it."[24] "It is difficult to find a doctor in the countryside when people are sick. They all believe Jesus is a great doctor (*da yisheng*) and accept the gospel. When someone is ill, they would trust and rely on (*xin kao*) Jesus [for treatment]; [the sick person] would usually recover."[25]

The practice of presenting the church as a local source for healing was sustained by a growing number of indigenous church leaders and preachers. The Protestant Church in Wenzhou was among the most thoroughly indigenized churches in China before 1949. Driven by a considerable group of volunteer native preachers and church leaders, a significant number of financially and administratively self-reliant Protestant communities came into being.

Partly for practical reasons, the Methodist Church and the CIM in Wenzhou were already emphasizing and promoting the self-administration and self-support of local Christian communities before the national wave of independent church movement in the 1920s and 1930s, "All missionaries live in the city of Wenzhou . . . by far the heavier burden of evangelizing this district lies upon the shoulder of the local preachers. These form the backbone of the mission,"[26]

---

[22] Chen Shangsheng, "Xiantan Xiang xiangzhang quanjia guizhu" (The whole family of Xiantan Township head converted). *Xiaduo yuekan* 1, no. 6 (1937): 36.

[23] Ibid.

[24] Lin Hongbin, "Wenzhou Aojiang Rui'an budao zhi jieguo" (The fruits of sermons in Aojiang and Rui'an of Wenzhou), *Tongwenbao: Yesujiao jiating xinwen*, 1550 (1933): 7.

[25] Ibid.

[26] A. H. Sharman, "Rural Evangelism in the Wenchow District," in *China Mission Year Book 1917* (Shanghai: The Christian Literature Society for China, 1917), 358–359.

wrote A. H. Sharman of the Methodist Church in 1917. "These local preachers chiefly represent the farmer class . . . not well educated. . . ." In addition, "another class of men that helps greatly in evangelizing the district is the 'church leader.' This is generally one to each church, appointed by the circuit meeting. He is consulted on all local matters, settles troubles between Christians and non-Christians, collects the offerings of the members for church expenses, and frequently preaches when the man appointed does not arrive. His work is always voluntary. He is in fact, as in name, the pillar of the church."[27] With this method, "it will be observed that while the churches of the district have more than doubled, the number of missionaries has not increased since 1900."[28] The CIM used very similar administrative structures, with the only difference being that they probably relied even more on voluntary preachers. In 1920, the CIM branch in Wenzhou had 211 voluntary preachers but only 44 salaried preachers.[29]

The first independent church in Wenzhou was the CJIC, established in the 1910s. The CJIC's membership and number of gathering places in Wenzhou made up nearly half of its national organization in the 1920s.[30] CJIC churches were financially and administratively independent. All church leaders and preachers were volunteers. Another independent church, the Assembly, adopted a similar system of voluntary preachers; its followers in Wenzhou in the early 1950s accounted for about a quarter of its national organization.[31] "Preachers et al. are all voluntary. They are dispatched to and take turns to preach in each place."[32]

Indigenization efforts before 1949 left Wenzhou Christianity with a history of financial self-reliance and a large pool of village church leaders, including church elders (*zhanglao*) and deacons (*zhishi*) in charge of administering Protestant communities, as well as preachers who were charged with evangelical work. Both financial independence and local leadership were crucial for Protestant churches to withstand the test of the turbulent Mao years, as I will show in the following chapters.

---

[27] Ibid., 360.

[28] Ibid., 364.

[29] "Work in the Wenchow Prefecture (Chekiang Province)," *China's Millions* (North American Edition) (Toronto: China Inland Mission, 1921), 86–87.

[30] Zhi Huaxin, ed., *Wenzhou Jidujiao* (Wenzhou Christianity) (Hangzhou: Zhejiang Sheng Jidujiao xiehui, 2000), 20.

[31] Zhu Yujing, "Guojia tongzhi, difang zhengzhi yu Wenzhou de Jidujiao" (State rule, local politics and Christianity in Wenzhou) (PhD dissertation, Chinese University of Hong Kong, 2011), 76–77.

[32] Yu Guozhen, *Zhongguo Yesujiao zilihui dagang* (The charter of China Jesus Independent Church), 26. Cited by Zhu Jianzhong, "Cong Wenzhou kan chuantong de jicheng he chuangxin" (The inheritance and innovation of tradition from the vantage of Wenzhou), http://www.chinesetheology.com/ZhuJZh/WenZhouChurchesNTraditions.htm#_ftn17 (accessed on May 4, 2018).

The Catholic Church in Wenzhou also relied very much on local catechists. Their approach developed during the tenure of French priest Cyprien Aroud of the Congregation of the Mission at Wenzhou parish from 1899 to 1929, and, like the Protestant reliance on local preachers, it proved successful.[33] However, unlike the Protestant approach, the Catholic strategy was not designed to encourage the self-administration of local Catholic communities. Most catechists started to be educated and trained as young children before being dispatched to out-stations; they were all paid workers, not volunteers selected among active members of the church. The Wenzhou parish set up a hierarchical system among the catechists, the stated purpose of which was to "guarantee complete control over the catechists."[34] In local Protestant communities, church elders played a pivotal role in administrative work and facilitating communication with non-Christians, but they played no role in the official Catholic approach. In finance, administration, and ritual services, all local Catholic groups and stations relied much more heavily on foreign churches in comparison to Protestant churches.

By 1949, Zhejiang had about 200,000 Christians, the largest number of any province in China, and 41.5 percent of these were concentrated in Wenzhou.[35] In Rui'an, the number of Catholic and Protestant churches jumped from 28 to 108 between 1911 and 1937.[36] By 1949, the six Protestant denominations had a total of 8,170 members spread across 59 churches (*tang*) and 37 gathering points (*dian*).[37] The Rui'an parish of the Catholic Church at the time had a parish church in the county seat and 19 branch churches in the countryside with a total of 3,093 members.[38]

Salvationist Tradition in Its Heyday

Trans-village and transregional sectarian traditions were not as visible as communal religious traditions, but for a long time they were also an important part of religious communities in late imperial Wenzhou. In the mid-nineteenth century, the crises provoked by the Taiping rebellion led to two local uprisings: the Qu

[33] Wenzhou parish was promoted to Wenzhou diocese in March 1949.

[34] Cyprien Aroud, "Catechist Work in Wenchow," *Catholic Missions*, 1917, 153. See also "Wenzhou jiaoqu de chuanjiao sishi" (Catechists of Wenzhou diocese). http://www.tzjwzjq.com/Look_History. aspx?MID=22 (accessed on May 4, 2018).

[35] Ying Fuk-Tsang, "Zhongguo Jidujiao de quyu fazhan: 1918, 1949, 2004" (The regional development of Protestant Christianity in China: 1918, 1949 and 2004), *Hanyu Jidujiao xueshu lunping* (Sino-Christian studies), 3: 171. Ying's data come from new local gazetteers published by the local government.

[36] Rui'an Xian xiuzhiju, *Rui'an Xian zhi gao* (Republican Rui'an gazetteer), daziben, 1–6.

[37] Rui'an jiaohui, *Rui'an jiaohui shi*, 11.

[38] "Tangqu lishi" (Parish history), http://www.tzjwzjq.com/Look_History.aspx?MID=30 (accessed on November 20, 2019).

Zhenhan uprising in Yueqing in 1855 and the Golden Coin Association (*jinqian hui*) in Pingyang in 1861. Both were connected to the sectarian traditions of southern Zhejiang.[39]

Then, in the first half of the twentieth century, "redemptive societies" burst onto the national stage, seeing immense growth in their number of followers, spheres of activity, and their engagement with local and national politics.[40] These new syncretic religious movements, like the Way of Former Heaven (*xiantian dao*) or the Fellowship of Goodness (*tongshan she*), inherited elements of the late imperial salvationist and millenarian traditions.[41] Yet they were also engaged in a deliberate renewal of Chinese tradition, appropriating and reinventing discourses of science, civilization, and philanthropy, especially from Christian churches.[42]

During the same period in Wenzhou, these new syncretic movements were flourishing alongside the direct heirs of the salvationist and millenarian traditions: the Seven Stars Teaching (*qixing hui*), the Yellow Yang Teaching (*huangyang jiao*), and the Big Sword Association (*dadao hui*), among others. Local salvationist groups accrued numerous followers, vastly extending their territory. Their growth throughout the Sino-Japanese War and the Civil War likely surpassed even the rapid expansion of Christianity. The Wenzhou government identified about forty sectarian movements that were active in the region in the early 1950s.[43]

Local branches of nation-wide redemptive societies developed in Wenzhou no earlier than the 1920s. The Way of Pervading Unity (*yiguan dao*), one of the largest redemptive societies flourishing over most of China, for instance, arrived in Wenzhou during the Anti-Japanese War (1937–1945). They were usually based in or near county seats. As elsewhere in the country, these societies engaged in

---

[39] Lo, "The Order of Local Things," Chapter 2.

[40] Chan, *Religious Trends in Modern China*; Thomas David Dubois, *The Sacred Village: Social Change and Religious Life in Rural North China* (Honolulu: University of Hawai'i Press, 2005); David A. Palmer, "Dao and Nation: Li Yujie—May Fourth Activist, Daoist Cultivator, and Redemptive Society Patriarch in Mainland China and Taiwan," in *Daoism in the Twentieth Century: Between Eternity and Modernity*, eds. David A. Palmer and Xun Liu (Berkeley: University of California Press, 2012), 173–195.

[41] Prasenjit Duara uses "redemptive societies" to refer to those syncretic religious movements in the twentieth centuries. See Prasenjit Duara, "The Discourse of Civilization and Pan-Asianism," *Journal of World History* 12, no. 1 (2000): 117–126. In this book I use "salvationist religion," suggested by David Palmer as an umbrella category to contain redemptive societies and traditional salvationist groups. Though both pursued self-salvation and held millenarian beliefs, they are significantly different, especially in ways of operation and proselytization, organizational structure, and theologies. For "salvationist religion," see David Palmer, "Chinese Redemptive Societies and Salvationist Religion: Historical Phenomenon or Sociological Category?" *Journal of Chinese Ritual, Theatre and Folklore* 172 (2011): 21–72.

[42] Ibid.

[43] *Longwan Qu shizhi bianzuan weiyuanhui* and *Longwan Qu zhi bianjibu, Longwan Qu zhi* (Longwan District gazetteer) (Beijing: Zhonghua shuju, 2013), 458.

meditation and the cultivation of morality and tended to appeal to businessmen and local gentry.[44]

In the countryside, among peasants, traditional salvationist groups enjoyed much greater popularity than redemptive societies. Peasants made up the bulk of believers in salvationist religions. Within each local group, these religious societies had hierarchical arrangements of various forms, such as center-altars (*zongtan*) and sub-altars (*fentan*),[45] but the groups were basically independent of each other, without close ties. The salvationist religious societies were loosely organized, without a coherent and unified hierarchical structure.

The Yellow Yang Teaching originated in Rui'an and was an important presence there. It also had many unaffiliated factions dispersed across several counties in Wenzhou. The Yellow Yang Teaching is said to have been created during the reign of Guangxu (1875–1908) in the late Qing period by Huang Yaopan, a former follower of the Non-Action Teaching (*wuwei jiao*) from Shantouxia Village in Mayu District, when Huang secluded himself for meditation in the Daluo Mountains of Tangxia District. In 1922 the Teaching split into two factions, the Zhu (Qimei) and the Li (Binwen), which both brought the teachings to nearby Yueqing County. In 1928, Peng Chongcai, a former follower of the Yellow Yang Teaching, formed his own teaching in Xianjiang District (the eponymous Peng Yang Teaching). In the late 1920s, another follower, Chen Changman, formed another faction in Mayu. Chen took over Tianfu Temple (*tianfu miao*) in Aodi Village, Shuntai Township, and rebuilt the temple into a regional center of pilgrimage.

Like the Yellow Tang Teaching, the Seven Stars Teaching also originated in Wenzhou. Its history traces back to at least the early nineteenth century. It was reportedly created in Dayang Temple (*dayang miao*) in the border region of Lishui, Jinyun, and Qingtian Counties in southern Zhejiang, where it initially appeared as the "Dayang Mountains Teaching" (*dayangshan jiao*), also known as the "Twelve Pace Teaching" (*shi'erbu jiao*) and the "Non-Action Teaching."[46] By the eve of the second Sino-Japanese War, several different denominations were active under the name "Seven Stars Teaching," each with its own network of

---

[44] Chen Murong et al., eds., *Qingtian Xian zhi* (Qingtian gazetteer) (Hangzhou: Zhejiang renmin chubanshe, 1990), 64; Yang Dianzhong et al., eds., *Yueqing Xian gong'an zhi* (A history of public security in Yueqing) (Beijing: Haiyan chubanshe, 1993), 34; Zhan Rujian et al., eds., *Qingtian Xian gong'an zhi* (History of public security in Qingtian County) (Hangzhou: Zhejiang renmin chubanshe, 2006), 176.

[45] *Tan* is literally an altar. Here it refers to a branch.

[46] It is unclear whether these names were self-referential or state-imposed labels. Most names of popular sects appearing in official documents of the late imperial period, according to Barend ter Haar, were just generic terms or labels. This discovery should apply to traditional salvationist groups in the twentieth century. See Barend J. ter Haar, *The White Lotus Teachings in Chinese Religious History* (Honolulu: University of Hawai'i Press, 1992).

altars covering the whole of the neighboring mountains of Wencheng, Qingtian, and Jingning.

Joining a local religious society was a simple process. To become a member of the Yellow Yang Teaching, one only had to take a vow before an incense table in the presence of an inductor, with a teacher's guidance. New disciples were sometimes asked to pay a membership fee. Members met at various dates, such as the birthdays of Guanyin, the Buddha, and the founder of the teaching, known as the Yellow Yang Master, to recite scriptures and hold a purification feast (*dazhai*).[47] Like the nation-wide salvationist and millenarian religions, teachers of indigenous societies used revelations, scriptures, and various other tools.

The eschatological messages of the Yellow Yang Teaching came from the famous apocalyptic *wugongjing* (the Scripture of the Five Lords) as well as from local culture, particularly the *shaobingge* ("Song of Baked Flatbread") allegedly written by Liu Ji (also known as Liu Bowen, 1311–1375), a famous minister and local dignitary of the early Ming dynasty (1368–1644). The major prophecy of the Yellow Yang Teaching was the ending of the three kalpas, a term originating in Buddhist cosmology to refer to a long period (an "era" or "epoch"). The Yellow Yang Teaching advertised itself as being able to help people avert the catastrophe that would come at the end of a kalpa. One Yellow Yang message read: "September 23 will be a gloomy day. The seven days and nights [thereafter will be] rainy and dark. Only the pious will be saved. Those who do not believe will lose their lives. A cave at the foot of the Yellow Yang Mountains can hide eighteen thousand people. Only those who arrive early will have a place; those who arrive late will die on the road."[48]

The Entanglement of Communist Forces with Religion

In the shifting political sands in the period leading up to 1949, we cannot neglect the rise of two major political players: the Nationalist and Communist parties. From 1911 to 1927, Zhejiang was under the control of warlords, though each region retained strong autonomy. Locals founded the county branches of the Nationalist and Communist parties almost simultaneously at the end of 1926, less than a year before the Northern Expedition army of the Nationalist Party entered Rui'an in early 1927. In this short period, the Communists and the

---

[47] "Pingyangkeng Qu fandong huidaomen qingkuang chubu diaocha zongjie baogao" (Concluding report on the preliminary investigation of reactionary societies, teachings and sects in Pingyangkeng District), October 30, 1952, Rui'an City Archives 45-2-4: 86–87. See also Zhan, *Qingtian Xian gong'an zhi*, 177–178.

[48] "Fandong Qixing hui cankao ziliao" (Reference materials on the counter-revolutionary Seven Stars Teaching), 1952, Wencheng County Archives 1-4-8: 56.

Nationalists worked hand in hand to attack established forces (in particular the powerful county chamber of commerce) and facilitate the arrival of the Northern Expedition army.

In April 1927, after Chiang Kai-shek unified China, he ordered a purge of Communist influence and leftists within Nationalist organizations. Some Communists in Wenzhou were arrested and killed. Many went into hiding in the mountains. Amid the famine and unrest of 1929 in southern Zhejiang, Communists eventually coordinated a group of peasant militias, the "Thirteenth Division of the Red Army." They staged a wide range of insurgencies and attacks in southern Zhejiang, including Taoshan and Mayu (Rui'an), before their main force was eliminated in May 1932. Organized Communist activities and guerrilla warfare resumed only when another stream of Communist guerrillas retreated from Jiangxi into the mountains of southern Zhejiang.

In late 1935, after the Nationalist Army defeated Red Army troops in the border area between Jiangxi and Fujian, a group of Communist forces led by Su Yu and Liu Ying went east into Zhejiang to wage guerrilla warfare. They eventually implanted themselves there, setting up revolutionary bases in the mountainous borders of a dozen counties in Wenzhou and Lishui, where there were fewer Nationalist garrisons and they had greater access to the people. Within Rui'an at the time, the Communists were most active in the Gaolou and Huling mountains of Mayu District and the Daluo Mountains north of Tangxia District. Then, in 1938, as the Communist and Nationalist parties joined forces to fight the Japanese, most of the southern Zhejiang guerrillas left to join the New Fourth Army. Liu Ying was imprisoned and died in Wenzhou in May 1942. In spite of this, Communist forces succeeded in expanding to the coastal plains of southern Zhejiang. By the eve of 1949, the southern Zhejiang guerrillas covered eleven counties in Wenzhou and Lishui, south of Taizhou, and a few counties in northern Fujian.[49]

When Nationalist and Communist forces put down roots in Wenzhou, the prevalence of religious followers and religious sites was such that they inevitably came into contact with them. Communist guerrillas extensively used public spaces, territorial temples, and Buddhist monasteries as a cover for their activities, especially in mountainous areas. Today one can easily find traces of the Communist forces' encounter with religion before 1949 in the histories of certain territorial temples, Buddhist monasteries, and Three-Self churches. Territorial temples and Buddhist monasteries openly celebrate the history of their engagement with Communism before 1949 (Photo 1.1). The Three-Self movement in some respects also celebrates the history of their engagement with

[49] Gregor Benton, *Mountain Fires: The Red Army's Three-Year War in South China, 1934–1938* (Berkeley: University of California Press, 1994), 209–233.

Photo 1.1. The Palace of Miraculous Blessing (*lingyou dian*), Yutan Village, Rui'an (2019). The sign on the center reads: "Site of the First Southern Zhejiang Congress of the Chinese Communist Party."
Source: Author.

Communism before 1949, though their engagement with the Nationalist Party or the Nationalist government is largely missing from the records.

Both Communist and Nationalist forces tended to keep religious communities at arm's length. Some Nationalist Party members even became fervent supporters of local anti-superstition campaigns, and caused the destruction of temples in Rui'an and Yueqing in 1928.[50] However, neither the Communists nor the Nationalists excluded members of religious organizations from joining their parties, nor did they refrain altogether from engaging with local religious communities. For instance, You Shuxun, one of the founding members of the CJIC in Wenzhou, was allegedly persuaded to become a member of the Communist Party and also a founding member of the party's independent division in Wenzhou in 1926. Zhang Dasheng, an Adventist who taught at the Three Cultivation (*sanyu*) school run by the Adventist Church, was a covert liaison officer for the

---

[50] Lo, "The Order of Local Things," Chapter 5, especially 226–227 and 265–272.

Communist guerrillas. In the 1930s and 1940s, he turned the Three Cultivation school and his own home into a virtual liaison point for the Communist guerrilla forces. He hosted numerous meetings of the Zhejiang Party Committee there and transferred resources and personnel to guerrilla bases in the mountains.[51]

The most noticeable interactions between religious communities and Communist forces occurred in Wenzhou's western mountains, where the Communists established guerrilla base camps in the 1930s and 1940s. In Huling, Gaolou, parts of Mayu, and Tangxia in Rui'an, Protestant preachers and salvationist groups frequently competed with the Communist guerrillas to expand in the same areas.

There was crossover between church membership and Communist activism. Lei Gaosheng, one of the founders of the Southern Zhejiang Red Army (formed in the Wenzhou region in 1928), was from a village in Mayu where Protestants were very active. Many of his family members were Christians. After Lei's death in 1930, his sons and their families also converted to Christianity.[52] In Zhuyuan Village in Huling District, some villagers were active in both the party and the church, and a few even became party cadres. It was not until 1949 that villagers in Zhuyuan had to choose between the church and the party. Five or six Christians eventually withdrew from the party.[53]

The encounters between Communist forces and salvationist groups were much more intricate. The emergence of the Communist guerrillas certainly eclipsed the expansion of local salvationist groups. When the Communist guerrillas became active in Shuntai Township in Mayu, they used Tianfu Temple in Aodi Village as a shelter and military base. Chen Changman, the founder of one of the Yellow Yang Teachings who had previously taken over the temple as faction headquarters, eventually abandoned the temple out of "anger against" the guerrillas. In 1946 he left for Dragon Pool Temple (*longtan si*), in the Daluo Mountains, Tangxia, where the Yellow Yang Teaching was said to have originated. One of his disciples, Xie Qingxian, soon followed Chen to the Daluo Mountains.[54] Shortly thereafter, Xie founded his own faction, which became the largest Yellow Yang Teaching faction after 1949.

The expansion of Communist guerrillas halted the growth of the Seven Stars Teaching in the region, as it did with the Yellow Yang Teaching, and even silenced

---

[51] http://www.wzscnxx.com/Art/Art_74/Art_74_2087.aspx (accessed on May 4, 2018).

[52] "Zhongguo Jidujiao xundao gonghui Wenzhou jiaoqu Pingyang lianqu ge hui dengjishu" (The register of churches of the Pingyang affiliated district of the Methodist Church's Wenzhou ecclesiastical district), July 24, 1954, Pingyang County Archives 10-6-100: 88–89. Lei's sons listed in this document have the surname of Shi, which is Lei's original surname.

[53] Shu Chengqian, *Wushi nian jiaohui shenghuo huiyi* (Memoirs of fifty years' life in the church), internal reference materials ("neibu cankao ziliao"), 2002, Chapter 15.

[54] Rui'an City Archives 45-2-4: 83–89.

the Seven Stars organization for a time. Huangliao Township in Nantian, where the Seven Stars Teaching had been most active, became a guerrilla base area in the mid-1930s. Long Yue and many other leaders of the southern Zhejiang Communist guerrillas had stayed there. As the Communists and salvationists competed for influence in the same area, both facing attacks by the Nationalists, their relationship was neither entirely hostile nor entirely collaborative. Each organization acted in its own interests. Therefore it was not surprising that some of the Seven Stars Teaching's leaders even joined the Communist guerrillas.[55]

Another local group, the Big Sword Association, had a highly dramatic entanglement with the Communist forces. The association was a militarized salvationist group which emerged from the 1940s uprising to resist excessive taxation and the military draft. It was most active in Pingyang (the present-day counties of Pingyang and Cangnan), but also spread to the districts of Mayu and Gaolou in the western and southern parts of Rui'an. As Prasenjit Duara and Joseph Esherick found in the north China plains,[56] the Big Sword Association was deeply rooted in the region's martial arts and sectarian traditions, especially from Pingyang.[57] The Nationalist government brutally suppressed the association and killed several thousand people. Following this, the remaining groups of the association split among the Nationalist government, the Communist guerrillas, and the Japanese occupation forces. Communist guerrillas made considerable efforts to absorb the remainder of the association's forces. They succeeded with part of the group led by Cai Yuexiang and maintained close relations with some of the association's other groups.[58]

Conclusion

In the first half of the twentieth century, nation-building efforts by regimes and political groups turned temples into a symbol of the decay of Chinese civilization and made them targets of political and military appropriation. As in much of China, this onslaught on religious activities shook the foundations of traditional communal religion in Rui'an and Wenzhou. Yet local religion continued to brim with vitality. Salvationist religious traditions broadly defined, both local and national, swept through the region at a remarkable pace—largely, perhaps,

---

[55] Wencheng County Archives 1-4-8: 51, 55.

[56] Prasenjit Duara, *Culture, Power and the State: Rural Society in North China, 1900–1942* (Stanford, CA: Stanford University Press, 1988), Chapter 5; Joseph W. Esherick, *The Origins of the Boxer Uprising* (Berkeley: University of California Press, 1988).

[57] Lo, "The Order of Local Things," 154–155 and Chapter 2.

[58] For a detailed history of the Big Sword Association, see Tao Dagong, ed., *Dadao hui shimo (Cangnan Xian wenshi ziliao di qi ji)* (A concise history of the Big Sword Association [Cangnan historical materials, volume 7]) (Cangnan: Cangnan Xian zhengxie wenshi ziliao weiyuanhui, 1992).

due to the greater social uncertainty brought about by political turbulence and wars. Protestant churches, the Catholic Church, traditional salvationist groups, and redemptive societies all found a niche. Their numbers of local followers rapidly grew.

Communist forces stayed close to local peasant society, including their religious communities. Though the Wenzhou region was not under Communist rule until 1949, it had been exposed to Communist influence since the late 1920s. The Communist guerrillas there operated like one of many players in a shifting local political ecology. As this chapter demonstrates, the Communists often used religious sites as shelter and competed with religious groups for followers. They both clashed and collaborated with religious groups, depending on the circumstances.

Many other parts of China that were not located in the Communist Party's major revolutionary bases may have been like Rui'an and Wenzhou at that time. The Communists were hostile to religious groups from an ideological standpoint, but they could not overpower them. Furthermore, they did not make it a priority to subdue religion. Strategically, they were willing to exploit the material and human resources of religious groups when they considered it necessary to do so. The 1949 Communist takeover on the national stage may not have essentially changed the ways that the Communist Party perceived religion. But as Chapter 2 will show, the revolution that it initiated soon brought about fundamental changes to the local religious sphere.

2

The Land Revolution and Religious Communities in the Early 1950s

On May 7, 1949, the Communist guerrilla force of southern Zhejiang, largely commanded by locals, entered the city of Wenzhou after peace negotiations with Nationalist forces, leaving behind the mountainous areas in the west where they had been entrenched for many years. Over the following days, Nationalist forces in the counties surrounding downtown Wenzhou followed suit, ceding ground to the Communist guerrillas. Rui'an was "liberated" on May 9. Soon after, someone informed the Communist forces against Jiang Songling, a former committee member of Lord Chen Temple (*chenfu miao*), a prominent religious site located outside the south gate of the county seat. Jiang had served on the temple management committee for many years, acting as its chairman from 1942 to 1948. He had also been the president of the county chamber of commerce and a member of the first county council elected in 1946.

The informer, perhaps another member of the temple management committee, accused Jiang of embezzlement and profiteering while serving on the committee. The accusation mainly involved contracts that Jiang signed with tenants of temple estates in 1942 and 1943, in the chaotic period when China was still fighting the war of resistance against Japan. Jiang was alleged to have taken money from negotiating and renewing contracts.[1] A request was made to investigate the property issue concerning Lord Chen Temple.

The new county government, formed days after the Communist forces entered the county, responded swiftly. They detained Jiang and ordered the temporary seizure of all of the temple's assets. In order to reorganize the temple's properties, the temple management committee invited Xu, the principal of a local elementary school situated on temple land, to join the committee as its new chairman. In October, after a dozen or so meetings, the new committee management invalidated all prior contracts signed with Jiang and asked tenants to sign new contracts with the temple under different terms. Enforcing the new contracts,

---

[1] "Rui'an Xian Chenfu miao miaochan zhengli weiyuanhui guanyu shenhe miaochan chubu juedingshu yu zuza hetong" (Rui'an County Lord Chen Temple property management committee's preliminary decision on temple property audit and rental agreement), October 1949, Rui'an City Archives 173-1-1.

Maoism and Grassroots Religion. Xiaoxuan Wang, Oxford University Press (2020). © Oxford University Press.
DOI: 10.1093/oso/9780190069384.001.0001

however, dragged on for a while and led to more board meetings. Some tenants refused to comply. In September 1950, almost a year after the establishment of the central Communist government in Beijing, the board was still meeting to discuss unresolved issues.

Those who informed on Jiang may have perceived the Communist takeover as an opportunity to settle old scores, to reshuffle temple leadership, or perhaps to revive temple activities. The war of resistance, followed by the civil war, had hit the temple hard. The tenants on the temple estates ran businesses in the south gate market, many of them dry goods shops or seafood stalls. Most members of the management committee, including Jiang, were also tenants of the temple estates. Yet few could have anticipated the fate that soon befell the temple, its properties, or the committee members themselves.

In April 1950, the new county government of Rui'an began experimenting with land reform in a few Rui'an townships. Then, in October of that year, about a month after the last recorded meeting of Lord Chen Temple board, the Rui'an County Government embarked on full-scale land reform. Within a few years, Lord Chen Temple fell into decay. Though what happened to its members is unclear, it appears that the board committee had ceased to function. The county's water transportation office took over the dilapidated temple buildings and turned them into a warehouse sometime around 1955. Neighborhood residents failed to claim back the temple in the 1990s due to the lack of legal standing of their claim—similar situations occurred in many other local communities at that time. They could only house the statue of Lord Chen in a cramped building not far from the south gate market.[2]

The issue of religious property, especially land, is central to "the religious question" in modern China. Land was also at the heart of Mao's revolution. This chapter explores the repercussions of the ferocious land reform campaign (1951–1952) for religious life in Rui'an. The intent of the campaign was to thoroughly restructure local society through the redistribution of land and wealth. As an economic revolution and political mobilization on a grand scale, land reform directly targeted the assets of religious organizations, jolting the foundations of communal religion in Wenzhou. The purge of traditional rural elites dealt a huge blow to the leadership and patronage of religious communities. Yet the effects of land reform on religious life were far from clear-cut and uniform. The uneven impact of the campaign pervaded various dimensions of religious life across the spectrum of religious affiliations and activities. This chapter follows

---

[2] "Jiang Xinmin weiyuan: Guanyu Damadao Xinfandianqian jumin laoxiehui huodong changsuo bixu geiyu jiejue" (Council member Jiang Xinmin: [The government] must settle activity space for elderly people associations in Damadao and Xinfandianqian), March 25, 1995, Rui'an City Archives 109-14-23: 78–80.

the trajectories of the major religious traditions in Rui'an in the early and mid-1950s, exploring the different ways in which they were affected by land reform and highlighting the factors that contributed to these differences.

Decay and Contraction of Communal Religious Traditions

As discussed in Chapter 1, campaigns against religion dated back to the turn of the twentieth century, including the appropriation and conversion of religious buildings and land assets to benefit secular institutions.[3] But the impact of land reform in the early 1950s was much more profound than that of any previous government encroachments on religion. The nascent Communist state saw communal religion and culture as "a principal obstacle to the establishment of a 'disenchanted' world of reason and plenty."[4] It also wanted to extract revenue from communal religion to finance its modernization programs.

However, there is another important difference. The Qing and Nationalist governments in the first half of the twentieth century never launched a concerted attack on all religions. They mainly targeted communal temple estates, and their appropriations of temple lands and buildings were carried out in the name of eliminating "superstition" and funding modern education. They were not overtly attempting to overturn the traditional structures of local society.

Under the late Qing and Nationalist governments, the conversion of communal temples and its properties was a much less violent process than it would be under the Communist government. It was spearheaded by local elites with government endorsement and encouragement. However, the Communist government, with the assistance of its extended bureaucratic system and peripheral organizations, targeted estates belonging to all religious organizations.

Countywide land reform in Rui'an began in October 1950 and continued until the end of 1951. The basic principle of the campaign was to classify households according to their class status and transfer wealth and land deemed to be "superfluous" from landlords and rich peasants to the poor peasant class. It is well known that land reform stripped individual families classified as landlords or rich peasants of land and properties. Yet what happened to land not owned by individual families is less studied. The Land Reform Act (*tudi gaige fa*) construed territorial temples, Buddhist monasteries, churches, ancestral halls, and other social organizations as corporate landowners. Chapter 3, section 2 of the

---

[3] Vincent Goossaert and David A. Palmer, *The Religious Question in Modern China* (Chicago: University of Chicago Press, 2011), 44–50.

[4] Prasenjit Duara, "Knowledge and Power in the Discourse of Modernity: The Campaigns against Popular Religion in Early 20th Century China," *Journal of Asian Studies* 50, no. 1 (1991): 75.

Act specifically stipulates the expropriation of "common land" (*gongdi*) held by ancestral halls, territorial temples, Buddhist monasteries, and other social organizations.[5]

According to statistical charts on changes to landholding before and after land reform in three districts in Rui'an, 80.89 percent of "common land" in Tangxia District, 66.2 percent in Xincheng District, and 87.93 percent in Mayu District was immediately distributed to villagers during land reform.[6] The rest was not untouched but instead was set aside for "the purposes of additional allocation" (*tiaoji zhi yong*). Common land saved for additional allocation made up 2.13 percent of total land in the district of Xincheng and 1.9 percent in Mayu.[7]

Monks and nuns (including some Daoist masters) who insisted on staying in their temples received on average 1.3 *mu* of paddy rice fields or other land per person.[8] Ultimate Tranquility Temple (*benji si*), a locally famous monastery in the suburb, had more than forty *mu* of fields in 1933. The fields provided not just for the monastics living in the temple, but also for more than two hundred children in a makeshift shelter that had been established on temple grounds during the second Sino-Japanese War.[9] After land reform, only two *mu* were left to two monks who resided in the temple and who were now expected to farm the land themselves.[10]

Before land reform, the ritual service economy had undergone a sort of recession. Members of the Municipal Wenzhou Buddhist Association, an independent organization of Buddhist monks with government approval,[11] had to initiate joint ritual services (*jingchan lianying*) to collectively weather the poor circumstances, after initial efforts to delimit their respective areas of operation failed to prevent different ritual service providers from competing in each other's

---

[5] Due to lack of records, it is unclear on what basis the common land was redistributed. As a general principle, the common land should be redistributed to residents of the villages where they were located regardless of the origins of former owners.

[6] "Tangxia Qu qige xiang tugai tongji zonghe cailiao" (Comprehensive statistical materials on land reform in seven town[ship]s in Tangxia District), August 1951, Rui'an City Archives 1-3-51: 12; Xincheng Qu ge xiang tugai zonghe tongji cailiao (Comprehensive statistical materials on land reform in town[ship]s in Xincheng District), September 30, 1951, Rui'an City Archives 1-3-52: 13; "Mayu Qu ba ge tugai xiang tongji cailiao" (Statistical materials on land reform in eight town[ship]s in Mayu District), December 31, 1951, Rui'an City Archives 1-3-55: 6. Some common land was likely not reflected in the statistics, given the complexity of land property rights before 1949.

[7] For the redistribution of monastery land in other regions, see Holmes Welch, *Buddhism under Mao* (Cambridge, MA: Harvard University Press, 1972), 46–47.

[8] The average land that each monk and nun acquired is based on data from "the register of Buddhist [monks and nuns] in districts in Rui'an County" in 1952 ("Rui'an Xian ge qu Fojiao jie fojiaotu mingce" (The register of Buddhist [monks and nuns] in districts in Rui'an County), 1952, Rui'an City Archives 4-4-74: 12–25.

[9] Li Bingjun et al., eds., *Qiannian gucha: Benji si* (A historical temple of a thousand years: Ultimate Tranquility Temple) (Rui'an Shi yuhai wenhua yanjiuhui Benjisizhi bianxiezu, 2009), 47.

[10] Ibid., 24.

[11] This was only an organization of Buddhist monks in the Wenzhou municipality. There was no Buddhist association at the regional level at that time.

territories. Ritual services were so essential to the livelihoods of monks and nuns that the association rejected the government's request for "scriptural ritual reform" (*jingchan gaige*) among its members in early 1950, which aimed to reduce and restrict ritual services. The association itself needed income from ritual services to fund its operations.[12] Following the decline in the ritual services market, the expropriation of corporate landholdings was another big blow to monasteries, monks, and nuns.

When land reform began, the government requested an end to activities in Buddhist temples and all other religious institutions, out of a concern that counterrevolutionary forces might use them as an opportunity for infiltration and manipulation. Few dared to openly challenge the government's requests. Jiaoxuan, then the head of the Buddhist Association in Yueqing County, was sentenced to five years in prison for "undermining" land reform solely because he printed copies of the land reform law to help monks and nuns better protect Buddhist temples and estates. Baihe Temple, where the association was located, was sealed on government orders.

In the years following land reform, there were signs of a recovery in Buddhist activities when the political atmosphere became less tense. The authorities noticed an increase in Buddhist rites (*fahui*), unsanctioned Buddhist organizations, and requests to repair damaged Buddhist temples in some regions of eastern China.[13] In the county seat of Rui'an, Buddhists organized a Rui'an Buddhism Study Group (*Rui'an Fojiao xuexihui*), which represented a large number of Buddhist temples in communications with the county authorities from its founding in 1953 until it disbanded in 1957.[14] Some rituals and ceremonies also resumed, such as the traditional Guanyin Ceremony (*guanyin hui*), which the Lotus Society for Nuns (*nu lian she*) hosted in the county seat, as well as the public ordination ceremony in Jianshan Hall (*jianshan tang*) in the Daluo Mountains of Xianyan District, a traditional center of Wenzhou Buddhism. Each of these two meetings drew a crowd of several hundred participants every day, according to authorities.

The purpose of resuming these ritual meetings was not just to revive the traditional religious calendar. As the official report found, much of the income from public ceremonies was used to repair damaged Buddhist sites. Because land

[12] "Gaige Wenzhou Shi Fojiao jingchan de jihuashu" (The proposal on scriptural ritual reform in Wenzhou municipality), March 1950, Wenzhou Prefectural Archives 51-1-33: 28–31.

[13] It was not just in Rui'an. In some other regions of eastern China, the central government too noticed that Buddhists sought to reorganize and repair monasteries without government approval. See "Huadongju guanyu chuli zuijin Fojiao huodong hunluan qingkuang de zhishi" (Directives of East China Party Committee on the handling of recent chaos in Buddhist activities), May 9, 1953, Longquan City Archives, 1-5-11: 61–67.

[14] "Guanyu xian fojiaotu huodong de han" (Report on Buddhist activities in our county), April 15, 1957, Rui'an City Archives, 4-9-121: 34–37.

reform had removed a major source of income, unsurprisingly, Buddhists had to rely on donations and ritual performance fees. Using funds from ritual meetings, the Buddhism Study Group repaired the Buddhist Hall in West Gate Street and succeeded in raising enough money to repair the Temple of Awakening to the Truth (*wuzhen si*), a major temple in the county seat, before authorities intervened to call off the restoration.[15]

On the whole, it became very hard to maintain monastic life with the loss of income from land and the decline of the ritual service economy. Indeed, "the decimation of the sangha was the most important of many consequences of land reform for Buddhism in China."[16] Monks and nuns were called upon to support themselves through labor by participating in production,[17] but this proved to be a difficult task. A 1955 government survey of 579 monks and nuns in Rui'an shows that 173 of them either claimed to have no capacity to farm their land or found it difficult to support themselves through agriculture.[18] In January 1951, in the midst of land reform, the Wenzhou Buddhist Association sent the government a list of items belonging to its member temples, mostly ritual instruments including drums, chimes, tripods, and tin wares, and asked for permission to sell them.[19] Due to restrictions on the performance of rituals, the 1951 survey likewise found that many temples "wanted to sell 'waste' (*feiwu*) like those ritual temple instruments to collect useful funds for members' production."[20]

The expropriation of land also removed a major source of income for territorial temples and ritual organizations. Membership in temple and ritual organizations in southern Zhejiang was traditionally based on certain inherited economic privileges, the most common of which was the right to farm and manage common fields. Wang Hengqing, a resident of Qiancang, Pingyang County (south of Rui'an), was a "head of affairs" (*shoushi*, a local name for temple and ritual managers) for both the Earth God Temple and the Five Manifestations Temple (*wuxian miao*) at Qiancang before the Communist takeover.[21] Wang

---

[15] Ibid., 36.

[16] Holmes Welch, *Buddhism under Mao*, 80.

[17] Holmes Welch, "Buddhism under the Communists," *The China Quarterly* 6 (1961): 1–3.

[18] Rui'an Xian Fojiao jiben qingkuang diaocha mingce (A preliminary investigational list of Buddhism in Rui'an County), July 1955, Rui'an City Archives 4-7-20: 105–149. This seemed to be a common phenomenon, also reported elsewhere. See Holmes Welch, *Buddhism under Mao*, 47–48, 54–55.

[19] For the letters of Wenzhou Buddhist Association to Wenzhou municipal government and the latter's reply, see Wenzhou Prefectural Archives 51-2-30: 2–21. The difficulties with maintaining monastic life partly explain the massive departure of monks and nuns from Buddhist temples. Holmes Welch estimated that the number of monks and nuns in Jiangsu and Zhejiang dropped by about 90 percent in the first eight years after liberation. See Holmes Welch, *Buddhism under Mao*, 80–81, 502–503n126.

[20] January 10, 1951, Wenzhou Prefectural Archives 51-2-30: 1.

[21] Zhang Fen, "Pingyang Qiancang chenghuang miaohui" (City god temple fair in Qiancang, Pingyang) in *Pingyang Xiang, Cangnan Xiang chuantong minsu wenhua yanjiu* (Studies of traditional

recalled that since the time of his grandfather, his family had farmed four *mu* of common lands belonging to the Earth God Temple (*tudi miao*).[22] They lost the land in the land reform campaign. The expropriation of common land made it nearly impossible to maintain temples or continue ritual activities. Temples and ritual organizations lost their economic foundation.

Yet land reform not only targeted the economic structures of religious life; it also attacked the traditional leadership of communal religion. Patrons of territorial temples and Buddhist monasteries were among the local elites purged in the revolutionary campaign. One example of this was the family of Jie Jiongsui.[23] For generations, the Jie family, who arose from organizing local militia against the Taiping Rebellion in the late nineteenth century, had been prominent patrons of Lord Jiang Palace (*jiangfu dian*), a temple in Dingtian, Xincheng District. Jiongsui's father had been the head of a township in the Republican period. In land reform, the family's land and properties were confiscated and redistributed to poor villagers. Then, shortly after the end of the campaign, Jiongsui's father was executed, allegedly for concealing weapons.

In the township of Meitou in Tangxia, the family of Ying Qiancheng suffered a similar fate. Qiancheng was a Daoist master and a successful businessman. He had been a constable (*baozhang*) for twelve years during the Republican era and was also an important patron of the East Peak Pavilion (*dongyue guan*) in Meitou. Ying was classified as a "businessman landlord" (*gongshangye dizhu*) and a "superstition boss" (*mixin touzi*). He lost all the lands he owned and most of his houses.[24]

Many territorial temples reopened following the end of the land reform campaign, though "the incense fire [or the incense smoke] had cooled" (*xiangyan/ huo lengluo*), to use a euphemism that often appears in historical accounts of local territorial temples.[25] [Great Emperor] Huaguang Temple (*huaguang miao*) in Xianyan, Tangxia District, formerly held a temple fair once every year on the seventeenth day of the first lunar month, when disciples made a tour of the neighborhood carrying the palanquin seating the statue of Emperor Huaguang, the temple's main deity. The temple survived the transition to a Communist government and the land reform campaign, but the annual temple fair ceased to take place. So did the temple's ritual activities for the Dragon Boat Festival. Only a

---

folk culture in Pingyang and Cangnan Counties), eds. Xu Hongtu and Kang Bao (Paul Katz) (Beijing: Minzu chubanshe, 2005), 108.

[22] Ibid.

[23] Interview with Jie Jiongsui, on August 18, 2012.

[24] Shi Shihu, *Ying Weixian zhuan* [Biography of Ying Weixian] (Xianggang chubanshe, 2009), 8–9; interview with Ying's grandson, Ying Weixian, on August 17, 2012. Ying Weixian has been the head of the Rui'an Daoist Association since 1992.

[25] Zhou Konghua and Ruan Zhensheng, eds., *Wenzhou Daojiao tonglan* (A general survey of Daoism in Wenzhou) (Hong Kong: Tianma Books, 1999).

few elderly people still frequented the temple, which the village government also used for its meetings and gatherings.[26]

Christian Churches: Laying Low and Relatively Safe Passage

After Communist guerrilla forces entered the county seat of Rui'an in May 1949, many local churches took steps to make their public presence less conspicuous. In Taoshan District, western Rui'an, the local China Inland Mission (CIM) church was building a new chapel. They had completed the auxiliary buildings but had yet to start building the main hall. Concerned by the militant political atmosphere, the church suspended the project as well as its church meetings. In 1950, the new Communist government executed Pan Bofeng, the pastor of CIM's main church in the eastern Rui'an plains, in Xincheng District, for being a land-lord and having served as town head for the Nationalist government.[27] Following his execution, the Xincheng Church also suspended gatherings for a year and half. But most churches did not immediately stop assembling. Some, such as the China Jesus Independent Church (CJIC) in the mountainous district of Gaolou in western Rui'an, reportedly even preached more actively.

Both during and after land reform, the buildings owned by churches were a frequent target of expropriation. During land reform, the Catholic Church in Baotian Township, Tangxia, was turned into housing for individuals. The Catholic Church in Zhangzhai Village was confiscated to house a kindergarten and a cultural center (*wenhuaguan*). The village clinic in Tangkou "borrowed" the village's Protestant Church. In Xiasheng Village in neighboring Xianyan, the Catholic Church was "borrowed" to house the local militia's offices as well as classrooms for the peasant night school.[28]

Nevertheless, in economic terms, the land reform campaign did not affect Christian groups as much as it did other religious institutions. Local churches, unlike Buddhist monasteries and territorial temples, did not rely heavily on rents as a source of income. Hence redistribution or confiscation of their land for government use had a much smaller impact on their economic structure.[29] The

---

[26] "Xianyan Qu Xianyan Cun Huaguang miao shijian diaocha" (Investigation of the Huaguang Temple incident in Xianyan Village, Xianyan District), July 1953, Rui'an City Archives 1-5-113: 17. The forced conversion of temples of such size and regional influence as Huaguang Temple could be much more damaging to Party-people relationship than the destruction of those small village temples. This may partly explain village cadres' attitude toward Huaguang Temple.

[27] Rui'an jiaohui, *Rui'an jiaohui shi* (A history of Rui'an church), internal document, 1998, 12.

[28] "Zhixing zongjiao zhengce diaocha baogao" (Investigational report on the implementation of religious policies), April 9, 1953, Rui'an City Archives 1-5-62: 13.

[29] The land data are from churches' registration forms with the government. It is not entirely impossible that some churches might have hidden some land possessions. The chance that they

United Methodist Church had 26.63 *mu* of land dispersed across four locations in the districts of Taoshan and Xianjiang. The income from these fields only made up 0.033 percent of its total income in 1948; that percentage went down to zero in 1950, when the lands must have been redistributed or repurposed.[30] The CIM owned three *mu* of vegetable gardens in front of its head church in the county seat, but these were "borrowed" by the People's Liberation Army (PLA) to build a training ground in 1949.[31] Catholic churches bought three *mu* of land in the Xianjiang District in 1944; in 1948 and 1950, the income from that land made up only 0.056 percent and 0.089 percent of the churches' total income, respectively.[32] Other denominations did not own any land or assets to finance church activities.[33]

For the vast majority of village churches, neither the 1949 transition nor land reform had much of an economic impact on their operations, as their finances came predominantly from member donations. Under the influence of the independent church movement, some rural branches of the Methodist Church and the CIM, such as West Gate (*Ximen*) Church in the county seat of Rui'an and the Xintian Church in Tangxia, maintained only a nominal affiliation with their denominations. Their finances and day-to-day operations were entirely independent. Both of these churches erected chapels in 1923 without the financial support of the CIM.[34] The Assembly and the CJIC had long cut off foreign connections and therefore had no foreign subsidies to speak of, nor did they own any land.

Most rural churches used a financing system very much like the Shayang Church, a branch of the Assembly in Rui'an. The church's financial records show that it held frequent collections to finance church activities, including a regular Sunday collection, a self-supporting fee, and a Thanksgiving collection. More

---

intentionally did not report large chunks of land possessions, however, is slim given the intensity of the political atmosphere.

[30] "Jidujiao xundao gonghui Wenzhou jiaoqu Rui'an lianqu dengji zongbiao" (The register of the Rui'an affiliated district of the Wenzhou ecclesiastical district of the Methodist Church), July 1951, Rui'an City Archives 4-3-12: 53–61.

[31] "Rui'an Xian Zhonghua Jidujiao zizhi Neidihui zonghui dengji zongbiao" (The register of the Autonomous Chinese Christian Inland Mission in Rui'an), July 11, 1951, Rui'an City Archives 4-3-12: 82–105.

[32] "Rui'an Xian Tianzhujiao dengji zongbiao" (The register of the Catholic Church in Rui'an), May 19, 1951, Rui'an City Archives 4-3-12: 123–131.

[33] "Yesujiao Zilihui Rui'an fenhui dengji zongbiao" (The register of the Rui'an division of the China Jesus Independent Church), July 1951, Rui'an City Archives 4-3-12: 45–52; "Jidu fulin Anxirihui Rui'an jiaohui dengji zongbiao" (The register of the Seventh-Day Adventist Church for the Return of Jesus in Rui'an), July 1951, Rui'an City Archives 4-3-12: 64–73.

[34] "Rui'an Ximen jiaohui 1950 nian jingji shouzhi qingkuang" (Financial statement of West Gate Church in Rui'an in 1950) and "Rui'an Ximen jiaohui dengji zongjiao" (The register of West Gate Church in Rui'an), July 14, 1951, Rui'an City Archives 4-3-12: 74–81, 134–135.

requests for donations could be made at any time if the church had additional needs.[35]

In 1949, many local churches did not yet have a permanent gathering place. While the Catholic Church in Rui'an had one parish church and nineteen branch churches, each with its own chapel (jiaotang, most of which were built before 1930), Protestant congregations were quite different. Only two of a total of nine branches of the Seventh-Day Adventist Church owned a formal church building. Among the twenty-one branches of the Assembly, only eleven owned a formal church building. Of the remaining ten branches, one held meetings in a cloth factory (which may have been run by Christians), while nine others met in members' homes.[36] Local Protestant churches' own historical records show that, as of 1949, fifty-nine of Protestant communities had "chapels" (tang) while the other thirty-seven were called "gathering points" (dian), suggesting that they had no permanent meeting place.[37]

Because of the reliance of local Protestant communities on home gatherings, even when they did have church buildings, Protestants still carried on various meetings in members' homes. Aside from attending Sunday worship at the church, members were also asked, for instance, to attend weekday Bible study or prayer meetings, which usually took place in members' homes. These were sometimes held on specific holy days, such as Holy Friday (sheng wu) or Holy Wednesday (sheng san).[38] Additionally, ad hoc prayer meetings were convened when a church member or one of their relatives became ill.[39]

The paucity of church estates and other church properties (and therefore limited economic effects of land reform on them) underlines the fact that Christianity in this region was a religion of the poor, which was not part of the social and political establishment that the land revolution targeted. The fact explains why, in spite of the changes brought about by the Communist takeover and the land reform campaign, the native leadership of Christian churches in Wenzhou was still largely in place by the early 1950s.

Most western missionaries had left within a few years of the establishment of a Communist government, and the land reform campaign thoroughly uprooted

---

[35] "Pingyang Xian Shayang jiaohui shehui tuanti chengli dengji shenqing shu" (Social organization registration form of the Shayang Church of Pingyang County), August 10, 1954, Pingyang County Archives 10-60-90:58. Shayang Church was located in Rui'an but for a short while had been under the administration of Pingyang ecclesiastical district of the CJIC because of its proximity to Pingyang.

[36] "Rui'an quan xian Anxirihui mingce" (The register of the Seventh-Day Adventist church in Rui'an), 1953, Rui'an City Archives 1-5-113: 29, 32.

[37] Rui'an jiaohui, Rui'an jiaohui shi, 11.

[38] Holy Friday and Holy Wednesday perhaps refer to Good Friday and Ash Wednesday.

[39] "Guanyu Mocheng xiang Yesujiao de huodong wenti qingkuang zonghe baogao" (Comprehensive report on Christian activities in Mocheng Township), November 4, 1955, Pingyang County Archives 1-7-164: 173–174.

local elites. Yet church leaders in Wenzhou were for the most part indigenous church members and rarely members of the Nationalist Party or the landed elite. Very few officials or members of established local families were attracted to the church.

However, the government did order the arrest and execution of a few church leaders with ties to the Nationalist regime. In addition to the aforementioned Methodist preacher Pan Bofeng, Shen Liangshi, a preacher for the Catholic Church in Meitou Township, Tangxia, was also arrested and executed for being the alleged ringleader of a Nationalist resistance force. In neighboring Pingyang County, Fang Jiesheng, a long-term leader of the CJIC, had to flee from his native Aojiang Town to avoid arrest. He came from a prominent local business family and acted as a standing commissary for the Nationalist government when it set up a local party committee in Pingyang in 1926.

The church leaders who remained felt a growing political pressure from none other than the government-backed Three-Self patriotic movement. In July 1950, the publication of the Three-Self Christian manifesto by Wu Yaozong (known in English-language sources as Y. T. Wu) and several other national church leaders set the tone for Communist government policies regarding Christianity. Thereafter, the government mobilized local churches to denounce imperialism and promote patriotism in a series of events such as the Resist America and Aid Korea movement, the land reform movement, and the Campaign to Suppress Counterrevolutionaries. In this climate, the Wenzhou Protestant Reform Committee was formed in January 1951. In November of that year, the Methodist Church in Rui'an rallied other Protestant denominations to found the Rui'an Protestant Three-Self Reform Preparation Committee. All six Protestant denominations had representatives on the committee.

In Pingyang County over a year earlier, in the summer of 1950, Pastor Chen Huimin of the CJIC returned to his native home of Lingxi Town and formed a Nangang District Three-Self Reform Committee, a move that church leaders in Pingyang, especially those from the CJIC, might consider an attempt to establish a power base on their home turf. Chen had spent almost his entire career outside of Pingyang. Months before coming home, he organized a Three-Self Preparation Committee in Anxi County, Fujian, where he served in the local CJIC. Chen repeatedly sent letters to the Pingyang County Government in June and July 1953 urging the government to take action against Ye Tingchao, a leader of the local CJIC, alleging that Ye had been implicated in criminal activity.[40] However, Chen's

---

[40] In the letters, Chen accused Ye of ten crimes, including embezzling donations in the Resist America and Aid Korea movement, convening church meetings privately without official permission, and funding the flight of Pastor Fan Jiesheng, who had a Nationalist background. See "Guanyu zuizheng quezao qing yi fa ban yili aiguo aijiao er yi sanzi gexin de cheng" (The evidence of [Ye's] crime is beyond doubt, please act in accordance with the law in order to promote patriotism and love

attempt to establish his own power sphere in Pingyang was unsuccessful. Ye was elected president of the Pingyang Protestant Reform Committee in 1954, while Chen did not obtain a formal position on the committee.

In spite of Chen's failure, incidents like this in the Three-Self movement sowed the seeds of discord within the church. These would ultimately bring about a much more harmful and far-reaching schism during the Anti-Rightist campaign of 1957 and the Great Leap Forward in 1958. Church leaders who had supported the Three-Self movement, as well as those who opposed it, would suffer bitter disillusionment when these political storms swept the church in the late 1950s, as I discuss in later chapters.

It is important to note that the Three-Self movement in the 1950s is significantly different from the Three-Self movement re-initiated in the 1980s. In Rui'an and Wenzhou, Three-Self committees were first organized at the prefecture and county levels, and were followed by Three-Self reform teams at the district level. But neither state archives nor church records indicate that the government at that time intended, as they did in the 1980s, to extend Three-Self organizations to the grassroots level, namely village churches. In other words, the government did not attempt to organizationally implement the Three-Self patriotic movement at the grassroots level. County governments indeed asked for the registration of churches, but they did not require village churches to register individually. Rather, each denomination registered collectively. A village church included in its denomination's collective registration was not pledging allegiance to the county Three-Self committee. Nor did it need county authority approval for its leadership choice.[41]

Salvationist Groups: An Ephemeral Surge

As the Communist government established strict measures to control religious groups after 1949, the militarized Big Sword Association was the first in Wenzhou to suffer a crackdown. In the early 1940s, the Big Sword Association's political

for church and therefore facilitate the Three-Self reform), June 16, 1953, Pingyang County Archives 10-5-20: 25–26. See also a historical account on the formation of Three-Self Church in Pingyang by Ling Konghua. Ling Konghua, "Heyi zhilu" (The path to unification), published online at https://www.meipian.cn/ojmgm5h (accessed on May 4, 2018).

[41] These suggest that in Wenzhou the Three-Self movement might not have created as much division in grassroots church organizations as it did among church leaders at and above the county level—something that partly explains the continued growth of some village churches in the early 1950s. That the government did not extend Three-Self organizations to the grassroots level implies that they were taking a top-down approach to the Three-Self movement, prioritizing the mobilization of church elites to support the Communist regime.

activities had begun to alarm Communist forces even more than its religious pursuits, at a time when the Communists were often aligned with the Nationalist government. The Dong Renzhang faction of the Big Sword Association in Pingyang was labeled a counterrevolutionary organization in June 1949 and suffered swift crackdown. The largest Big Sword Association group in Rui'an, the Ye Jilang faction in Gaolou District, refused to disband and was crushed in a battle against government forces in September of that same year.

For the time being, the government did not make it a priority to dismantle the non-militarized religious societies, though they were on the radar. With their eschatological messages, these societies seemed to view the 1949 transition as another opportunity for expansion. Of all the salvationist groups, the Yellow Yang Teaching had the most rapid expansion after 1949. Shortly after the Communist takeover in May of that year, Xie Qingxian established a new altar for preaching in Pingyangkeng Village, Mayu. Four of his disciples opened new altars in Jianglong Township in October 1949 and in Fengxiang Township, Gaolou, in March 1950. The expansion of Xie's group, however, soon ended after concerned local authorities raided one of their meetings in the spring of 1950 and arrested Xie. By then, Xie's organization was estimated to have over seven thousand followers in Tangxia District alone.[42] If true, this would have meant that more than 10 percent of the population of Tangxia belonged to Xie's group.

The Seven Stars Teaching and the May 9 incident

In neighboring Wencheng (formerly the Western Region [xiqu] of Rui'an County until the 1940s), another of the traditional salvationist groups, the Seven Stars Teaching, oddly kept growing even during and after the ferocious land reform campaign, albeit only for a short time.

When Communist guerrilla forces moved from the western mountains into the newly liberated areas in the plains, various groups belonging to the Seven Stars Teaching made a resurgence to occupy the mountains once again. A sectarian leader named Zhou Shouzhen re-established a central altar with several other members of the Seven Stars Teaching in Kutou Village, Huangtan District, in Wencheng. There they created a new technique called kexianjin, "inscribing divine turbans" (with talismans), and had soon established six sub-altars in Huangtan District.

Li Rongyin's faction, based in Huangliao Township, Nantian District, expanded even more quickly. By April 1950, the success of the faction was such

---

[42] "Rui'an Xian renmin zhengfu bannian minzheng gongzuo zongjie" (Semiannual summary of civil affairs by the Rui'an County Government), 1950, Rui'an City Archives 4-2-6: 7.

that Li had to upgrade the original central altar to a master altar (*zhutan*) plus four central altars, which oversaw twenty-six sub-altars and two minor altars (*xiaotan*). Li was even enthroned by his assistants and disciples. When land reform was at its height in late 1951, the government accused Zhou and several other leaders of attempting to incite an uprising. They were arrested and executed for their alleged crime. Yet Li was able to continue his operations, and his faction, as well as other Seven Stars groups, continued to expand,[43] like the group affiliated with Hu Zhilong and Hu Zhiping of Jinyan Township, Nantian, whose network of altars—established in Puzhou Township, in the Beishan District of Qingtian County, in November 1951—soon extended to thirty-two townships.[44]

Local authorities did not see the expansion of the Seven Stars Teaching as a cause for any serious concern. Cadres knew very little about it and considered it at most a "superstition" group, less harmful than others.[45] However, the dramatic events of May 9, 1952, only a few months after land reform, changed the game.

On that day, hundreds of followers of the Seven Stars Teaching marched from the border regions of Wencheng, Qingtian, and Jingning from all directions toward the Liu Ji Temple in Nantian. They wore white vests and white turbans inscribed with talismans, carrying Seven Stars flags and shouting slogans referring to Liu Bowen, also known as Liu Ji, a Ming minister and native of the region, whom they believed had descended to save people and the world. "We will offer sacrifices to the great master Liu who will bestow upon us precious swords and open the *jinnang* [the embroidered pouch which was supposed to contain Liu's revelations]."[46] While they were carrying out rituals within the temple, it was besieged by soldiers and public security officers.

The incident had a rather peaceful end. The Seven Stars followers were hardly armed and unprepared to resist. Most of those who marched to Liu Ji's temple were arrested. A few were injured; only one was killed, when he attempted to flee.

It is unclear who actually coordinated the May 9 action. In official propaganda, the May 9 incident was classified as a landlord-manipulated counterrevolutionary riot for the political purpose of stigmatizing the Seven Stars Teaching, although the government never found any direct evidence to implicate those former landlords.[47] Yet internal investigation reports acknowledged that it was

---

[43] "Fandong Qixing hui cankao ziliao" (Reference materials on the counterrevolutionary Seven Stars Teaching), 1952, Wencheng County Archives 1-4-8: 51–52.

[44] Zhan, *Qingtian Xian gong'an zhi*, 173.

[45] During the crackdown after the incident, superior officials had to explain to village and town cadres why the teaching was counterrevolutionary. See "Guanyu Wencheng, Qingtian, Jingning san xian fandao diqu xiang ganbu kuoda huiyi zongjie" (Summary of the expanded meeting of district and town[ship] cadres on anti-religious society work at three counties of Wencheng, Qingtian, and Jingning), August 6, 1952, Wencheng County Archives 1-4-9: 16–19.

[46] Zhan, *Qingtian Xian gong'an zhi*, 174.

[47] *Wencheng County gazetteer* says that Li Rongyin and an ex-KMT military Fu Shaodai at Nantian, Wencheng, masterminded the entire incident. *Qingtian County public security gazetteer*, however,

other factors, including discontent with the Communist Party among local residents, which were mainly responsible for driving people to join the Seven Stars Teaching, eventually leading to the May 9 incident.

Villagers in the mountains had a very strong sense of being left behind when the Communist guerrillas moved to the cities in the plains. People in the border regions of Wencheng, Qingtian, and Jingning supported the guerrillas and participated in militias and peasant associations, hoping that the revolution would improve their impoverished lives. But their lives did not get better after 1949. During village visits, officials learned of ballads such as: "Thunder hit the mountains, but the rain fell on the plain areas [instead]." "The Nationalist Party could not provide for us, the Communist Party could not support us, to survive we can only depend on Buddha and submit our-selves to the will of Heaven."[48]

The investigators found that mountain villagers were even more distressed at the disparities of land reform. In many cases, cadres dominated the distri-bution of land to favor their own families while not giving a fair share to other villagers. Other cadres used land reform to launch personal attacks against other villagers.[49] A growing sense of disillusionment pushed local residents to embrace salvationist religion.

The messages of the Seven Stars Teaching appealed to many inhabitants of the mountain areas. Some of their slogans spoke directly to the disadvan-taged: "Believing in [the power] of Heaven would win you [women] the status of eighteen celestial beings," "bring you [the sick] peace" and "help you [poor peas-ants] cross over to Jingzhou [a mythical land in ancient Chinese myth) to have a life of great peace."[50] They assured the relatives of PLA soldiers that joining the Seven Stars Teaching would bless their sons and prevent them from being killed in battle. Some Seven Stars propaganda directly commented on the campaigns and policies of the Communist government. On land reform: "Landlords' land resulted from the good deeds of their ancestors. Thus we should not take away [their land] . . . you would not be able to eat grains grown in the distributed land." On the counterrevolutionary campaign: "We should behave with a good heart.

---

shows that the incident was "manipulated" (*caozong*) by Hu Zhilong and Hu Zhiping, two "counter-revolutionaries" in Beishan District of Qingtian. The discrepancies between these versions suggest that the May 9 incident was perhaps deliberately used to frame the Seven Stars Teaching as a political group with the intention of subverting the communist regime. See Zhu Li et al., eds., *Wencheng Xian zhi* (Wencheng County gazetteer) (Beijing: Zhonghua shuju, 1996), 723; Zhan, *Qingtian Xian gong'an zhi*, 173–174; and Chen, *Qingtian Xian zhi*, 540.

[48] "Liuyue ershi zhi liuyue ershiwu ri qingkuang baogao" (Report on the circumstances between June 20 and June 25), June 25, 1952, Wencheng County Archives 1-4-9: 85.
[49] Wencheng County Archives 1-4-9: 61.
[50] Wencheng County Archives 1-4-8: 56–57.

Do not hurt others." And on taxation: "the Communist Party imposes ten thousand [types of] taxes. In the past, we farmed for landlords, but now we farm for the Communist Party."[51]

The brutality against followers of the Seven Stars Teaching during land reform might even have catalyzed the movement's proliferation, officials implied. A report pointed out that land reform work teams "seriously violated policy, [and mistakenly] expanded the scope of the attacks."[52] In the "encirclement and elimination" (weijiao) campaign that was concurrent with land reform, they arrested and executed some sectarian leaders as "bandits." Followers were coerced to confess and condemn sectarian leaders in struggle meetings. There were "excessive arrests and excessive strikes."[53] Even some villagers who seemed to have no history with the Seven Stars Teaching were under attack. Many of those affected, whether or not they were members of a Seven Stars group, were frightened and fled to hide together in the mountains.

The Massive Crackdown on Salvationist Groups and Its Aftermath

After the May 9 incident, the Wenzhou Prefectural Commission, which by then had become aware of how serious the situation was, immediately sent its cadres out to the region. There they joined top county officials to form a fandao ("anti-religious society") command center. More fandao groups were established at various administrative levels, from district to village, to ask followers to register with the government and mobilize villagers to inform on members of religious societies. Supervision and training camps (guanxunban) were organized to brainwash sect leaders. The most creative and interesting propaganda measure was a propaganda play with a script based on the May 9 incident. This theatrical performance toured the affected villages, with some former top leaders of the Seven Stars Teaching appearing as themselves. [54]

By the end of September, the government had made massive arrests and had organized public struggle meetings. Official records state that 1,433 people were either arrested or killed.[55] By the spring of 1953, all salvationist groups

---

[51] Ibid.

[52] Ibid.: 53; Wencheng County Archives 1-4-9: 61.

[53] Wencheng County Archives 1-4-8: 56.

[54] Zhao Shaozhong, "Yi zhi tebie 'xuanchuandui'" (A special propaganda team), in Wencheng wenshi ziliao di san ji (Wencheng historical materials volume 3), ed. Wencheng Xian zhengxie wenshi weiyuanhui (Wencheng Xian zhengxie wenshi weiyuanhui, 1987), 54–60.

[55] Wencheng County Archives 1-4-9: 30.

were outlawed in southern Zhejiang. At the end of that year, a total of 3,163 society leaders and approximately 61,500 followers were registered with the government in twelve counties under the jurisdiction of the Wenzhou Prefectural
Commission.[56]

Conclusion

In the years immediately following 1949, the Communist government did not
have a systematic program to crack down on religion. Yet land reform—Mao's
core revolutionary agenda—dealt a huge blow to religious communities. The
permanent, full-scale expropriation of religious land under Mao followed a logic
similar to prior modernization efforts from 1898 onward, in which religious
properties were commandeered to serve as public buildings. Yet the sweeping
breadth of land reform, driven by the Communist government's capacity to reach
to the heart of rural society, went far beyond the "temple to school" movement or
previous anti-superstition campaigns. It marked the peak of state efforts to take
over the operation of religious sites, effectively restructuring the economic basis
of communal temples and constraining their day-to-day operations.

Yet land reform did not have the same effects on all religious traditions.
During and immediately after the land reform campaign, land seizures removed
one of the main sources of livelihood for Buddhist and territorial temples, while
"ways of organizing actions" less bound by locality—the salvationist groups
and Christian churches—were less hard hit economically. More to the point,
Christian churches were largely not part of the social and political establishment
in local society, which explains why they were less economically and politically
affected for the time being. Yet Christian groups were also under pressure to
submit to the new regime because of the political campaigns concurrent with
land reform, sowing the seeds of discord among church leaders.

The most significant consequence of land reform's uneven effects on religious life
may have been the dramatic expansion of indigenous salvationist groups during
land reform, followed shortly thereafter by their swift downfall. This marked a critical shift in the local religious landscape. In a broader context, the downfall of salvationist groups was tied to the Campaign to Suppress Counterrevolutionaries to
consolidate the Communist Party's power. Yet the downfall of salvationist groups
should also be understood in relation to local history before 1949. For decades,
salvationist groups and Communist forces had been powerful players who both

[56] Zhao Jiazhu, ed., *Zhongguo huidaomen shiliao jicheng* (A comprehensive compilation of historical materials on reactionary societies, teachings and sects in China) (Beijing: Zhongguo shehui
kexue chubanshe, 2004), 465.

competed and collaborated with each other in the local politics of Rui'an. The crackdown marked a brutal end to this relationship, as well as the fifty-year rise of salvationist groups in the local religious landscape.

After the massive clampdown of the early 1950s, traditional salvationist groups did not disappear, and still exist today.[57] Yet the political stigma of "reactionary societies, teachings and sects" made it difficult for them to gain traction in the local ideological landscape (though we do not know if this may happen in the future). Local gazetteers show pockets of Yellow Yang Teaching activities still taking place during the rest of the Mao era. In the autumn of 1953, less than a year after the crackdown, nine central altars resumed activities involving 1,081 followers. A year later, in the autumn of 1954, Li Xiuzhuo, a former teacher of the Seven Stars Teaching, launched sixteen "central altars of the world" (shijie zongtan) that amassed hundreds or possibly thousands of followers.[58]

Zhang Dechang, one of the most important early leaders of the Seven Stars Teaching, was released from prison and returned to his hometown in Zhangdan Brigade in Qingtian in February 1961, coinciding with the Great Famine. He soon reconnected with old teachers and followers. They absorbed more than 180 new followers in seven brigades and one town across three districts before they were suppressed. In early 1967, Wu Qingyan, a self-styled "emperor" of the Seven Stars Teaching and the leader of a central altar, interpreted the outburst of the Cultural Revolution as a message from Heaven (tianji) that he should secretly resume activities. His organization spread to fourteen brigades across four districts until it was exterminated by the government in October 1977. In the final years of the Cultural Revolution, followers in Qingtian, after undergoing meditation training in neighboring Ouhai County, returned to revive the Twelve Steps Teaching, a faction of the Seven Stars Teaching. They created new altars and attracted disciples in the name of "religious freedom." Their activities involved five districts and towns in Qingtian until early 1987, when the county government again ordered a clampdown.[59]

In the early 1980s, there was a brief surge in the Yellow Yang Teaching in parts of Yueqing. Revelation teacher Chen Libin of Haiyu Township mobilized three hundred followers in seven towns and townships to rebuild a series of local temples: the "Jade Emperor Palace" (yuhuang dian), the "Saint Mother of Black Dragon Palace" (wulong shengmu gong), and the "Evergreen Pavilion" (changqing guan).[60] They took advantage of these temples to open altars for preaching and

---

[57] For the survival of salvationist religion in the Mao years in China, see Steve A. Smith, "Redemptive Religious Societies and the Communist State, 1949 to the 1980s," in Maoism at the Grassroots: Everyday Life in China's Era of High Socialism, eds. Jeremy Brown and Matthew Johnson (Cambridge, MA: Harvard University Press, 2015), 340–364.

[58] Zhu, Wencheng xianzhi, 724.

[59] Zhan, Qingtian Xian gong'anzhi, 179–180.

[60] Yang Dianzhong et al., eds., Yueqing Xian gong'anzhi (A history of public security in Yueqing) (Beijing: Haiyan chubanshe, 1993), 36.

practicing exorcism to cure illnesses for village residents. Although the attempt to use communal temples for salvationist religion in Yueqing did not last long, it indicates a tendency to integrate two traditions that is worth further study.

Unlike salvationist religion, communal religion never had to face a massive militarized crackdown. As Chapter 3 shows, communal religion was the largest religious tradition and was much less politically sensitive, giving followers much more room to maneuver—though having suffered a huge loss of properties and leadership, they continued to be bound by political constraints throughout the rest of the Mao years.

3

The Contests for Communal Temples in the Early 1950s to the Mid-1970s

With land reform completed, in 1952 the Rui'an County Government started promoting mutual-aid teams (*huzhuzu*) in rural areas. From then on, most of the temples that survived land reform had to face increasingly frequent encroachments on ritual space. The land reform statute did not stipulate the expropriation of religious property other than land, but unsurprisingly, the other assets of religious organizations were often a target of plunder and violence provoked by the mass mobilization of land reform. As collectivization unfolded, trespasses on temple and temple property became routine. More buildings belonging to territorial temples and Buddhist monasteries were expropriated under the pretext of various state and local initiatives. The government seized temples in the name of setting up state granaries (linked to grain requisitions), government offices, and supply-and-sell co-ops (*gongxiaoshe*). Local communities themselves also converted temples for various non-religious purposes such as hosting schools of various types, offices for the village government, and warehouses for collectives or communes.

This chapter explores the struggle to preserve communal temples and carry on traditional religious practices in the years following the end of land reform. Expressions of religiosity continued to find an outlet even during the Cultural Revolution. Even as most temples were eventually shut down, attempts to revive them came to be at the center of religious politics in the ensuing decades. Here I delve into the reasons for this, exploring the challenges facing communal religion in spite of the continuation of public religious practices.

The Collectivization of Communal Temples

Temple of Pacified Nation: Occupation and Loss

In the late 1930s and throughout the 1940s, Temple of Pacified Nation (*anguo si*) (Photo 3.1), a Buddhist convent in Upper Village (*shang cun*), Xincheng District, often served as the command center for underground Communist

Maoism and Grassroots Religion. Xiaoxuan Wang, Oxford University Press (2020). © Oxford University Press.
DOI: 10.1093/oso/9780190069384.001.0001

Photo 3.1. Temple of Pacified Nation (2012).
Source: Author.

forces in eastern Rui'an. Liaoxing (Photo 3.2) was the temple abbess throughout the Communists' stay. In addition to providing a cover for Communist activities, members of her family and many other families in the village signed up to join the party before 1949, including a few women. In the years immediately following land reform, the convent continued to hold ceremonies on the first, eighth, fifteenth, and twenty-third day of each lunar month to recite Pure Land scriptures. In October 1955, the convent even started hosting a Lotus Pool Buddhism study group meeting with around 140 participants.

When Upper Village formed cooperatives, the village government began requesting the use of Temple of Pacified Nation housing. Liaoxing seemed to have reached an informal verbal agreement with the village head to allow the front row of the temple complex to store farm tools for the village's Lianguang cooperative and three rooms in the middle row to house a village night school. But the cooperative did not want to wait and did not consider Liaoxing's informal offer to be generous enough.

On October 8, 1956, dozens of villagers belonging to the Lianguang cooperative broke into the west wing of the rear row, the main section of the temple complex. Tossing away all the items in the west wing rooms, they claimed to have a government order to turn the temple into a night school to develop cultural

Photo 3.2. Photo of Abbess Liaoxing on display at Upper Village revolutionary memorial hall, along with a photo of Anguo Temple (2012).
Source: Author.

industry and improve the peasants' level of education. The village head did not appear.[1]

Furious, Liaoxing sent a letter to the county government that very day. Accusing the cooperative members of manipulating state policy for their own purposes, she asked, "Didn't they hear what Chairman Mao said, 'the Chinese Communist Party's policy is to protect religion?' People have religious freedom, which the constitution clearly stipulates. . . . They should not have used such a repressive means to offend Buddhist properties, because today, under the sagacious leadership of Chairman Mao and the Chinese Communist Party, there should no phenomenon of people oppressing people."[2]

The letter did not seem to have an immediate effect, as on October 12 the cooperative further occupied and remodeled the main hall of the temple set in the rear section of the complex, turning it into their accounts office. After Liaoxing again sent letters via the Rui'an Buddhism Study Group, the county government

[1] October 9, 1956, Rui'an City Archives 4-8-111: 35.
[2] Ibid.

did send a reply, but without offering any substantial measures in response. They only asked village and town cadres to educate those young cooperative members responsible for any excesses, to negotiate first and to refrain from causing damage in the future if they needed to use temple buildings, to avoid complaints from Buddhist communities.[3]

Liaoxing eventually gave in to the cooperative's encroachment on convent property. As I learned on my visit to Upper Village, she had to vacate the temple which had been her home for sixty-some years, along with the temple's remaining nuns, and for the remainder of her life she lived with a relative in the village.

With collectivization progressing rapidly in the mid-1950s, many other religious institutions faced the same fate as Temple of Pacified Nation. In 1956, the same year that Liaoxing wrote letters to protest the invasion of the temple, the Rui'an Buddhism Study Group made a formal complaint to the county government that twenty-eight other temples had been partly or wholly taken over by cooperatives. Most of them were converted to livestock pens and storage in response to the government's call for cooperatives to develop animal husbandry. Monks and nuns were also asked to participate in cooperative agriculture.[4] The twenty-eight temples that sought help from Buddhism Study Group were very likely not the only temples taken over by cooperatives. A 1955 government survey indicates that the number of temples with housing for monks and nuns had shrunk from 383 in 1949 to only 256 in 1955.[5]

Even Sagacious Longevity Temple (*shengshou si*) in Xianyan Town, Tangxia—one of the most famous Buddhist temples in the Wenzhou region, which supposedly enjoyed protected status as a legal religious site—was helpless to prevent encroachments on its property. Since land reform, lower level cadres and some residents had willfully taken things from the temple. Then in 1952, a village school was set up inside the temple. Villagers turned wooden engravings into chairs and blackboards and sold iron cauldrons (valuable ritual objects) to fund the school.[6] In the following years, more educational institutions took over parts of the temple: first Xianyan High School, then Xinyan Elementary School, some

---

[3] "Rui'an Xian Fojiao Xuexihui baogao" (A report from Rui'an Buddhism Study Group), October 12, 1956, Rui'an City Archives 4-8-111: 28, 79.

[4] "Wei ju gedi siyuan deng baogao ge qu xiangcun nongyeshe wei xiangying zhengfu fazhan xumu haozhao, fenfen jiang gedi siyuan fangshe renyi shunhuai qingxing yanzhong, kaiju xiangqing qing xunsu zhizhi yimian kuoda jiufen you" (On rural agricultural cooperatives that, according to monks and nuns living in the temples in the respective districts covered thereby, recklessly damaged temples one after another in response to the governmental call to develop animal husbandry. [We] list details [below], please promptly stop [them] in order to prevent further disputes), August 11, 1956, Rui'an City Archives 4-8-109: 81–92.

[5] "Guanyu Fojiao qingkuang diaocha baogao" (Investigational report on Buddhism), July 14, 1955, Rui'an City Archives 1-7-137: 38.

[6] "Guanyu Xianyan si dahuo sunshi qingkuang baogao" (Report on fire in Xianyan Temple and losses), 1953, Rui'an City Archives 1-5-113: 4–7.

Photo 3.3. Sagacious Longevity Temple (ca. 1975).
Source: Courtesy of Mr. Liu Xianyou.

cadre schools, and a night school successively set up classrooms in the temple complex. Eventually, by the early 1970s, the temple became barely recognizable (see Photos 3.3 and 3.4).

Resistance: The Unsettled Summer of 1953

In contrast with land reform, when the extraordinarily tense political atmosphere silenced almost all dissent, in the mid-1950s some communities openly resisted the appropriation of temples. This was especially the case in 1953, when several factors converged to bring about a string of collective actions to take back temples.

This is the year that county authorities began to implement the unified purchase-and-sale policy (*tonggou tongxiao*), a key economic program aiming at nationalizing the grain market. Food shortages appeared in some areas when people did not have enough grain left over for their own consumption. Rumors

Photo 3.4. Sagacious Longevity Temple (2012).
Source: Author.

criticizing the unified purchase-and-sale policy abounded. Villagers attacked cadres and demanded grain in several towns in the western mountains and along the southern bank of the Feiyun River.

Efforts to promote collectivization were not going well. Some rural households quit the cooperatives. By the summer of 1953, only 20 percent of rural households were participating in mutual aid teams. Then, between June and mid-August, a prolonged drought ravaged all of Zhejiang Province. It was the first major natural disaster since liberation.

The drought finally pushed tensions to boiling point: many villagers believed that it was caused by deities upset by the reckless destruction and closure of temples. This set off what local authorities named the "superstition riots": a series of attempts to retake local temples, beginning with the attempted restoration of dragon boat racing in the eastern plains, in the basin of the Tang canal.

The yearly Dragon Boat Festival (*duanwu*) still took place, but the dragon boat races, a central part of the festival, had been disrupted since 1949. In May 1953, as villagers were preparing for the ritual procession, they recalled how dragon boats stored in temples and ancestral halls had been dismantled for the construction of schools and government offices. A rage held back for years suddenly

Photo 3.5. Huaguang Temple (2012).
Source: Author.

erupted to the surface.[7] Many villagers asked village governments to compensate them for the dragon boats that were destroyed. Some went to beat up village and town cadres in retaliation for demolishing the dragon boats. In Xiasheng, Li'ao Township, Tangxia, some villagers even threatened to drown local school principal Lin Fuzhen (drowning was a traditional local method of punishing criminals), because Lin was accused of ordering the dragon boats sawn into pieces to make stools for the township school.[8]

In the night of June 13, two days before the date of the Dragon Boat Festival, villagers in Xianyan Village, Tangxia, assembled to ask for the restoration of Huaguang Temple (see Chapter 2) (Photo 3.5). Two months earlier, Wang Muyong, the principal of Xianyan Elementary School, began work to convert the temple into a school in collusion with cadres from the southern part of the village. Cadres from the northern part of the village, who had long been at odds

[7] "Wei xi chaming Yueqing Xian suo fasheng zongjiao wenti chuli bao shu you" (On elucidating the handling of the religious incidents in Yueqing County and reporting to the [Wenzhou regional] Commission), September 12, 1951, Yueqing City Archives, 26-3-2: 15–17.

[8] "Tangxia Qu hualongzhou qingkuang jianbao" (Briefing on the situation of dragon boat racing in Tangxia), June 1, Rui'an City Archives 49-5-1: 97–100.

with their southern counterparts, did not agree. Nevertheless, in April 1953, Wang covertly brought in students and local militias to demolish almost all of the statues in Huaguang Temple in April and turn the temple into an elementary school.

Most villagers believed the government had ordered the takeover, so they did not dare protest. The atmosphere changed in early June, after a worker from a rock-mining company based in nearby Qingtian County had a vision while staying in Huaguang Temple overnight. The next day, he told the residential temple manager that he had a dream in which he saw a man wearing a white robe and heard the sound of horses. The story spread panic through the community, as villagers feared that Lord Huaguang (*Huaguangye*) had abandoned the temple and the community.

In the night of June 13, over 140 people flocked to Wang's school, most of them elderly residents of the village. When he heard the news, Wang fled. According to official reports, most village cadres did not intervene; they simply stood by and looked on. A few of them even joined the crowds.

Over the next two days, villagers flocked to the Xianyan town government to demand a solution. They searched for Wang but could not find him. On the third day of their search, villagers destroyed all the elementary school facilities that Wang had set up within the temple. The incident startled county officials. The county culture and education chief and several town cadres who had gone to investigate the incident could not appease the villagers until 3 a.m. on the fourth day, when Wang reappeared and performed a self-criticism in the temple in front of the assembled villagers. He agreed to take responsibility for all damages and guaranteed that the school was not going to move in.[9]

In July and August, as drought set in, people made ritual processions to ask for rain, carrying statues of their gods on village tours. Many residents of Rui'an ascribed the drought to the destruction of temples and statues of divinities. An official report quotes one villager as saying: "*Pusa* [deities] do exist. The government is wrong not to believe in *pusa* . . . the lack of rain in the past [months] is due to the fact that the government did not believe in *pusa* and destroyed too many *pusa* [statues]."[10] Similar words were heard throughout the county.

---

[9] Rui'an City Archives 1-5-113: 17–23. Government documents did not indicate later developments around Huaguang Temple. Yet what I learned during my visit to the temple in 2012 was that the triumph of the villagers did not last long. After a while the school still moved into the temple.

[10] "Guanyu benxian gedi fasheng qunzhongxing zhaofo qiuyu ji saodong shijian de baogao" (Report on (the incidents of) conjuring up deities to make rain and disturbances throughout the county), August 5, 1953, Rui'an City Archives 1-5-3: 77. Throughout the province, people similarly held the party responsible for the drought. In Yongkang County of Jinhua, for instance, people held rainmaking ceremonies, also blaming the Communist Party for causing the severe drought. See Lü Shanxin, "Taiping Xiang qiuyu mixin shijian huigui" (Memoir of the incident of rainmaking superstition at Taiping Town), in *Wushi niandai de Yongkang* (*Yongkang wenshi ziliao di shisan ji*) (Yongkang Shi zhengxie wenshi weiyuanhui, 2001), 357.

Photo 3.6. East Hall Palace (2012). Rebuilt multiple times since 1980s, the temple today, which includes a park, is several times bigger than it was before 1949.
Source: Author.

As people were preparing for the rainmaking ceremony, they demanded that the temples be restored. In Lower Village (*xia cun*), Xincheng, near Upper Village where Temple of Pacified Nation was located, the government set up a granary in the former village temple of East Hall Palace (*dongtang dian*) (Photo 3.6). Rumors spread that "the milled wheat has choked the gods and sent them away" (*longkang ba fo mengzoule*).[11] On July 26, villagers meeting in East Hall Palace for a ceremony to call out the moon (a local custom to make the moon reappear after a lunar eclipse) tore down the clapboards on the granary walls. They subsequently asked to remove the stored grain from the temple in order to stage a rainmaking ceremony. When vice district head Xie Duyin arrived to inspect the temple and discuss solutions, the situation almost escalated into violence. Xie had to fire a gun in the air to stop an excited villager who wanted to grab his gun.[12]

---

[11] "Xincheng Qu guanyu Dongtang miao bei pohuai de baogao" (Report on the damage to East Hall Palace), July 30, 1953, Rui'an City Archives 32-4-7: 5.
[12] Rui'an City Archives 1-5-113: 17–23; Rui'an City Archives 32-4-7: 4–6. For superstition riots in Rui'an, see also "Mayu Qu Caocun xiang mixin saodong shijian de baogao" (Report on

In response, the county government was curiously accommodating. They did not issue a prohibition order to stop the dragon boat races. With tensions running high due to the unpopular policies of collectivization, officials may have wished to avoid further resentment. The county government ordered that when villagers went to pray for rain, they should first be "educated" (*jiaoyu*), and if persuasion was futile, they should be allowed to perform the ritual.[13] They even stressed that cadres should not impose uncompromising prohibitions, but should instead make it clear that "there is no prohibition on the belief in deities and there is also freedom not to believe in religion."[14] Xie Duyin was later asked to write a self-criticism for firing his gun in the air to "dispel the masses" and "attacking" a ritual organizer in Lower Village.[15] Finally, the county government decided to restore both East Hall Palace in Xincheng District and Brook-side Palace (*xiwei gong*) in Mayu District, removing granaries and returning the temples to their respective communities—though, as it turns out, this would prove to be only a temporary measure.[16]

These accommodations were certainly not typical of the way local governments handled "superstition riots," but they reflect the difficulties that local officials were only beginning to face in their relations with villagers. As land reform left a vacuum in the leadership of communal religious practices, grassroots cadres had to confront religious activities mainly led by the "revolutionary masses" (*geming qunzhong*), the landless peasants, poor peasants, and middle peasants whom the Communist Party relied upon for the revolution and the construction of a socialist state.

For many cadres, dealing with the revolutionary masses was more difficult than ousting traditional elites. Unlike the activities of salvationist groups, the government typically avoided labeling the religious activities of the "revolutionary masses" as counterrevolutionary. Moreover, it was not a secret that in some villages, a number of local cadres themselves, including village heads and Youth League secretaries, organized rainmaking ceremonies.[17] Where grassroots

the superstition riot in Caocun Township, Mayu District), August 27, 1953, Rui'an City Archives, 4-5-63: 78–81.

[13] The county government in Yongkang, Zhejiang, even allowed all the county officials except for administrative heads (i.e., county head, district head, etc.) to participate in rainmaking ceremonies in order to better "educate" people. See Lü Shanxin, "Taiping xiang qiuyu mixin shijian huigui," 360.

[14] Rui'an City Archives 1-5-3: 81.

[15] See "Guanyu Xincheng Qu Xinzhou Xiang saodong shijian geren jiantao" (Self-criticism on the riot of Xinzhou Town, Xincheng District), August 31, 1953, Rui'an City Archives, 1-5-90: 23–29.

[16] "Wei baogao benxian Xincheng Qu liangku feng zhun chexiao bao qing bei cha you." (On the request for permission to revoke the Xincheng granary), August 25, 1953, Rui'an City Archives 32-4-3: 2; Rui'an City Archives, 4-5-63: 78–81. East Hall Palace, villagers told me, was later used for various non-religious purposes. At least one of the leaders who the government believed instigated the riots in East Hall Palace was sentenced to jail.

[17] Rui'an City Archives 1-5-3: 72–81.

cadres were involved in "superstitious" activities, county officials had a difficult time obtaining effective support for the ban on illegal religious practices. Indeed, when political campaigns did not demand a drastic approach, county officials preferred to maintain a certain flexibility.

Adapting to the Constriction of Ritual Spaces

In spite of these concessions, the closure and expropriation of village temples continued over the following months and years. Unlike the sudden, drastic confiscation of religious estates during land reform, these encroachments were often a gradual process. In many temples, ritual and secular activities occurred side by side, sometimes maintaining a fragile peace. The most typical case was the coexistence of ritual and educational sites. Schools might occupy the majority of a temple building, while the worship of deities was allowed to continue, confined to a smaller part of the temple.

The coexistence of religious and secular activities very much depended on whether religious practitioners and occupying institutions were able to avoid conflict. Tensions sometimes mounted to the point where the county government was required to intervene. Hongyan Palace (*hongyan dian*) in Middle Village (*zhong cun*), Xincheng, was turned into a township school after 1949. Nevertheless, villagers continued to use the school's auditorium as ritual space, sweeping up the cabinet previously built for divine statues and setting up incense tables. The auditorium had been the temple's main hall before the conversion. The school principal made multiple requests for various levels of local government to intervene, but the problem was only solved with the involvement of the county government in 1954. Though it still took four months of negotiations with the villagers, the school and the township government were finally able to remove the incense tables.[18]

The outcome of the dispute over the incense tables was not ideal for religious practitioners, because it meant that even limited religious practices were no longer possible on temple sites. This transformation of ritual spaces to public spaces precluding any kind of religious activity was a widespread occurrence, with government orders to confiscate or expropriate temple buildings and construct granaries, county-level schools or factories in their stead. In such cases,

---

[18] "Wei benxiang xiangxiao litang shang baiman fogui yuanbaozhuo fang'ai xuesheng jihui bufen mixin nongmin zhishi xuesheng kangyi yidong qing zhengfu xiezhu jiejue you" (On shrines and sacrifice tables occupying the auditorium of a town elementary school in Xinzhou Town, Xincheng, that obstructed school meetings; some superstitious peasants instigated students to protest against the action to remove shrines and sacrifice tables, we ask for the assistance of the government in settling [the problem]), 1954, Rui'an City Archives 4-6-69: 135–136.

the occupying institutions tended to restructure and demolish the temple itself or to construct entirely new buildings. In the 1950s and early 1960s, the county Buddhism Study Group, on behalf of the Sagacious Longevity Temple in Xianyan (see earlier discussion), filed multiple reports requesting that the schools move out, but local authorities ultimately rebuffed all their requests in the name of developing education. There was not much local communities could do to salvage traditional ritual sites.

Nevertheless, some religious and secular sites coexisted for many years, in some instances even for the entire duration of the Mao era. The Great Yin Palace (*taiyin gong*) in the northeastern district of Huling, dedicated to the worship of the deity Princess Chen Shisi (known as Lady Linshui in her home region of Fujian), continued to hold religious activities even after liberation when a school was set up on the premises. According to the Great Yin Palace's own historical account, "for forty years, the palace's religious activities and the school's educational activities were constantly in tension." Nevertheless, school and temple coexisted until 1979 when a new Great Yin Palace was built at the entrance of the village to resolve the problem.[19]

When the conditions were such that religious practitioners could not carry on even minimal worship in a repurposed temple, a common solution was to make a substitute space. Local residents worshipped statues of gods and other religious objects, secretly or semi-publicly, often in remote locations. Such arrangements sometimes persisted until the end of the Cultural Revolution or even later. When Liujia Palace (*liujia gong*) in Liujia, Taoshan District, was closed down in 1952, people took the statue of the main deity Lord Yang to another location, where people continued to worship him discreetly until the reconstruction of Liujia Palace in 1979.[20]

The Great Leap Forward and the Massive Destruction and Closure of Temples

The Great Leap Forward, beginning in 1958, was the biggest blow to communal temples in Rui'an after land reform. The Great Leap, like the land reform campaign, did not directly target religious issues. But the frenzy of agricultural and industrial production led to the wholesale closure and massive destruction of temples, a "great leap in religious work," as local cadres called it, the details of which will be discussed in the following chapter. The harsh political

[19] Zhou Konghua and Ruan Zhensheng, eds., *Wenzhou Daojiao tonglan* (A general survey of Daoism in Wenzhou) (Hong Kong: Tianma Books, 1999), 219–220.
[20] Ibid., 213.

climate made it impossible to engage in open resistance or even negotiation over religious space.

Following a socialist education class in April 1958 attended by religious leaders and activists in the county seat, with similar "struggle meetings" held in other districts, many monks and nuns in Rui'an came out to condemn the old society and renounce their Buddhist faith.[21] Those who had asked for the return of monasteries admitted their "mistakes." An official report described the party position: "The government borrowed monasteries for socialist construction, which is beneficial to all people. We should never consider monasteries as the private property of the religious sector."[22] Subsequently, "ninety percent of temples and churches were voluntarily donated to brigades," with monks and nuns choosing to return to secular life and participate in agricultural production.[23] A government survey boasted that zero Buddhist monasteries were active in 1960,[24] in sharp contrast with the 400 or so Buddhist monasteries that had been active in Rui'an in 1949, and the 256 monasteries still housing monks and nuns in 1955, according to a government survey.[25]

It is impossible to state the exact number of territorial temples shut down or destroyed during the Great Leap Forward due to the lack of statistical data. Most of the temples which were already closed likely suffered further damage, while yet more temples were shut down.[26] In the movement to collect iron for smelting, a program that was occurring throughout China as part of the Great Leap Forward, temples and monasteries became a source of raw materials: metal, timber, and bricks.[27]

Temples were also torn down to make way for the construction of reservoirs and dams, another important local program of the Great Leap Forward. Reservoirs were typically built in mountainous areas, leading to the destruction of a number of mountain temples. Temples near dam sites were sometimes entirely torn down to supply raw materials for construction.[28]

[21] For how the 1958 campaign affected Buddhist monks and nuns elsewhere in China, see Holmes Welch, *Buddhism under Mao* (Cambridge, MA: Harvard University Press, 1972), 91–92, 235–237.

[22] "Guanyu zongjiaojie shehuizhuyi jiaoyu yundong zongjie baogao" (Concluding report on socialist education movement in the religious sector), April 1958, Rui'an City Archives, 1-10-161: 51.

[23] "Guanyu 1958 nian zongjiao gongzuo zongjie baogao" (Conclusion report on religious work in 1958), April 24, 1959, Rui'an City Archives 1-11-183: 108.

[24] "Zongjiaotu bianhua qingkuang" (Changes in the number of religious believers), June 5, 1961, Rui'an City Archives, 4-13-42: 25–26.

[25] We should not take these numbers literally, especially the 1960 number, as I learned in my fieldwork. In Jianshan Hall (*jianshan tang*) of Jian Mountain near Luonan Township, Tangxia, for instance, throughout much of the 1960s, a small number of monks remained and worked together with a work team sent to open up a tea plantation and living in the temple. The 1960 number, however, does suggest the heavy blow to Buddhist monasteries from the Great Leap Forward.

[26] Most senior residents confirmed further destruction of temples and statues of divinities during the Great Leap Forward, though they could rarely give details.

[27] Zhou and Ruan, *Wenzhou Daojiao tonglan*, 53, 150, 226, 254.

[28] Ibid., 56, 12, 400.

A small number of territorial temples apparently survived the storms of the Great Leap Forward. In Zi'ao Commune in 1963, not far from the district center of Tangxia, the work team sent down by the Wenzhou regional government for the Socialist Education Movement discovered that all of the territorial temples and Buddhist monasteries remained "fully preserved" (*baocun wanzhengde*) in the commune's Shen'ao Brigade. The brigade had also kept seven roadside shrines (*xiaoshenmiao*). In a neighboring brigade, the temple of Shan'gen Palace (*shan'gen dian*), dedicated to the worship of the Monkey King (*qitian dasheng*, a famous figure in Chinese mythology), welcomed crowds to light candles and recite scriptures for blessings (*dian fodeng*) every first and fifteenth day of the lunar month.[29]

A Religious Resurgence in the Early 1960s

The policies of the Great Leap Forward led to severe famine throughout China lasting two to three years. During this period, religious activities in Rui'an fell into a near-total silence, at least according to government records. Yet as early as 1960, "superstitious activities" such as reciting scriptures, worshipping deities, and building temples and divine statues reportedly re-emerged in eleven communes of Xincheng, Tangxia, Gaolou, Xikeng and Nantian,[30] along with many rumors about catastrophes and the end of time.[31] After 1961, local authorities estimated that most "superstition professionals" (*mixin zhiye fenzi*) in Zhejiang had resumed their activities, including sorcerers, diviners, and occultists (male or female). In Pingyang, a county adjoining Rui'an, as well as several other counties in southeastern Zhejiang, nearly all "superstition professionals" were reported to have resumed their former roles after the end of the Great Leap Forward.[32]

[29] "Guanyu Tangxia Shen'ao dadui liangda shili zhengduo qingshaonian de qingkuang diaocha" (Investigation of two major forces competing for youth in Shen'ao Brigade, Tangxia), July 7, 1963, Rui'an City Archives, 1-15-143: [1–3].

[30] Xikeng and Nantian are districts of Wencheng County which fell under the same administrative division as Rui'an from 1958 to 1961.

[31] "Guanyu liji caiqu cuoshi jiaqiang fanghuo he zhizhi mixin huodong de yijian" (Opinions on immediately taking measures to reinforce the work of fire prevention and to stop superstitious activities), July 6, 1960, Rui'an City Archives, 4-13-12: 17.

[32] To name only a few numbers in Zhejiang: the percentage of superstition professionals who resumed the old profession is 69 percent in Xinchang (northern Zhejiang), 98 percent in Ninghai (eastern Zhejiang), and 98 percent in Pingyang (southern Zhejiang). See Cheng Shicen, ed., *Pingyang Xian gong'an zhi* (Pingyang county public security gazetteer) (Tianjin: Nankai daxue chubanshe, 1997), 98; Gao Shuibiao, ed., *Xinchang Xian gong'an zhi* (Xinchang county public security gazetteer) (Beijing: Dangdai Zhongguo chubanshe, 1994), 139; Zhang Zhebin, ed., *Ninghai Xian gong'an zhi* (Ninghai county public security gazetteer) (Beijing: Zhonghua shuju, 2001), 256. Those "superstition professionals" in the statistics should have been under the radar previously. But other than that, we have no way to know exactly how local authorities generated the numbers. So we should not read these data too literally and they can only give some basic sense of the renewal of religious activities.

As county officials in Rui'an noted, an important step in the restoration of communal religious practices was the re-creation of traditional spaces required for large-scale communal rituals. Surveys in Tangxia District in 1963 indicated that more than a thousand villagers were involved in renovating temples, rebuilding statues of divinities, and gathering for purification rites (*jingdu*) on the first and fifteenth day of the lunar month. Twenty-two territorial temples and Buddhist monasteries were renovated.[33] Thirty-two lineages in twenty-seven brigades, covering a total of more than 20,000 people, were engaged in compiling genealogies.[34] In Hongqiao District of Yueqing County, ten of the district's 161 brigades renovated their ancestral halls, twenty-nine of them restored territorial temples, and fourteen compiled new genealogies.[35]

The resurgence of religious life was such that in June 1961, villagers held dragon boat races once more. The revival was initially led by none other than the party secretary of Lingxia Brigade and vice head of the County Seat Commune, Wu Zhenqian. It quickly spread to other districts. Concerned with the increase in "superstition activities," the Rui'an County Government reiterated the ban on dragon boat racing in May 1963.[36]

Then, in 1964, in the midst of the Socialist Education Movement, the Zhejiang provincial government issued a special anti-feudal-superstition notice, worrying that "superstition activities" would affect social stability and might become a vehicle for counterrevolutionary activity.[37] It may have been the first wide-scale ban on "superstition" in Zhejiang. The county government prohibited dragon boat races again in spring 1966, referring to "rampant feudal superstitious activities in the guise of dragon boat races, which have caused multiple disputes and even fights between villages."[38]

[33] "Tangxia Qu dangqian jieji douzheng qingkuang" (Current situation of class struggle in Tangxia District), December 15, 1962, Rui'an City Archives, 49-14-16: 64.

[34] "Pizhuan zhengfa dangzu guanyu zhizhi fengjian canyu de gezhong fubi huodong de yijian" (Approving and circulating Party committee of [county] political and legal office's notification on stopping restoration activities of various residual feudal forces), May 5, 1963, Rui'an City Archives, 1-15-69: 18.

[35] "Hongqiao Qu guanyu dang de gugan zhengfeng xuexihui qingkuang de jianbao" (Brief report on rectification study cession of backbone Party members in Hongqiao District), February 18, 1963, Yueqing City Archives: 1-15-27: 42.

[36] "Guanyu Duanwujie hualongzhou huodong de tongzhi" (Notice on dragon boat race during Dragon Boat Festival), June 14, 1961, Rui'an City Archives, 1-13-108: 28–30; "Rui'an Xian Lingxia shengchan dadui nao longzhou" (Lingxia Production Brigade of Rui'an County to hold dragon boat [race]), June 13, 1961, Wenling City Archives, J79-1-48: 77–78.

[37] "Zhejiang Sheng renmin weiyuanhui guanyu fandui fengjian mixin huodong de tongzhi" (The Zhejiang People's Committee's notice on opposing feudal superstitious activities), December 26, 1964, Rui'an City Archives, 49-16-41: 19–20.

[38] Zhang Chaoyin, ed., *Rui'an Shi longzhou huodong jianshi* (A concise history of dragon boat racing in Rui'an) (Rui'an Shi shiwei dangshi yanjiushi, Difangzhi bangongshi, internal document, 2002), 8.

Grassroots cadres were, perhaps not surprisingly, implicated in most cases of temple restoration. During the Socialist Education Movement (also known as the Four Clears Movement), work teams found that in Rui'an County and the periphery of Wenzhou, many grassroots cadres either directly organized or tacitly agreed to religious activities like temple reconstruction and genealogy compilation, the latter being a critical aspect of local lineages.

Zhang Buwang, the party secretary of the embroidery (handicraft) brigade in Tangxia Commune, arranged a large-scale funeral for his mother, who passed away on December 28, 1965. He invited a group of liturgists and Daoists to host a complete set of elaborate rituals, some of which, it was said, had only been seen before 1949. Hundreds of relatives and neighbors, including "landlords, rich peasants, counterrevolutionaries and bad elements" (di fu fan huai), attended the funeral and the immense banquet that followed.[39]

In another case, Shao Yongsheng, the vice head of Zi'ao Brigade in Tangxia, was invited to lead members of the Shao lineage in Shaozhai Brigade of Tangxia Commune in compiling a new genealogy for the entire Shao lineage in Tangxia District (Photo 3.7).[40] In the new genealogy, which I saw in 2012, Shao Yongsheng's name was listed alongside that of chief editor Shao Yanliu, a former landlord, who was also the chief editor of the previous genealogy. Cadres in Donglian Brigade, Hongqiao District, Yueqing, even used the brigade's money to fund temple reconstruction and genealogy compilation.[41]

More surprising yet is the case of the Mountain God Temple (shangong miao) in Meishukeng Brigade, Yaozhuang Commune, Huling, which borders Qingtian County and Wenzhou municipality. When the Mountain God Temple was rebuilt in 1961, county officials learned that brigade party secretary Chen Zhaorao not only initiated the restoration of the temple, but also was a spirit medium. In the opening ceremony of the restored Mountain God Temple, Chen allegedly entered a trance state and gave a speech condemning the government. In reference to the destruction of the temple, he said, "the Communist Party (previously) forced me to have no place to live."[42]

---

[39] "Pizhuan xianwei jianwei guanyu Tangxia Zhang Buwang tongzhi jinxing fengjian mixin huodong dasi huihuo langfei de diaocha baogao" (Issuing the investigational report by the county Party supervision committee on comrade Zhang Buwang of Tangxia's engagement in feudal superstitious activities and extravagant expenditures), January 14, 1966, Rui'an City Archives, 1-18-8: 35.

[40] "Guanyu Tangxia Shao Yongsheng tongzhi canyu lingdao 'xiu jiapu' wenti de taolun" (Discussion on comrade Shao Yongsheng of Tangxia District's involvement in organizing "genealogy compilation" activities), June 15, 1963, Rui'an City Archives, 1-15-143: [1–6].

[41] "Guanyu Donglian Gongshe fengjian mixin huodong qingkuang de diaocha baogao" (Investigational report on the situation of feudal superstitious activities in Donglian Commune), May 6, 1963, Yueqing City Archives, 1-15-27: 162–182.

[42] "Guanyu Yaozhuang Gongshe dubo he mixin huodong qingkuang de diaocha baogao" (Investigational report on gambling and superstitious activities in Yaozhuang Commune), December 26, 1961, Rui'an City Archives 82-11-8: 31–32. Similar waves of religious restoration were seen in Shannxi, Fujian, and Hebei in the early 1960s. See Elizabeth J. Perry, Challenging the Mandate of

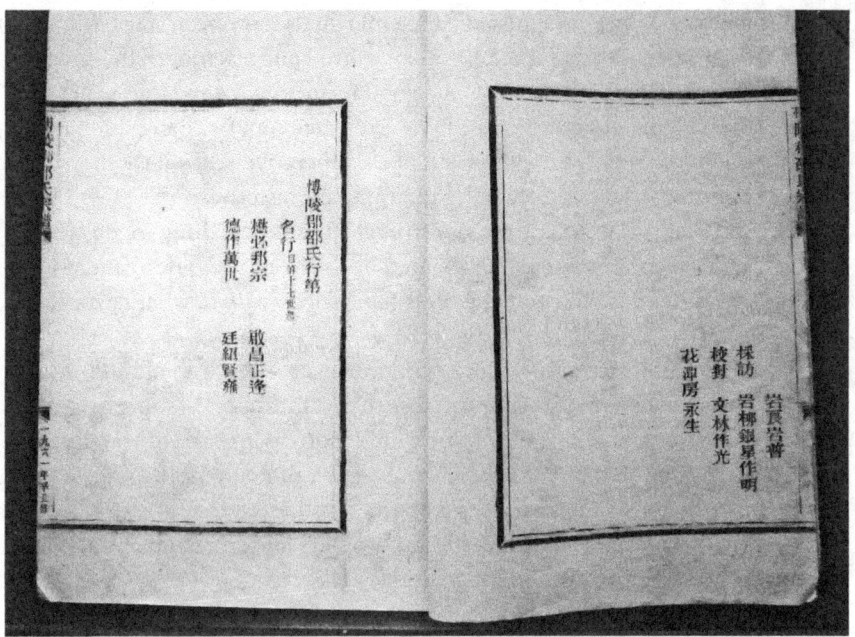

Photo 3.7 A page from the 1961 genealogy of the Shao lineage, which listed Yongsheng as a member of the editorial board. Yongsheng also appears in the editorial broad of the 1976 genealogy of the Shao family.
Source: Author.

Both Zhang and Shao became the targets of criticism in cadre meetings ostensibly held to educate other cadres, teaching "correct" attitudes and understandings of issues like lineage and feudal superstition. During the meetings, however, many cadres expressed overt sympathy toward Shao and Zhang. Regarding Shao, some cadres believed it was necessary to compile a genealogy because without it "the five relations (*wulun*) would get messy. We would not be able to recognize our ancestors, or a great aunt would not realize that she married her grandnephew . . . all things have a system. A nation is constituted of the center, province, county and commune level by level. So human relations should also be ordered generation by generation."[43]

Heaven: Social Protest and State Power in China (London: M. E. Sharpe, 2002), 289; Adam Yuet Chau, "Popular Religion in Shannbei, North-Central China," *Journal of Chinese Religions* 31 (2003): 41–42; Stephen Jones, *Plucking the Winds: Lives of Village Musicians in Old and New China* (Leiden: CHIME Foundation, 2004), 135–138.

[43] Rui'an City Archives, 1-15-143: [1].

In Zhang's case, one person said: "Funeral rituals have been our customs for thousands of years. Zhang's mother was long-lived and a senior in the genealogical ranking (*beifen*). [She also had] the good fortune of having four generations [in her family] living together in one house (*sishitongtang*). [Zhang's] son is party secretary and his grandson is the head of a cooperative. They have money and there is nothing wrong with making the funeral boisterous (*'re'nao'*)." The observer continued, "If a funeral is class struggle, then everything in village life is class struggle! It is an old custom handed down from the older generation. If somebody's funeral is cold and cheerless (*lenglengqingqing*), what flavor does it have?"[44]

As brigade and commune cadres continued to engage in traditional religious practices and other local customs, their ambivalence suggests that the difficulties in suppressing "superstition" did not disappear with collectivization. Collectivization may even have made it more difficult for the state to tackle communal religious activities. As the new commune leaders, grassroots cadres were now largely responsible for community affairs, becoming an obstacle to the state's efforts to clamp down on superstition.

Indeed, after collectivization, local cadres became both the targets and the enforcers of anti-superstition policies. Superior officials were at pains to inculcate brigade and commune cadres with politically correct notions of religious and lineage activities. However, these cadres shared ideas of religion and lineage similar to those of ordinary villagers. They certainly behaved differently during political campaigns or when an important directive was sent down from above (even if they privately considered communal religious and lineage activities as harmless customs). However, as the county government discovered in its investigations, they could secretly permit, support, or even directly participate in religious and lineage activities.

The Cultural Revolution and the Conundrum of Temple Restoration

In the summer of 1966, when calls for the great proletarian Cultural Revolution reached Rui'an, work teams were sent to the countryside. They were tasked with mobilizing commune youths to "Clear the Four Olds" (old customs, old culture, old habits, and old ideas) and sweep away the "ox demons and snake deities" (*niu gui she shen*, a derogatory term loosely referring to class enemies). Religious

---

[44] "Guanyu dui Tangxia Zhang Buwang tongzhi jinxing fengjian fubi huodong de diaocha qingkuang he bianlun qingkuang" (Investigation and discussion of comrade Zhang Buwang's engagement in restoration of feudal order) January 17, 1966, Rui'an City Archives, 49-18-1: 82.

sites and religious followers were faced with further attacks. But the Red Guards might not find many things to destroy in communal temples, as most of them had already been emptied during previous political campaigns. Thus religious objects belonging to households and families bore the brunt of the onslaught.

A report from a work team stationed in Caocun Township, Mayu, summarized a scene of the destruction of the Four Olds:

> Within only a few days, ancestral altars, stovetop shrines, old tablets, clay statues of divinities, old doorplates have all been destroyed spontaneously. . . . Nu'ao Brigade, for instance, has spontaneously destroyed a thousand and more old incense holders and amassed more than seven hundred old books and "dirty novels". . . now all 150 households in the Brigade have put up Chairman Mao's poster in each of their homes. They [also] turned the tablets that used to hold ancestral altars into Chairman [Mao] quotation boards. Every house has hung one up. Members of Xu'nan and Xubei Brigade voluntarily demolished thirty-five clay and wooden statues of divinities in Mani Temple (*mingjiao si*) and Xu'ao Palace (*xu'ao gong*). The Great Yin Palace of Shangdu Brigade has been turned into a club.[45]

Incense holders and tablets were common household objects for the worship of deities and ancestors in traditional Chinese families. In October 1966 in Mayu alone, Red Guards confiscated 7,484.5 taels of tin and 57,698 incense holders. They destroyed 180 statues of divinities and burned 1,060 volumes of genealogy.[46]

In the wake of these ferocious attacks by Red Guards, the vast majority of temples, if not all of them, must have ceased to operate. Po Yiha, a former head of the Rui'an Buddhist Association which was established in the early 1980s, witnessed all of the Mao-era attacks on Buddhism in the region and confirmed that throughout Rui'an, very few Buddhist temples were still active or had any monks present during the Cultural Revolution.[47]

But in these fraught early years of the Cultural Revolution, villagers still found ways to save their deities and, where possible, carry on public worship. Sacred objects were sometimes salvaged and hidden elsewhere to allow villagers to covertly pursue religious activities elsewhere, as in the case of the Temple of the

[45] "Rui'an xianwei Caocun gongzuodui gongzuo qingkuang jianbao" (Bulletin of work of Rui'an County Party Committee Caocun work team, volume one), September 10, Rui'an City Archives 1-18-37: 2–3.

[46] "Xincheng Qu zongjiao qingkuang diaocha tongjibiao" (Statistical tables from investigations into the religious situation in Xincheng District), 1991, Rui'an City Archives 72-24-10: 56–57. Tin was commonly used to make religious artifacts in traditional Chinese society.

[47] Po Yiha, interview by author. Rui'an, May 15, 2013.

True Body (*zhenshen si*) in Baotian Commune, Tangxia District. The temple is dedicated to a local woman from the Dai lineage who was deified after death. Her statue, the Princess of the True Body (*zhenshen taigu*), is famously the temple's main deity and once contained her mummified remains. In 1968, the Red Guards stormed the temple and removed the statue. They paraded it through the streets of Baotian before setting it on fire in front of the Dai lineage's ancestral hall next to the temple. While those Red Guards most likely came from one of the local communes and may even have been members the Dai lineage, some members of the Dai lineage managed to collect the statue's damaged remains, including the deity's bones. They reburied the damaged relics behind a small shrine in nearby Fenghuang Mountain until the end of the Cultural Revolution.[48]

As the political atmosphere made it nearly impossible to publicly worship statues of divinities, resourceful villagers turned to more discreet means. In traditional Chinese religion, burning incense is a means of communicating with deities, offering them deference and inviting their presence. Furthermore, incense fire (*xianghuo*) is understood as a symbol of a territorial unit, family, or village. Thus burning incense is not just a religious act but also a way to reaffirm the bond between the community, the family, and their deities.[49] Burning incense became especially important when it was not possible to engage in public worship in front of statues of gods.

Burning incense could be a means of engaging with religious sites, even after temples and buildings had been destroyed. The Temple of the Eastern Marchmount (*dongyue miao*), located at the center of the town of Tangxia, was first occupied by a supply-and-sale co-op and then was used as a timber shop. The worship of deities probably continued despite the occupation of the temple. Therefore, when the temple building was torn down to build a food market in 1970, a corner was left to erect an incense burner for worship. Incense fire, it was said, was still needed on the first and fifteenth day of every lunar month for prosperity. When even an incense burner was not allowed, people simply inserted incense sticks into the ground outside the temple.[50] Villagers in the Lower Brigade of Xincheng did the same during the early years of the Cultural Revolution when the East Hall Palace was completely locked up.[51]

Whether public worship continued had a lot to do with varied local political environments and the inconsistency of social control across different levels of the state. The "Clear the Four Olds" campaign in 1966 and the armed fighting

---

[48]   Ying Weixian and Shi Shihu, eds., *Liangchu guan yu Zhaoming taizi* (Pavilion of Liang [dynasty] crown prince and crown prince Zhaoming) (Shenzhen: Haitian chubanshe, 2008), 74–75.

[49]   Stephan Feuchtwang, *Popular Religion in China: The Imperial Metaphor* (Richmond, Surrey: Curzon Press, 2001), 133–136.

[50]   Zhou and Ruan, *Wenzhou Daojiao tonglan*, 158.

[51]   Zhan Songlen, interview by author. Xincheng, May 1, 2013.

that occurred over the next few years were the most severe disruptions to religious life. The county seat remained at the center of political campaigns when armed fights began, whereas the vast rural areas, especially those away from town centers or the county seat, were relatively quiet in the remaining years of the Cultural Revolution.

In the summer of 1967, the Red Guard movement erupted in countywide armed fights of rival factions. General Headquarters (*lianzong*), a rebel group who held the county seat, began fighting another faction mainly made up of peasants, the loyalist United Headquarters (*lianzhan*), who besieged the county seat for three months.

In a pamphlet published in August 1967, General Headquarters accused United Headquarters of encouraging "superstitious activities" throughout Rui'an:

The burning of incense and worshipping of deities have resurfaced in Xincheng, Tangxia, and Mayu. People once again set up candles and incense holders in temples. "Superstitious" goods such as paper money and candles were available on the market for sale in large quantities. Those who were in power (*dangquanpai*, incumbent cadres) in Shangwang Commune openly told relatives of [their] soldiers [referring to those commune members mobilized to rescue incumbent cadres in the county seat]: "you can recite scriptures and worship deities as much as you wish." The mother of Pan Shixing, team head of Shangwang, the mother of militia commander Yu Naibao, and the wife of party secretary Zhang Busong (who was fighting the war in Long Mountain [in the urban areas surrounding Rui'an]) all went to worship deities and light candles.[52]

This General Headquarters pamphlet may have been propaganda to defame United Headquarters. It was possible, however, that factional leaders who were not Maoist ideologues did give some leeway to public religious practices.

In the summer of 1967, at the height of the violent conflict, the county suffered its most severe drought since 1953.[53] Senior residents of nearby villages flocked into the East Hall Palace in Xincheng (described earlier) and prepared to pray for rain. United Headquarters apparently allowed the rainmaking ceremony, but it was soon halted by General Headquarters. Fights broke out between the two

[52] "Xuezhai leilei zuixing taotian" ([United Headquarters'] mountains of blood debts and towering crimes), November 1967, Rui'an City Archives 42-1-15: 39.
[53] There was almost no rain for eighty-three days starting from mid-July. Even Tang River, the longest river in the Wenrui plains, dried up.

factions, claiming two lives: a General Headquarters soldier and an elderly villager who was shot one night by the temple guard.[54]

As the Cultural Revolution crippled the regular functions of government, the control of religious activities fell to grassroots cadres, and their attitude toward religion gained a greater importance. In spite of the extreme political atmosphere, grassroots cadres behaved much as they had done in the 1950s and early 1960s. Not surprisingly, there were numerous accounts of brigade and commune cadres dispersing religious gatherings, reporting them to the county government, and making arrests. But there were also many instances where cadres tacitly allowed religious activities or directly participated in them.

In the early and mid-1970s, there were clear signs of attempts to bring back communal religious activities. A collection of brief histories of 170 village temples in Rui'an states that eleven of these were renovated or rebuilt between 1970 and 1978.[55] This gives us a sense of the extent of the restoration of temple activities in the later stage of the Cultural Revolution. The records of the Rui'an County Revolutionary Committee at the time also noted instances of what they termed the "restoration of feudal superstition" (*fengjian mixin fubi*).

In Chengshanping Brigade, Lumu Commune, Huling, in February 1973, a medium called Chen Shicong and his son Chen Wenzhu claimed to be possessed by Lord Yang and helped the brigade identify the thief who had stolen fertilizer from its forest group. The Chens subsequently asked for the reconstruction of Lord Yang's Palace, the temple that had been turned into an elementary school. In the name of the deity, the Chens even appointed Feng Zongde, the brigade secretary, as the manager of the project and asked him to collect donations to fund the reconstruction. However, less than a month later, both father and son were arrested, ending efforts to rebuild the temple.[56]

In another attempted revival of communal religion in the Huling District, which occurred in the Datong Brigade of Huling Commune in the winter of 1974, the Zheng family—under the leadership of a certain Zheng Qingzan—successfully forced the brigade's agricultural machinery workshop to move out from the Zheng ancestral hall and got the brigade to agree to repair it. The county government only discovered the restoration of their ancestral hall when they were alerted by an informant, perhaps someone who did not belong to the Zheng family and resented Zheng Qingzan's frequent interference with brigade issues

[54] Interview with Jie Zisong at Lower Village on July 26, 2012. Tang Yijun, ed., *Xincheng Zhen zhi* (Xincheng town gazetteer) (Huangshan shushe, 1998), 280.

[55] Ying Weixian, ed., *Rui'an Shi Daojiao zhi* (History of Daoism in Rui'an) (Rui'an Daojiao xiehui, 2011).

[56] "Guanyu Huling Qu Zheng Qingzan jinxing fengjian fubi de chuli jueding" (Decision on the handling of the case of feudal restoration of Zheng Qingzan in Huling District), July 8, 1977, Rui'an City Archives 82-27-1: 260–261.

using "lineage force" (*zongzu shili*). Zheng was subsequently convicted of being a "counterrevolutionary."[57]

Much as in other stages of the Mao era, attempts to restore communal temples during the Cultural Revolution could not overcome a fundamental problem: Even when a temple was successfully rebuilt and rituals were restored, how could religious practitioners ensure its continued stable existence?

This conundrum stemmed from three difficulties. First, communal religious activities lacked a stable leadership to shield them from political retaliation and relentless political onslaughts. The examples of Shao and Zhang in the mid-1960s and Chen and Zheng in the late 1970s all suggest that regardless of one's position, whether as a spirit medium, family elder, or cadre, one could not openly lead temple activities without incurring the wrath of higher authorities. Cadres sometimes shut their eyes to communal religion, and sometimes even secretly supported it, but when they took the lead in regular temple activities, they risked their political careers and the swift retaliation of higher officials.

A further leadership problem affected Buddhism in particular. In Rui'an, the vast majority of monks and nuns had returned to secular life after 1958 and ordination had been prohibited since then. Most ordained monks and nuns who were still alive in the early 1970s were already in their seventies.[58] Though Buddhist gatherings did resurface around that time, these monks and nuns were simply too old to take an active leadership role, resulting in many Buddhist gatherings being organized and led by young lay followers. Due to the lack of clergy, collective ritual services became rare, and Buddhist gatherings were limited mainly to scripture chanting in the mountainous areas near villages, such as in the Daluo Mountains, Tangxia, a traditional center of Buddhism in southern Zhejiang, and in Jin'ao Mountain, Xincheng.[59]

The second major difficulty facing communal religion in the Mao era was financing. Performing rituals and maintaining territorial temples and Buddhist monasteries consumed a great deal of money and labor, which is why local cadres constantly criticized communal religious activities for being extravagant. The commune system removed money and production materials from individuals and concentrated them in the hands of the collective. As observed in the religious resurgence of the mid-1960s in Rui'an and Yueqing, people had to ask for commune leaders' permission to use money and other materials belonging

---

[57] "Guanyu dui Huling Qu Chen Wencong, Chen Wenzhu fengjian fubi an de chuli yijian baogao" (Opinions on handling the feudal restoration case of Chen Shicong and Chen Wenzhu of Huling District), March 30, 1973, Rui'an City Archives 1-21-9: 30–31.

[58] The average age of monks and nuns in the entire county was fifty-two, based on a 1955 survey of residential Buddhist monks and nuns. See "Guanyu Fojiao qingkuang diaocha baogao" (Investigational report on Buddhism), July 14, 1955, Rui'an City Archives 1-7-137: 38.

[59] Po Yiha, interview by author. Rui'an, May 15, 2013.

to the collective if they wished to stage a communal ritual or repair a temple or ancestral hall.

To overcome this problem, people sometimes went door to door asking for donations (*aihu tankuan*) from individual families, a traditional way of collecting funds for communal affairs, such as when Shengjing Temple (*shengjing dian*) was repaired in 1955. The problem, however, was how to secure reliable funding from members of communes and collectives. Using collective money would risk attracting the attention of local authorities, which would have a political cost for commune leaders.

Finally, even when communal rituals resumed or temples were successfully repaired, their existence was constantly interrupted by local and national political campaigns. Villagers in some cases did take back or rebuild temples and ancestral halls or resume the annual ritual of dragon boat racing. However, communal religion could rarely survive the onslaught of political attacks. With new campaigns, statues of divinities were smashed and temples were once again shut down. Their destruction could not prevent people from trying again, which is why there were always attempts to rebuild temples following waves of destruction. But followers of communal religion were never able to break the cycle of destruction during the Mao years.

Conclusion

From collectivization to the Cultural Revolution, communal temples deprived of land routinely came under attack by political campaigns and encroachments on their property and religious sites. Unlike the expropriation of temple estates during land reform, the loss of traditional communal religious space did not happen all at once. It occurred at a varied pace, with many temples going through periodic revivals before being shut down. By the early 1970s, the vast majority of communal temples belonging to territorial cults, Buddhism, and Daoism in Rui'an were either shut down, occupied, or destroyed, a massive deterritorialization on a truly unprecedented scale in local history.

The temples that disappeared under Mao and have not already been rebuilt are unlikely to be restored. Conversely, the temples that were rebuilt after the end of the Mao era were often rebuilt in new locations and in different forms. Whether temples were lost or rebuilt in new forms, their disappearance and transformation marked a permanent change in the local religious landscape. For the time being, though, as this chapter demonstrates, followers quickly learned to face up to the expropriation of traditional communal religious space through resistance, negotiation, and compromise, sometimes finding alternative spaces where they could continue to worship.

The prolonged struggle for communal religious space indicates that entrenched beliefs in local society continued to guide everyday life even as Maoist ideology took root in the minds of local residents. The political environment, which became more and more hostile in the decades following land reform, in fact pushed some people to cling to traditional practices. When facing intrusive sociopolitical and economic policies and their consequences, some people increasingly turned to religious explanations of natural and man-made disasters, sometimes culminating in public expressions of discontent, like the "superstition riots" of 1953. This type of collective action is essentially the same as other social protests, such as the widespread resistance against agricultural cooperativization in the mid-1950s, rejecting the Maoist imposition of social units and space.

Mao once famously wrote, "Peasants themselves erected gods [*pusa*, literally "Bodhisattvas"] and eventually they will use their own hands to cast aside [these] gods."[60] Yet the reverse is also true: the hands that cast aside their gods could erect them again. From the 1950s to the 1970s, the same rural residents of Rui'an who closed temples or even smashed statues of divinities would sometimes rebuild statues or temples and resume worship when they felt the time was right. The restoration of temples did not lack the support of party cadres, the new village leadership, in spite of the purge of traditional local elites who were leaders and major patrons of temples before 1949.

Brigade and commune cadres were far from being Maoist ideologues. On religious issues they often thought like other commune members, though their actions very much depended on their own interests. Village cadres' backing of communal religion took a much less visible form than the support of traditional rural elites, but it was pervasive, as we see in the superstition riots or the "feudal restoration" occurring in the early 1960s and 1970s.

Communal movements to retain or restore traditional religious spaces ebbed and flowed following the currents of Maoist policies, with the intervals between major political campaigns at times allowing attempts at temple restoration to resume—at the beginning of collectivization, after the Great Famine, and in the later stage of the Cultural Revolution, as we see in Rui'an. This is because the political climate to a great extent determined the behaviors of ordinary community members and community leaders as well as the resources that people could mobilize. The wave of restoration of temples and ancestral halls in the early 1960s, for instance, was facilitated by the increased autonomy of local brigades, which the central government had allowed in the aftermath of the Great Famine.

[60] Mao Zedong, "Hunan nongmin yundong de kaocha baogao" (Report on the peasant movement in Hunan), in *Mao Zedong xuanji di yi juan* (Anthology of Mao Zedong, volume one) (Beijing: Renmin chubanshe, 1991), 33. Officials often quoted this sentence in dealing with the issue of "superstition" during the Maoist period.

During this era, most cases of temple restoration occurred with the leadership and material support of the collective. It is difficult to imagine a similar scenario at the height of the Great Leap Forward or the Cultural Revolution.

Therefore, during the Mao era, as the political climate affected the stability of religious spaces as well as the material foundations and leadership of communal religious activities, attempts to restore temples and temple practices could only persist at a minimal level. But this persistence, as subdued as it was, had a crucial role in laying the groundwork for the post-Mao revival of communal temples. The cycle of frustration, when attempts at communal religious revival were rebuffed and worship was once again halted or pushed underground, only came to an end in the post-Mao era, when the collective dissolved and the political environment became more permissive toward religion (explored in Chapter 7).

Traditional communal religious space is fundamentally territorial in nature: bound to land and to temples serving local communities. Thus it can only be reterritorialized within the communities that it serves. Its importance in the life of local communities lent it some resilience amid the political storms of the Mao era. How, therefore, did the political climate affect Christian churches, which had a distinct way of operating, much less bound to local religious sites? The trans-communal connections and organizational networks of the church made for a very different set of challenges during collectivization, as I discuss in the next chapter.

4

Destruction and Renewal

Christian Churches from the Early 1950s to the Mid-1960s

A few years after land reform, Christian activities publicly re-emerged. For the Catholic Church, it was a slow recovery. As was the case for communal religion, the end of land reform did not put a stop to state's efforts to circumscribe or even eliminate the role of religion in local society. As part of the Campaign to Suppress Counterrevolutionaries, the central government launched a nationwide crackdown on the Legion of Mary, an organization affiliated with the Catholic Church.[1] In Wenzhou, the suppression of the Legion of Mary took place from the winter of 1951 to the spring of the following year. The Rui'an County Government clamped down on two branches of the Legion of Mary, forcing its twenty-two members to disband, and arrested Priest Lin Mingzhu of Rui'an parish in 1952 for his alleged involvement with the group.

The suppression of the Legion of Mary occurred on a relatively small scale, but it created a horrific atmosphere among local Catholics. They were afraid of being associated with a group now labeled as "counterrevolutionary," and these fears were probably not without reason.[2] A report from a police station in the neighborhood where the Rui'an parish church was located shows that every church activist was under close surveillance. The report listed detailed information about the backgrounds, social relations, and personal characteristics of Catholic activists.[3] Many Catholics did not dare rejoin their congregations after land reform for fear of political consequences. By January 1953, only ten out of the region's twenty Catholic churches were reported to have resumed their activities. Five more became active again sometime in the next two years, but as of July 1955, the remaining five were still closed.

---

[1] For a history of the Legion of Mary in China and the Communist government's crackdown on the Legion of Mary, see Paul P. Mariani, *Church Militant: Bishop Kung and Catholic Resistance in Communist Shanghai* (Cambridge, MA: Harvard University Press, 2011), 46–53, 75–87.

[2] "Zhixing zongjiao zhengce diaocha baogao" (Investigational report on the implementation of religious policies), April 9, 1953, Rui'an City Archives 1-5-62: 14–15.

[3] "Dongmen paichusuo Tianzhujiaotu paidui" (Profiling Catholics under the jurisdiction of East Gate police station), 1953, Rui'an City Archives 1-5-113: 6–14.

Maoism and Grassroots Religion. Xiaoxuan Wang, Oxford University Press (2020). © Oxford University Press.
DOI: 10.1093/oso/9780190069384.001.0001

In contrast, Protestant churches made a much faster recovery. Many became active again soon after land reform without asking local authorities for permission. A few congregations did not resume their gatherings because they could not find a meeting place or their ministers had not returned. But by January 1953, almost all Protestant congregations had taken up their routine activities once more.

This chapter follows the evolution of Christianity in Wenzhou from the early 1950s to the mid-1960s, with a focus on Protestantism. I start by tracing the development of Protestant churches up to 1957 and the tensions surrounding the growth of the church. I then move on to the "great leap in religious work" as it affected the church and explain why 1958 was such a critical moment for Protestants under Mao. The last part of the chapter explores the aftermath of the Great Leap Forward and how it transformed the landscape of Christianity in Wenzhou.

1950–1957: Protestant Growth, Catholic Stagnation

From 1952 to 1957, the central government implemented two crucial policies: collectivization and "unified purchase and sale." These policies encountered fierce resistance in Rui'an, including riots and a massive exodus from collective farms along the southern bank of the Feiyun River and in the western mountains. These happened to be the areas where Protestant churches were the most active at the time. The root of the conflict was not quite the same as in communal religion, which had seen massive expropriations of land and then temple buildings. As with temples "borrowed" or taken for public purposes, collectivization and other political directives certainly supplied more pretexts to take over religious buildings belonging to Protestants. But the ongoing expropriation of religious properties did not have the same effect on Protestant congregations, as they had long housed gatherings in members' homes and other convenient meeting places. In fact, Protestant communities throughout Rui'an continued to form new branches and gain new converts in the early stage of collectivization.

The Methodist Church is the only Protestant denomination that did not establish new branches after 1949. All of the other Protestant denominations formed at least one or two new branches during this period.[4] The expansion of the Assembly was even more rapid. Solely in Chuanhe Township, Huling, from the second half of 1954 to July 1957, its gatherings increased from three to six.

---

[4] Rui'an City Archives 1-7-35: 2.

Between 1951 and 1958, the Assembly established a total of eleven new gathering places (*juhuidian*) in Huling, Tangxia, Xianjiang, and Mayu districts.[5]

Some Protestant communities were preparing to build new churches. In Zhuyuan Village, Huling, Protestants became the majority population in 1957, and the village's Adventist community had collected all the necessary construction materials for a new church as of 1957.[6] Ou Fachen, a founding member of the Assembly in Qianbu, Xincheng, recalled that the cloth factory where they met was no longer big enough to accommodate their membership, so they sought a bigger permanent meeting place in 1953.[7] They collected donations amounting to 100,000,000 RMB (*yiyi renminbi,* about 10,000 RMB after the currency reform in 1953),[8] and the new church was about half-built in 1958 when the Great Leap Forward put a stop to construction.

The government carried out multiple surveys in the 1950s in order to track changes in the religious landscape.[9] Though colored by state discourse, these surveys lend some insight into Christianity in Rui'an from land reform to the Great Leap Forward.[10]

---

[5] Rui'an jiaohui, *Rui'an jiaohui shi*, 13.

[6] Shu Chengqian, *Wushi nian jiaohui shenghuo huiyi* (Memoirs of fifty years' life in the church), internal reference materials ("neibu cankao ziliao"), 2002, Chapter 15 (section 1). When the Great Leap Forward came early next year, the government confiscated all their materials and even took the land that they intended to use to build the church. The materials and the land were distributed to villagers to build new houses.

[7] Ou Fachen, interview by author, Rui'an, May 7, 2013.

[8] Xianwei pizhuan xianwei xuanchuanbu xian gong'anju dui Tianzhujiao shengmu nian huodong de ji dian yijian (The county party committee issues several opinions by the propaganda department and public security department on the Catholic Church's celebration of the Assumption of Mary), June 1, 1954, Rui'an City Archives 1-6-12: 4.

[9] See "Guanyu minzheng gongzuo zhuanti baogao he Chengguan, Xianjiang Jidujiao, Tianzhujiao jiben qingkuang dengjibiao" (Special report on civil affairs, registers of Protestant churches and Catholic Church in the county seat and Xianjiang), 1951, Rui'an City Archives 4-3-12: 45–135; "Guanyu zongjiao gongzuo wenjian cailiao" (Documents on religious work), January 1953, Rui'an City Archives 1-5-113: 29–33; "Guanyu zongjiao gongzuo, zhengyong simiao wenti, ji jiaohui ganbu, jiaotu mingce" (Report on religious work and expropriation of temples, and registers of church leaders and followers), 1958, Rui'an City Archives 4-10-75: 14–28.

[10] Three comprehensive surveys of local Christian groups were taken in 1951, 1953, and 1957. A further survey of the China Jesus Independent Church was taken on the eve of the Great Leap Forward. These religious surveys vary in levels of detail. The most detailed surveys include a brief history of each individual church, the name of its leader, the church's financial statement, a summary of recent events, and information about membership (e.g., total number, each member's origin [village name], gender, age, baptized or not, family relations, class, education and occupation). Less detailed surveys only contain the location of individual churches, the leader's name, and the total membership of the church. These surveys may not be accurate and can even be problematic for various reasons. It is unknown if officials edited these surveys and made any adjustments, especially of the membership numbers, before putting them together into final form to present to their superiors. The definition of "church member" (*xintu* or *jiaotu*) also raised ambiguities. In spite of these reservations, these surveys, when supplemented with the historical records kept by local churches and information provided by witnesses in interviews, can provide a basic sense of the trajectories of different Christian denominations.

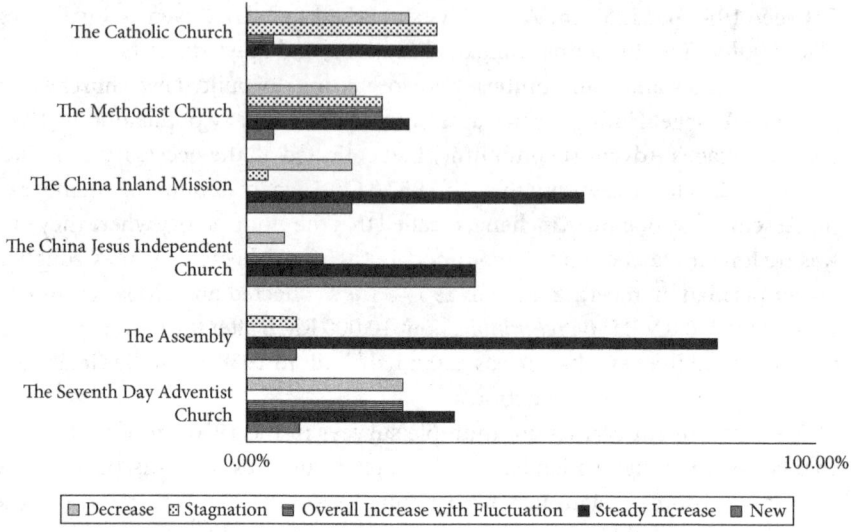

Figure 4.1. The trend of Protestant populations, 1950–1957.

We can broadly class changes in church membership over this period into five categories: decrease, stagnation, fluctuation but overall increase, steady increase, and newly created communities. These categories cover ninety-two Christian communities in Rui'an. "Decrease" includes Christian groups whose membership fell more than 20 percent. "Stagnation" refers to Christian groups whose membership fluctuated less than 20 percent. Groups whose membership increased more than 20 percent fall in the categories "steady increase" or "fluctuation but overall increase."[11] Figure 4.1 depicts the trend of Protestant populations between 1950 and 1957, using the above five categories.

The Methodist Church and the China Inland Mission (CIM) were the two oldest and largest Protestant denominations before 1949. As Figure 4.1 shows, both grew after 1949, though in slightly different ways. Nine out of a total of twenty-one Methodist churches either stagnated or decreased in membership, whereas six Methodist churches showed a steady increase. Membership in the other five Methodist churches dropped in 1956 but increased overall. Sixteen of the seventeen branches of the CIM whose membership can be traced show a steady increase in numbers. By contrast, ten of a total of nineteen local Catholic

[11] The 20-percent mark reflects the fact that every group falling within the "stagnation" category generally witnessed a membership fluctuation of far less than 20 percent (generally tending to fluctuate only slightly above or below zero percent, with a maximum fluctuation of around 16 percent).

churches either stagnated or decreased, while eight experienced steady increases in membership between 1951 and 1957.

The Seventh-Day Adventist Church seems to have lost ground after land reform. Of its eleven branches, two, the Jiaopu Church in Pingyangkeng and the Dongkeng Church in Huling, did not restore activities. However, membership in its seven other churches nearly doubled or even tripled. Among the fourteen China Jesus Independent churches (CJICs) listed in the surveys, seven experienced a steady increase in membership and one experienced fluctuations in membership, but there was an overall increase. The CJIC's remaining six churches, which only appeared in government surveys after 1953, were mostly new establishments. Finally, nineteen of the Assembly's twenty-three churches experienced steady increases in membership. Between 1951 and 1956, total membership in the Assembly increased by 86 percent.

The appearance of new converts in several villages of the western mountain areas is surprising. Some were even party members, a fact that concerned the authorities. "Protestant families in Duikeng Village in this township [Chuanhe] grew from one family before 1949 to fifty-five families with a total of 234 people [in 1955]. What is even more worrying is that [Christianity] infiltrated our party's grassroots organizations in the countryside. Five party members and nine Youth League members joined Protestant churches."[12]

In Huang'ao, Xianfang Township, the CJIC had set up a gathering place in 1938. There were only seventeen Christian families in the village in 1951. However, by March 1955, the number had increased to eighty-one families with a total of 348 members, making up more than half the population in the village. Three of the eight party members converted to Christianity.[13]

We see similar trends in some parts of Pingyang County bordering Rui'an to the south. The Protestant population in the towns of Qiaodun, Lingxi, and Zaoxi went from 237 before land reform to 352 in 1954.[14] Comparing 1951 and 1954 membership numbers in the Assembly in Mocheng Township (in the suburbs of the Pingyang county seat) also shows an increase. Before 1954, Protestant gatherings were only active in a few villages, but after 1954, small groups started holding regular meetings throughout the township. Two Assembly churches in Mocheng had 308 baptized members and 305 inquirers (*mudaoyou*) in 1951. The

[12] Rui'an City Archives 1-7-35: 3–4. This number (234) likely included all non-Christian family members. The number that this church provided for the religious survey in 1955 is fifty. In the registers submitted by individual local churches, they did not include the family members of Christians among their church constituents.

[13] Rui'an City Archives 1-7-35: 6.

[14] "Pingyang Xian zongjiao gongzuo yijian" (Opinions on religious affairs in Pingyang), July 19, 1954, Rui'an City Archives 1-6-70: 28.

number rose to 363 baptized members and 414 inquirers in 1954; 111 of these, most of them inquirers, participated in the Church's activities after 1951.[15]

Socialist Production and Religious Freedom

As Protestant churches resumed and expanded their activities, their growth led to mounting tension with the state. During the Great Leap Forward, friction with local cadres, even local communities, would soon have a high price for the church. Government reports noted the Christian background of some of the individuals who took part in the riots (e.g., Protestants in the riots in Lingya Township, Huling, in 1953, and Catholics in the petitions for grain in Mayu in 1954) as well as those who quit collectives.[16] Local authorities did not explicitly blame the church for the riots and the exodus from the collective, yet official documents were full of rhetoric denouncing church meetings for "obstructing production"—which may have worried grassroots cadres more than the church's political or ideological dimensions.

From a structural perspective, religious activities almost inevitably collided with state-imposed collective units, from mutual aid teams to primary and advanced cooperatives (*chujishe/gaojishe*). These made up an ordered hierarchy of collective units that the state had created to exert full control over rural society. As the state reorganized traditional communities from the ground up, it came into conflict with religion, which was integrated into the rhythm and order of rural life. When religious activities continued to exist outside of state-imposed institutions, they unsurprisingly met with intervention and suppression, though the extent of this varied in different contexts.

In different communities, the state showed various degrees of tolerance toward religious life depending on its local influence and the extent to which local cadres perceived it as a threat to the collective order, especially the calendar of agricultural production. Collective religious activities, from Christian gatherings to Buddhist meetings and rituals in territorial temples, were all accused of "obstructing production." Official propaganda often criticized dragon boat racing for wasting time and money that could be put toward production.

Grassroots cadres probably cared more about religious followers complying with agricultural production and the general order of the collective than the ideological and political issues surrounding religious activities. This was a real

---

[15] "Guanyu Mocheng xiang Yesujiao de huodong wenti qingkuang zonghe baogao" (Comprehensive report on Christian activities in Mocheng Township), November 4, 1955, Pingyang County Archives 1-7-164: 173–174.

[16] Rui'an City Archives 1-7-35: 2.

issue that they saw and had to deal with in everyday life. Some grassroots cadres felt that Christian activities interrupted collective production much more frequently than Buddhist meetings or territorial religious activities. Traditional communal rituals such as dragon boat rowing were usually annual or seasonal, while Christian gatherings took place on a much more frequent basis. In addition to Sunday worship (or Saturday for Adventists), small groups met for worship on weekdays. Together with annual festivals and gatherings, weekly Christian meetings formed a dense schedule that interfered with collective production. Thus, local cadres who wished to maintain the rhythm of collective life saw church meetings as an obstacle.

Some mutual aid teams or cooperatives mainly made up of Christians were willing to cooperate with the production aims of village cadres. Cadres did not harass them and turned a blind eye to church meetings.[17] However, in official reports, numerous complaints by village cadres suggest that it was common for Christians not to cooperate with the schedule of agricultural production. Cadres from the coarse cloth cooperative in the town of Xincheng complained, "When Sundays came, Christians all went to church. [We] therefore could not complete the cooperative's production plan. Their slogan is, 'traditionally there are only six days [of work], there is no tradition of [working] seven days. Sunday is only a day of rest'. . . [We] could not implement the core programs of our party. They did not want to attend all kinds of meetings. Those who attended sometimes left in the middle [of a meeting]."[18]

In cases like this, retaliation was swift. Local cadres in Pingyang County quickly "intervened in religious life," according to an official report:

> Agricultural production cooperatives forced Christians to give up their faith as the prerequisite for participating in the cooperative. Some Christians suffered discrimination and exclusion in cooperatives. There were cadres who considered Christians "bad people" and treated them differently. They intentionally arrange more work on Sundays, wanting to prevent Christians from going to worship. . . . Christians complained that there was no freedom in the cooperatives. . . . The Christians of Lubian Village all quit the advanced cooperatives of Nanping Township and formed a separate basic cooperative.[19]

[17] Zhu Yujing, "Guojia tongzhi, difang zhengzhi yu Wenzhou de Jidujiao" (State rule, local politics and Christianity in Wenzhou) (PhD Dissertation, Chinese University of Hong Kong, 2011), 92–93.
[18] "Zhengzhi guashuai, pochu mixin" (Politics in command, eradicating superstition), July 27, Rui'an City Archives 3-1-5: 82.
[19] "Zhonggong Zhejiang Shengwei zhuanfa shengwei zongjiao gongzuo weiyuanhui guanyu Pingyang Xian Yishan, Jinshan liang qu zhixing zongjiao zhengce qingkuang de jiancha baogao" (Zhejiang Communist Party Committee issuing Religious Work Committee of Zhejiang Party Committee's investigation report on the implementation of religious policies in Yishan and Jinxiang Districts, Pingyang County), *Zhejiang Tongxun* 30 (1956): 15–16.

When cadres interfered with church meetings, Christians often cited the principle of religious freedom to fend them off.[20] In Xijie Village (Qianku Town) and Linjiayuan Village (Puqian Township) in neighboring Pingyang County, officials reported:

> On Easter, the Qianku parish of the Catholic Church seized the opportunity to hold a meeting with the managers and followers of all nineteen branches. More than [one or two—unclear] thousand people attended and the meeting lasted for three days, which seriously affected spring plowing and production. Town cadres went to ask [them to join in]. Instead [of joining], they cited the "religious freedom of the Common Program" to reject [the request] of our cadres, who could only stare at them angrily. Grumbling that "the Catholics are rebelling," they still had to hold in their rage. A member of Qianku Town militia said to the town head: "if you agree, I can use one bullet to shoot down the head [of the statue of Christ]!"[21]

Many grassroots cadres felt frustrated not only because of the resistance from below, but also because of the criticism they received from their superiors, putting them in an impossible position. County officials often construed village and town cadres' responses to religious activity as inadequate or too divisive. According to an official report from 1955:

> Our cadres are not willing to confront [religious issues], afraid of violating freedom of religious belief and making [political] mistakes. Some cadres even believed that any move would constitute interference with religion. . . . Therefore they did not dare ask about [religious activities]. . . . In some other areas, [cadres] use different approaches. . . . Some cadres in the district [of Huling] . . . consider all religious activities as counterrevolutionary. . . [They] arrest religious leaders in the middle of religious activities and interrogate them [as criminals]. Some places confiscated the Bible. Mayu seized church land for cooperatives to farm. Some places use verbal harassment (*pilao baogao*) to disturb festival activities . . . causing discontent among religious followers.[22]

---

[20] Followers of other religious traditions, for instance Buddhist monks and nuns, similarly used official policies to serve their purposes. See Holmes Welch, *Buddhism under Mao* (Cambridge, MA: Harvard University Press, 1972), 257–266.

[21] "Pingyang Qianku Zhen Xijie Cun Puqian Xiang Linjiayuan Cun zongjiao qingkuang baogao" (Report on the religious situation in Xijie Village of Qianku Town and Linjiayuan Village of Puqian Township, Pingyang), June 7, Pingyang County Archives, 1-7-164: 182.

[22] Rui'an City Archives 1-7-35: 5.

The pent-up anger and frustration of cadres could quickly turn into something worse. The "great leap in religious work," which I discuss in the next section, represents the culmination of local cadres' grievances against Christians and the momentary triumph of the hard-line approach. Though it was an attack on all religious traditions, it hit Christianity the hardest. For Protestant churches, it was the first such attack since 1949. The "great leap in religious work" was so extreme that it even caught the attention of some officials in the central government, as I describe in the following section.

The "Great Leap in Religious Work" and Its Aftermath, 1958–1960

In late 1957, religious control in southern Zhejiang tightened once again in the midst of the national Anti-Rightist Campaign. In October 1957, the Ministry of United Front Work formulated a plan to urge religious leaders to follow the socialist path and to accept the leadership of the Communist Party through debate. Yet when this plan was brought to execution in Wenzhou in 1958, local officials went much further than United Front officials in Beijing expected. Driven by the frenzied atmosphere of the Great Leap Forward, local governments promoted a local campaign of a "great leap in religious work" (*zongjiao gongzuo dayuejin*).

To Wenzhou Christians, the Great Leap marks a turning point in their relations with the state. While the brutal repression of Christianity is often associated with the start of the Cultural Revolution in 1966, it was in 1958 that local officials implemented new drastic measures throughout the region of Wenzhou to minimize the presence and influence of religion.

Prefectural officials in Wenzhou believed that if agricultural and industrial production could leap forward, so "certainly could religious work because it is the same as other works" (*zongjiao gongzuo yu qita gongzuo yiyang shi wanquan neng dayuejin de*).[23] A local campaign of "great leap in religious work" was therefore launched against religion in conjunction with the great leap forward of agricultural and industrial production. Almost all churches and gathering places were shut down or seized during the campaign. Local churches became deeply divided as many followers were coerced to abandon their Christian faith and even attack other members of the church.

---

[23] "Wenzhou diwei guanyu quanqu zongjiao gongzuo xianchanghui qingkuang baogao he Pingyang Huqian xiang dui zongjiao douzheng shidian zongjie baogao" (Wenzhou Party Committee's report on the regional on-the-spot religious affairs meeting and summary of the experiment on the struggle against religion at Huqian Township, Pingyang County), November 1, 1958, Longquan City Archives 1-5-172: 76–79.

The Ministry of Public Security and the National Bureau of Religious Affairs apparently favored the extremism displayed by local governments in Wenzhou. Officials from both departments, including He Chengxiang, the head of the National Bureau of Religious Affairs, held a special on-the-spot meeting in Pingyang in September, without officials from the United Front Work Ministry, to praise and popularize the Wenzhou experience.[24]

The new drastic measures temporarily put a stop to church expansion. In April 1958, the Rui'an County Government convened a ten-day socialist education movement study class, which could be considered a prelude to the "great leap in religious work." Two hundred and sixteen people attended the class, including Protestant and Catholic clergy, "core lay Christians" (hexin xintu), and Buddhist monks and nuns from all over the county. Among those summoned was Preacher Shu Chengqian of the Seventh-Day Adventist Church in the town of Mayu, ten miles away from the county seat. County officials considered "restraining and weakening religious activities" as a complementary measure to "support [the great leap in] industrial and agricultural production."[25] But Shu, who wrote a memoir about his experiences, described the study class essentially as "a measure to exterminate religion (miejiao).[26]

In the class, religious leaders and adherents were mobilized to denounce the "crimes" of imperialism and missionary enterprises in meetings and big-character posters. They were also asked to sign the "patriotic convention" (aiguo gongyue), agreeing to reduce the length of church meetings and restrict themselves to one gathering per week. Many religious leaders complied, apparently under great pressure from local officials. Some even " 'voluntarily' canceled" weekly worship and "donated houses and church facilities to the commune,"[27] as officials reported.

The small group meetings were what Preacher Shu found most painful. Organizers distributed materials containing evidence of the "crimes" committed by religious leaders and activists, and attendees were asked to confess and denounce others, particularly fellow participants whose "crimes" were listed in the materials. Some made self-criticisms "admitting their problems." Pastor You

---

[24] "Longquan City Archives 1-5-172: 76–89.

[25] "Guanyu 1958 nian zongjiao gongzuo zongjie baogao" (Conclusion report on religious work in 1958), April 24, 1959, Rui'an City Archives 1-11-183: 109.

[26] Whether the government planned to immediately stamp out religion is debatable (Zhu 2011, 94–95). The central government did not issue a formal policy of eliminating religion, even though the radical steps by the local government in Wenzhou were endorsed by some officials in Beijing and Hangzhou (e.g., officials of the Department of Public Security and the National Religious Affairs Bureau) who had once intended to popularize the Wenzhou experience in the country. Documents of county governments did not place "exterminating religion" as a concrete goal to be accomplished.

[27] Rui'an City Archives, 1-10-161: 42–61; Rui'an City Archives 1-11-183: 107–111; "Xincheng Town zhengzhi guashuai, pochu mixin" (Putting politics in command, abolishing superstition in Xincheng Town), July 27, 1958, Rui'an City Archives 72-5-2: 82–84.

Daoshu of the Methodist Church, for instance, said: "While I pray to God all day and entrust my hope to empty delusion, [other] people are actively participating in the Great Leap of production and construction . . . I am useless to the construction of our country. I want to break away from the church and participate in production." People like Shu tended to remain silent during the meetings. Shu was condemned for instigating villagers to withdraw from the cooperative in 1957 and was even accused of rape. According to his memoir, he did not respond to any of these charges.[28]

In a similar case, Preacher Ye Zhiqing, a major leader of the Assembly in Rui'an, was also charged with several crimes. Ye was publicly attacked by some other Christians attending the study class for "throwing himself into the lap of imperialism" (toukao diguozhuyi), referring to his close relations with foreign missionaries before 1949. Liao Zhensheng, a fellow preacher who had been a close friend of his for over twenty years, even requested that Ye be sent to a labor camp.

Ye denied all accusations and refused to renounce his faith, but he and several other church leaders and activists were nevertheless convicted as rightists and counterrevolutionaries.[29] Shortly thereafter, at the Rui'an Christian meeting that the government convened, Ye and three others were formally expelled from the church.[30] We do not know whether the people who expelled them had any motives other than political pressure from the government. What is clear is that the attacks on Ye and other church leaders fomented divisions and distrust within the church.

Conditions became worse in the second half of 1958 when the entire Wenzhou region was swept up in the fury of the Great Leap Forward. The Wenzhou Three-Self committee meeting in May decided to abolish denominations and form joint services (lianhe libai).[31] This, as Fuk-tsang Ying points out, was an extremist move that was intended to reinforce the power of the Three-Self organizations. It would further weaken traditional denominations and their leadership over

---

[28] For Shu's accounts of the study class, see Shu, Wushi nian jiaohui shenghuo huiyi, Chapter 4. As elsewhere in the country, the wave of withdrawal from the cooperative, which swept mountainous areas of the county in 1957, included villages with the presence of Adventists. Adventists constituted the majority population in Zhuyuan Village, Huling, where church leaders Du Zhulai and Du Zhuxiong allegedly led the withdrawal campaign. See Rui'an City Archives 1-11-183: 108.

[29] "Rightist" and "counterrevolutionary" were polyvalent concepts during the Maoist era. These church leaders were likely convicted as rightists or counterrevolutionaries because they refused to cooperate with the government. As such, they received penalties varying from self-criticism, "re-education through labor" (laodong gaizao), to execution in some cases.

[30] Rui'an City Archives 1-11-183: 110; Rui'an City Archives, 1-10-161: 58.

[31] "Wenzhou jiaohui shixing hebing" (Wenzhou church to carry out a merger), Tianfeng 9 (1958): 20–21.

Protestant communities.[32] Nine hundred and eighty-two churches and gathering places were consequently shut down in Wenzhou (and Lishui, which was then under the jurisdiction of the Wenzhou Prefectural Commission). From July onward, only five churches in Wenzhou prefecture, Lishui prefecture, and the county seat of Qingtian were kept open for weekly half-day joint services for all denominations.[33] The shuttered churches were mostly taken over by communes and production teams. Some were remodeled or even demolished.

As churches and temples were shut down, most church leaders and members of the clergy were labeled as rightists and counterrevolutionaries. Some were forced to publicly renounce their faith and give up religious items. Preacher Shu was once brought to a mass meeting held at the playground of a school in Mayu along with lay Christians and the leaders of other congregations. They were forced to "donate" Bibles, hymn books, churches, and other property to the collective, but Shu refused to comply. He was tortured by being made to kneel on sharp pebbles with a heavy slate on his calves. A young man stood on the slate, grabbed Shu by the shoulder and repeatedly pushed him down for two to three hours, asking him to surrender, until the end of the struggle session.[34] Similar meetings were held throughout Rui'an.

In the frenzy of attacks against religion, even the Three-Self organization was destroyed. An official report claimed that "90 percent of temples and churches were voluntarily donated to brigades,"[35] though as in the struggle meetings described by Shu, these "donations" inevitably took place under conditions of violence or duress. In April 1958, Pastor Chen Zhehai of the Methodist Church, who was also the president of the county's Patriotic Protestant Association, was convicted of being a rightist and counterrevolutionary and was arrested along with several other Christian leaders. He died in prison about a year later. Cao Yongqi, an elder (zhanglao) of the CJIC, also died in prison.[36] Many church leaders were sent down to the countryside to "support agricultural production." Cadres urged Shu Chengqian to go back to Wenzhou municipality, his registered hometown, but he insisted on staying in Mayu. He was driven from the church to a neighboring village, where he was assigned to supervised labor (jiandu laodong) until the start of the Cultural Revolution.

---

[32] Ying Fuk-Tsang, Fandi, aiguo, shulingren: Ni Tuosheng yu jidutu juhuichu yanjiu (Anti-Imperialism, patriotism and the spiritual man: a study on Watchman Nee and the "Little Flock") (Hong Kong: The Christian Study Centre on Chinese Religion and Culture, 2005), 178–183.

[33] "Guanyu Wenzhou diqu zongjiao zhengce zhixing qingkuang de baogao" (Report on the implementation of religious policies in the Wenzhou region), June 26, 1959, Rui'an City Archives 1-11-248: 18.

[34] Shu, Wushi nian jiaohui shenghuo huiyi, Chapter 4 and Chapter 5 (section 1).

[35] Rui'an City Archives 1-11-183: 108.

[36] Rui'an jiaohui, Rui'an jiaohui shi, 14–15.

Regrouping of Protestant Gatherings, 1961–1965

Some United Front officials in Wenzhou were concerned that the "great leap in religious work" would sharply antagonize local communities. Considering that it had deviated from normal religious policy, they did not endorse the campaign. In 1959, the Zhejiang Provincial United Front Work Department issued an investigation on the implementation of religious policy in Wenzhou and asked for excessive measures to be rectified.[37] Yet their efforts were too little and too late.

Christian congregations, both Protestant and Catholic, had largely though not entirely disbanded between late 1958 and late 1960. In addition to the "great leap in religious work," other factors conspired to temporarily silence religion, notably the Great Famine of 1959–1961. The famine hit the southeast coast less severely than other regions of China, but there were still about 141,000 recorded "abnormal" deaths in Zhejiang.[38] In August 1959 alone, the Rui'an government reported 10,895 cases of "swelling sickness" (fuzhong bing), referring to dystrophia caused by hunger.[39] It seems likely that the famine contributed to ending house meetings for a time.

The "great leap in religious work" marked a turning point for Christian churches under Mao. When Christian congregations re-emerged in the wake of the campaign, they began to hold church meetings entirely in private homes. Before 1958, a majority of Protestant communities were already congregating in members' homes, but beginning with the Great Leap, Christians had to devise new strategies to hold any meetings in an increasingly hostile political environment.

The top priority for Protestants was to sustain group meetings in secrecy, or at least keep a low profile. They began to develop a new set of patterns for worship. The dates and times of gatherings were not fixed. Members sometimes had to take turns participating in worship. Meetings were generally held at night time in order to evade the attention of local cadres as well as allowing participants to join from afar.[40] The challenge of dealing with the difficult political climate also influenced their choice of locations and led them to keep congregations small. It is from these maneuvers that we see the beginning of a reinvention in the church.

[37] "Guanyu Wenzhou diqu zongjiao zhengce zhixing qingkuang de baogao" (Report on the implementation of religious policies in the Wenzhou region), June 26, 1959, Rui'an City Archives, 1-11-248: 17–19.
[38] See Cao Shuji, Dajihuang—1959 nian—1961 nian de Zhongguo renkou (Chinese population between 1959 and 1961) (Hong Kong: Shidai guoji chubangongsi, 2005), 282.
[39] See Yang Jisheng, Mubei—Zhongguo liushi niandai dajihuang jishi (Tombstone—a historical record of the Great Chinese Famine in the 1960s) (Hong Kong: Tiandi tushu chuban gongsi, 2008), 246.
[40] "Guanyu zongjiao huodong qingkuang de diaocha" (Investigation of religious activities), August 1, 1962, Rui'an City Archives 1-4-207: 177.

In Mayu, as early as 1959, some Adventists who used to belong to the Adventist Church in the town center joined services in nearby Wujia Brigade, with the encouragement of Preacher Shu Chengqian. About a dozen people took turns attending the meetings and they limited the number of participants to ten.[41] Preacher Shu, who was undergoing supervised labor and was restricted from traveling or communicating with villagers outside of agricultural production, probably did not attend meetings in the new locations until these restrictions were lifted in 1961.[42]

Protestant congregations became larger again starting in the fall of 1960 when conditions gradually improved.[43] In the district of Tangxia, Pan Jinyou, the former resident manager (zhutang) of Shangma CIM church at Baotian Commune, along with his wife, visited former church members under the guise of seeing friends and sick people in Baotian and neighboring communes (though the official report did not indicate whether the couple were doctors or not). They eventually got together a group of more than forty people, which was unusually large for a congregation at the time. Some participants came from as far as Yongqiang Commune in Wenzhou Prefecture.[44] Separately, some churchgoers who used to meet at the Methodist Church in Tangxia Commune dispersed to four nearby villages to hold secret meetings coordinated by Preacher Zhao Hongtian and Deacon Zhao Hongzhu. According to official documents at the time, they had assembled a group of eighty-two Protestants by 1965.[45]

In eight county districts, local authorities noted that all five Protestant denominations showed signs of a revival.[46] Gatherings were held in Christians' homes. Most were simply prayer meetings without pastors or other members of the clergy, many of whom had either been imprisoned or were too intimidated to lead services. By the fall of 1962, according to an estimate by the county government, about twenty Protestant gathering places had appeared in the county, with about eight hundred participants in total.[47] In an unusual occurrence in early 1962, adherents of the CJIC in Lingxi Commune in the mountainous Huling District even started holding public services in their old church. That same year, after learning about the central government's "Sixty Articles on Agriculture" (nongye liushi tiao, issued in 1961),[48] Zhao Hongxu (a deacon of the Methodist

---

[41] Rui'an City Archives 4-13-42: 4.

[42] Shu, Wushi nian jiaohui shenghuo huiyi, Chapter 5 (section 2).

[43] "Guanyu muqian zongjiao huodong qingkuang" (On current religious activities), November 16, 1961, Rui'an City Archives 4-13-42: 5.

[44] Rui'an City Archives 4-13-42: 16–19.

[45] "Ruhe zhizhi Tangxia Yesujiao jiating juhui" (How to prevent Protestant house gatherings in Tangxia), November 6, 1965, Rui'an City Archives 49-17-12: 116–117.

[46] Rui'an City Archives 1-4-207: 170.

[47] Ibid.

[48] "Sixty Articles on Agriculture" is short for "nongcun renmin gongshe gongzuo tiaoli cao'an" (A draft of the regulations on the work of the people's commune), which were new central guidelines on the management of communes that gave more rights to brigades and reintroduced private plots.

Church in Tangxia), Yang Chisheng (a CIM preacher in Hai'an), and Zhu Shunli (an elder of the Assembly in Taofeng Commune) spontaneously convened about thirty Christians to go to the county government and demand the reopening of churches.[49]

As local authorities noted the re-emergence of Christian meetings in private homes, they saw no change in Christian strategies to engage members, which they described as "expelling demons to cure patients."[50] In the 1950s, officials reported several incidents where preachers persuaded patients not to take medicine or consult a doctor, allegedly delaying treatment and leading to death.[51] Whether or not this is accurate, it is clear that prayer as a tool against disease was a powerful means for evangelists to attract new members to the church. When underground gatherings were established in Tangxia in the early 1960s, Protestants typically used the same methods to make new converts and bring back former members of the church, visiting the families of sick people and performing exorcisms to rid them of disease.[52]

An exorcism was typically hosted by a preacher who would convene a group of Protestants to pray in front of the invalid. Many Protestants believed that the patients in question were possessed by Satan or were polluted because of contact with idols, meaning any object related to the worship of local deities. Sometimes, they grabbed the sick person's shoulders or hands in order for the power of God to work directly on their bodies. Such prayer sessions lasted several hours or more. Participants sometimes prayed day and night without pause until they believed that the demons had been driven away.

Shu Chengqian often hosted collective prayer sessions to expel demons in patients' homes.[53] Some active organizers of Protestant gatherings in Tangxia also received patients and organized prayers in their own homes. Ten house gatherings in Tangxia in 1962 led to sixteen new converts, all reportedly due to illness.[54] There were even cases where brigade cadres gave Protestants permission to say prayers to cure illness and expel demons.[55]

With the issuing of "Sixty Articles on Agriculture" in 1961, the Great Leap Forward quietly came to an end. Although those sixty articles were not about religion, for religious followers at that time it might be read as a sign of the state loosening control of rural society.

[49] Rui'an City Archives 1-4-207: 170–171.
[50] Rui'an City Archives 4-13-42: 6.
[51] "Wei Yesujiao chuanjiao renshi zuzhi bingren yanyi fuyao zaocheng shengming siwang" (Protestant preachers obstructed patients from seeing doctors and taking medicine, leading to death of lives), 1957, Rui'an City Archives 4-9-79: 67.
[52] Rui'an City Archives 4-13-42: 9–19; Rui'an City Archives 1-4-207:173; Rui'an City Archives 49-17-12: 116; Rui'an City Archives 4-21-27: 96–97, 117.
[53] Shu, *Wushi nian jiaohui shenghuo huiyi*, Chapter 5 (section 2) and Chapter 6 (sections 2 and 7).
[54] Rui'an City Archives 1-4-207: 179.
[55] Shu, *Wushi nian jiaohui shenghuo huiyi*, Chapter 5 (section 2).

To a lesser extent, official reports also accused Christian preachers of luring people to church by spreading eschatological messages like those heard before 1958. As elsewhere in China,[56] eschatological redemption features prominently in indigenous Protestant Christianity in Wenzhou in the twentieth century. In the early 1950s, the authorities denounced Christian "rumors" such as: "the end of the world is coming. When the second millennium of Christ's calendar [begins], a raging fire will consume the earth and humans will all die out. [Those who] believe in Jesus Christ will be saved;"[57] or "those who do not believe in Jesus will die on the road with birds pecking [their] bodies and dogs eating [their] bones."[58] According to county officials, Christian preachers started spreading the same sorts of messages in the early 1960s. Seizing opportunities to preach, such as when people were resting, sitting on a bridge or under the shade of a tree, Deacon Zhao Hongxu of the Methodist Church, Zhaozhai Brigade, Tangxia, claimed that "we have disaster this year, [you] would do better to change course and believe in Christ . . . then [you] will be saved."[59]

Concerns about the resurgence of Christian churches and their messages led to a few arrests in Rui'an. For instance, Teacher (*jiaoshi*) Chen Dengyong of the Adventist Church ignored warnings and insisted on organizing house meetings in multiple locations in the county seat. He was arrested and put into a labor camp in a remote inland province in 1960. Chen's wife carried on the congregations after his arrest until she was arrested as well.[60] Neither of them was released until 1980. Nevertheless, from the early 1960s until the start of the Cultural Revolution, state hostility toward Christian activities never reached the same height as in 1958.

Provincial and prefectural officials in Wenzhou who had not favored the radical movements against religion in 1958 took measures to reduce the impact of the crackdown starting in the early 1960s.[61] Their preference was to avoid provoking further tensions. For instance, concerned about the growth in Christian activities, the Zhejiang provincial government sent officials to investigate the religious situation in Wenzhou in 1960 and 1962 but did not launch any major operations.[62] The Wenzhou Regional Committee drew up a list of

---

[56] Xi Lian, *Redeemed by Fire: The Rise of Popular Christianity in Modern China* (New Haven, CT: Yale University Press, 2010).

[57] "Pingyang Xian zongjiao gongzuo yijian" (Opinions on religious work in Pingyang County), July 19, 1954, Pingyang County Archives 1-6-70: 33.

[58] Pingyang County Archives 1-7-164: 174.

[59] "Guanyu muqian zongjiao huodong qingkuang" (On current religious activities), November 16, 1961, Rui'an City Archives 4-13-42: 176.

[60] Rui'an City Archives 1-4-207: 175–176.

[61] Zhu, "Guojia tongzhi," 96–97.

[62] The news of the coming of provincial officials to villages was ironically advertised by leaders of Christian communities as a sign of the loosening of restrictions on Christian gatherings (though county officials seemed to suggest that the Christians were in fact misled by provincial officials into believing that the provincial government had more religious tolerance). County officials accused

"counterrevolutionary bad elements" within religious organizations in the spring of 1964, but it seems that the plan was never carried out.[63]

More importantly, though Christian communities were recovering, their scale and scope were incomparable to what they had been before the 1958 crackdown. Therefore, it was less urgent for local officials to impose drastic measures. In this context, superior officials observed that brigade and commune cadres once more adopted a passive attitude toward religious work, as they had done in the early 1950s. County officials criticized brigade and commune cadres for "being short of methods [in dealing with religion]."[64] Brigade and commune cadres, in their defense, complained that religious affairs were difficult to handle. The head of Xincheng Commune said in a meeting, "if we did not handle [religious affairs] well, it would affect religious freedom. However, if we do not interfere, religious activities will gradually expand, which would affect production and the development of socialism. We are caught in the middle. It is better for superiors to provide [us] with some solutions (chuzhuyi)."[65]

As described in official reports, the typical responses of brigade and commune cadres in the early 1960s were either "crude actions" (cubaozuofa) or "letting things drift" (fangrenziliu). "Crude actions" could mean "simply calling together Christians to force them to write confessions or educating them together with thieves, landlords or counterrevolutionaries and asking them to write guarantees (baozheng) [to promise to abandon their religious activities]."[66] At the other end of the spectrum, "letting things drift" meant that some cadres simply did not interfere. An investigation of Protestant gatherings in Shangma Brigade, Tangxia, in 1961 found that "brigade cadres neither took any measures regarding those [Protestant] gatherings nor did they report it to their superiors."[67] Vice brigade secretary Chen Liangkui even claimed that without directives from above, they lacked the means to control Christian activities. Brigade and commune cadres would also give permission to religious activities. The same investigation in Shangma also discovered that Chen Liangkui's father mobilized village elders to rebuild a *sanbaodian*

"sent-down" provincial officials of being "out of touch with reality" and only relying on "policy directives from above." See Rui'an City Archives 1-4-207: 175.

[63] "Guanyu daji zongjiao neibu fanhuaifenzi de yijian baogao" (Opinions on strikes against counterrevolutionaries and bad elements inside religious sector), June 1, 1964, Rui'an City Archives 1-16-80: 76–77.

[64] Rui'an City Archives, 4-13-42: 4.

[65] "Guanyu muqian zongjiao huodong qingkuang" (On current religious activities), November 16, 1961, Rui'an City Archives, 4-13-42: 7.

[66] "1961 nian zongjiao huodong qingkuang" (Situation of religious activities in 1961), November, 1961, Rui'an City Archives, 4-13-42: 4.

[67] "Guanyu Meitou, Changqiao, Baotian, sange gongshe zongjiao huodong qingkuang de diaocha" (Investigation of religious activities in three communes: Meitou, Changqiao, and Baotian), October 12, 1961, Rui'an City Archives 4-13-42: 19.

(literally a Buddhist temple, but possibly referring to a village temple instead). This initiative was said to have received tacit permission from Chen.[68]

Preacher Shu Chengqian wrote in his memoir that when he was still doing supervised labor in 1963, a man living in Mayu Town center got very sick, allegedly possessed by demons. His wife went to ask the brigade cadres' permission to get help from Shu, and the cadres then came to Shu and asked him for help curing the possessed man.[69] It is worth noting that at least in the early 1960s, some Christians retained positions as brigade and commune cadres. For instance, Ou Mensan was from a family that had been Protestant for three generations and was baptized in early 1958. But he was still selected as brigade party secretary and remained in his position throughout the Cultural Revolution. He told me that he stopped going to Protestant meetings until his retirement in the mid-1990s.[70]

Conclusion

The period from the beginning of collectivization to the eve of the Cultural Revolution saw that Christian communities lost almost all churches and turned completely to house gatherings, a turn that would have profound impacts on the power dynamics in the Christian community in Rui'an today. But the process unfolded in radically different ways between the Catholic Church and Protestant churches. Whereas the politically charged "counterrevolutionary" stigma overshadowed the Catholic Church until the end of the Mao era, most Protestant churches were less heavily stigmatized, allowing them to resume services and even evangelical activities. Many village churches welcomed new converts, and new church groups were founded, resuming the expansion of Protestantism that occurred from the 1940s to late 1957.

These developments were made possible partly by the mobility of Protestant gatherings. By comparison, the activities of communal temples or Catholic churches in Rui'an were traditionally tied to a permanent sacred space. Additionally, the extensive native leadership of Protestant denominations allowed many Protestant communities to regroup in the early 1960s, even in the absence of pastors and other formal clergy. Crucially, in the worsening political atmosphere, shifts in policy created an environment that sometimes allowed Protestant communities to employ the discourse of religious freedom to shield their activities from the interference of local cadres, who were often bewildered by policy changes and adopted a passive stance.

---

[68] Ibid.
[69] Shu Chengqian, *Wushi nian jiaohui shenghuo huiyi*, Chapter 5.
[70] Interview by author, Tangkou Village, May 12, 2013.

The increase in the number of Protestants in the early to mid-1950s was certainly not limited to Rui'an and Wenzhou. A study shows that between 1951 and 1958, the Protestant population in Yunnan Province increased from about 100,000 around 1949 to more than 120,000 in 1958.[71] An internal state report also noted a growth in Protestantism in at least four counties of Jiangsu Province in 1957.[72] In Hunan Province, from 1954 to 1955, membership of the Anyang Assembly increased by more than 50 percent, from 1563 to 2467. In 1954, all eleven assemblies in Fujian Province saw a threefold increase in their church membership.[73]

This ongoing growth before 1958 had consequences, however, creating friction with state programs, local cadres, and even non-Christian villagers. As Protestants invoked the principle of religious freedom and the government's conciliatory measures to defend churches and worship, grassroots cadres increasingly came to see them as unruly subjects who posed an obstacle to the reorganization of rural life. Thus in Wenzhou, the Great Leap Forward, which was intended to promote industrial and agricultural development through radical collectivization, was manipulated to launch a "great leap in religious work," shutting down all churches and forcing many Christians to renounce their faith. To make sense of why a national development campaign generated another local campaign against religion, one must consider the tension between local cadres and church members, as cadres encountered resistance to strict production schedules and political gatherings. In this sense, the extreme violence against religion in 1958, particularly against Christianity, appears to be an unintended consequence of the Great Leap Forward.

The campaign left Protestant communities deeply divided, with fresh wounds and old feuds mixed with new ones. Cracks appeared in church communities. Yet the destructiveness of the Great Leap triggered a renewal in Protestant churches. The departure of clergy members and old leaders meant that others had to fill the vacuum if church life were to continue. The hostile political climate led to clandestine house gatherings and new ways of operating for Christian communities. This shift would bring about a much more dramatic transformation during the Cultural Revolution, explored in the next chapter.

---

[71] Su Cuiwei and Xiong Guocai, eds., "Yunnan Jidujiao fazhan kuai, huodong luan wenti fenxi ji duice" (Analysis and resolution for rapid growth and chaotic activities of Christianity in Yunnan), in *Yunnan zongjiao qingshi baogao 2003-2004* (A Report on Religious Conditions in Yunnan, 2003-2004), eds. Xiong Shengxiang and Yang Guozheng (Kunming: Yunnan daxue chubanshe, 2004), 73-74.

[72] "Jiangsu xinjiao renshu juzeng" (Number of new converts to Protestant Christianity grew rapidly in Jiangsu), *Neibu cankao*, the Xinhua Agency, May 17, 1957.

[73] Joseph Tse-Hei Lee, "Politics of Faith: Patterns of Church-State Relations in Maoist China (1949-1976)," *Historia Actual Online* 17 (2008), 133.

5

Diversification and Unification

Protestant Churches during the Cultural Revolution

When the Cultural Revolution broke out in the summer of 1966, Christians were once again caught up in a political storm. Christianity, though never officially prohibited, was ubiquitously denounced as "superstition" or "religious superstition" (*zongjiao mixin*). The Red Guards ransacked church buildings and Christian homes. Shouting the slogan, "Clear the Four Olds," they destroyed church facilities and burned anything they objected to, from Bibles and hymn books to church magazines and crosses. Preacher Shu Chengqian and other religious leaders were taken to struggle meetings and parades. Their bodies pressed together, they were forced to wear plaques hanging from their necks with labels like "counterrevolutionary," "leader of superstition," or "special agent of imperialism." To humiliate him as a Christian, Preacher Shu was made to wear the gown of a local deity that militias had looted from a village temple, and had his face scribbled in ink. Late one night, several young people abruptly marched him off to the Mayu theatre, where they attacked him with kicks and blows, nearly beating him to death.[1]

When it broke out, the high pitch of the Cultural Revolution inflicted a new level of misery on Christians and indeed adherents of all religions. The Great Leap in 1958 mainly targeted religious leaders,[2] but at the start of the Cultural Revolution, anyone with a Christian background could become a target of the Red Guards, regardless of his or her status in the church. Ni Guangdao of Lower Village, Xincheng, who was then a lay Protestant in his mid-twenties, recalled that in July 1967 he was hung from the beam of a farm tool shed in a nearby brigade and tortured for thirteen days.[3] Even people who had renounced their faith in 1958 could not avoid being attacked. Lin Youdi of Changqiao, Tangxia, said

---

[1] Shu Chengqian, *Wushi nian jiaohui shenghuo huiyi* (Memoirs of fifty years' life in the church), internal reference materials ("neibu cankao ziliao"), 2002, Chapter 4. Note that during the Cultural Revolution, activists often used theatres as sites to imprison and torture "counterrevolutionaries" and other enemies of the state.

[2] Rui'an jiaohui, *Rui'an jiaohui shi* (A history of Rui'an church), internal document, 1998, 16.

[3] Ni Guangdao, "1978 nian qianhou de jiaohui shenghuo" (Church life before and after 1978), *Tianfeng* 11 (2008): 8–9, and Ni's testimony, http://www.jidujiao.com/shuku/files/article/html/0/505/12332.html (accessed on May 4, 2018). Ni later became the president of Zhejiang Three-Self Patriotic Association in the reform period.

Maoism and Grassroots Religion. Xiaoxuan Wang, Oxford University Press (2020). © Oxford University Press.
DOI: 10.1093/oso/9780190069384.001.0001

she was ashamed of renouncing Christianity in 1958, but after being paraded through the streets in 1966, she felt that God had not abandoned her and believed again.[4]

The Red Guard movement in 1966 brought house gatherings to a halt throughout Rui'an County, silencing local churches for a second time after the Great Leap of 1958–1960. As local Christians described it, churches in Rui'an entered the "three nos" period: no church, no clergy, and no Bible.[5]

Yet the attacks that started in the summer of 1966, as one Christian interviewee commented, were just "a gust of wind" (*yizhenfeng*).[6] They were intensely violent but also short-lived. Unlike the attacks on religion in 1958, which were "policy-driven" (*zhengcexingde*) and directly carried out by the government,[7] the frantic attacks on religious followers in 1966–1967 soon died down as the Red Guard movement lost momentum. In retrospect, local Christians even celebrated these years as a time of solidarity. A history of Christians in Rui'an explains, "During the 'exterminating religion' period of 1958, shepherds were assaulted and sheep were, without question, dispersed. Yet [home] searches and struggles during the Cultural Revolution pushed every adherent into the same corner. We all shared the feeling of being on the same boat."[8]

This chapter picks up the story where Chapter 4 left off and follows the evolution of Protestant churches in Rui'an and Wenzhou during the Cultural Revolution. During this period, religious repression dramatically empowered the territorial expansion, institutionalization, and unification of Protestant organizations, which added to the importance and availability of Protestantism both as part of a "cultural toolkit" and as a set of organizational resources for local society, paving the way for the subsequent boom and nationwide expansion of Christianity after the Cultural Revolution.[9]

Factional Politics and Loosening Social Control

The Red Guard movement quickly turned into countywide factional battles beginning in the summer of 1967. Armed fights broke out between two major mass organizations: the so-called loyalist group (United Headquarters) and the rebel group (General Headquarters). The conflict would last two years. Between July

    [4] Rui'an jiaohui, *Rui'an jiaohui shi*, 16.
    [5] Ibid.
    [6] Ou Fachen, interview by author. Rui'an, May 7, 2013.
    [7] Ibid.
    [8] Rui'an jiaohui, *Rui'an jiaohui shi*, 16.
    [9] Ann Swidler, "Culture in Action: Symbols and Strategies," *American Sociological Review* 51, no. 2 (1986): 273–286.

and September 1967, battles for control of the county seat left dozens, if not hundreds, of dead bodies floating in the nearby Feiyun River.[10] The apparatus of state, including the county government, party committee, public security bureau, and the court system, ground to a halt. The large-scale conflict ended in September 1969 when the loyalist group, United Headquarters, officially disbanded.[11]

Factional politics continued to dominate social and political life in Rui'an and Zhejiang for the remainder of the Cultural Revolution.[12] There were recurrent clashes between military-appointed officials who had no former ties to Wenzhou, rebels who had been incorporated into the local leadership, and rehabilitated "old cadres." The reshuffling of local leadership in Zhejiang and Wenzhou after the anti-Confucius, anti-Lin campaign further destabilized the political and social order. State structures were in disarray, with constant conflicts between opposing groups and organizations.[13]

In spite of the massive disruption of religious life at the start of the Cultural Revolution, factional conflicts and the ensuing factional politics ironically created a space for religious activities, as they loosened the government's ideological grip on religion. When county authorities were overthrown in 1968, they turned to rural residents for help. Many young villagers joined the loyalist United Headquarters and were mobilized to participate in battles in the county seat and its surroundings. The major armed fights took place in urban areas, while rural areas were relatively quiet. The period of factional politics that followed did not focus on rural areas either.[14]

It was difficult for local authorities to oversee and control everyday life, especially in the vast rural areas, to the same extent as before the Cultural Revolution, because the upheaval of factional conflicts seriously weakened the governmental apparatus at the county level. The Rui'an Party Committee was restored in July 1971, five years after the start of the Red Guard movement, and lower level party committees were restored around the same time. The county public security

---

[10] "Rui'an Xian Lianzhan he Lianzong" (United Headquarters and General Headquarters in Rui'an), September 25, 1967, Rui'an City Archives 4-28-13: 92–107; "Rui'an Xian wuchanjieji wenhua dageming dashi jiyao 66 nian 6 yue zhi 67 nian 12 yue" (Summary chronicle of major events during the Great Proletarian Cultural Revolution in Rui'an, June 1966–December 1967), 1967, Rui'an City Archives 4-28-13: 56–91.

[11] Zhonggong Rui'an shiwei dangwei yanjiushi, ed., *Zhongguo Gongchandang Rui'an lishi dashiji 1949–1999* (A chronicle of the Chinese Communist Party in Rui'an 1949–1999) (Beijing: Zhonggong dangshi chubanshe, 2001), 78–83.

[12] Miao Zhitong, *Wenzhou qu jiaohui shi* (Church history in Wenzhou), internal document, 2005–2006(?), 137–139.

[13] Keith Forster, *Rebellion and Factionalism in a Chinese Province: Zhejiang, 1966–1976* (Armonk, NY: M. E. Sharpe, 1990), Chapters 5–8.

[14] In Shanxi of north China, Henrietta Harrison (Harrison, *The Missionary's Curse*, 167) similarly observed that the Cultural Revolution was not focused on the Catholic villages, whereas the Socialist Education Movement in the early 1960s hit these villages the most.

bureau and the county court were not restored until April and March of 1973, respectively.[15]

Factional conflicts pulled many young people into political campaigns in the county seat, making it difficult for the communes to organize collective agricultural production. Though conflicts ended after a few years, a significant number of the youths who had left the countryside ended up moving elsewhere to make a living, an experience shared by many of my interviewees. Zou Zeiyi, of Tangkou Brigade, Tangxia, left the cooperative around 1969 and spent a few years as a beekeeper in several distant provinces, including Yunnan.[16] Deng Benkuo of Lower Brigade, Xincheng, became an itinerant salesman. He traveled the mountains of Rui'an and neighboring counties exchanging malted candy for junk wares throughout the 1970s.[17] Some residents of Yantou and the nearby villages of Mayu secretly started lumber businesses in the early 1970s, buying lumber in the mountains of neighboring Taishun and Wencheng and selling it on the black market of Yantou Brigade.[18]

For Christians, as for everyone else, the lax collective order meant that brigade and commune leaders were much less motivated to push villagers to follow a rigid schedule of collective production, which had previously caused friction between Christians and cadres. For the remaining years of the Cultural Revolution, Protestant churches and other religious traditions in Rui'an and Wenzhou re-emerged and even thrived, much like the private economy.[19]

In the villages with the most Protestant gatherings, Christians continued to encounter interference from grassroots cadres, who had a greater say in commune and brigade affairs now that county authorities were consumed by factional politics. The tense political environment made grassroots cadres lean toward suppressive approaches to religious activities. According to my interviews with local Christians and numerous other accounts, grassroots cadres dispersed their gatherings, beat them, sent them to study classes, and sometimes reported them to county authorities.

Nevertheless, there were still times when cadres protected or deliberately ignored Christian activities, or even directly participated in church activities. A report of the Zhejiang Party Committee in 1973 shows that in brigades across nine different counties with historically strong Christian presence, nineteen brigade party secretaries and heads of the Youth League converted to Christianity.

---

[15] Zhonggong Rui'an shiwei dangwei yanjiushi, *Zhongguo Gongchandang Rui'an lishi dashiji*, 91.
[16] Interview by author. Tangkou Village, May 12, 2013.
[17] Interview by author, Lower Village, May 12, 2013.
[18] Ou Zhanwu, interview by author. Mayan Village, July 23, 2012.
[19] Wang Ping, "Fengwozhuang jingji zhong de huise shichang—1978 nian yiqian de Wenzhou minying jingji mengya" (Gray market in cellular economy—the sprouts of private economy in Wenzhou before 1978), *Zhongguo Yanjiu* 13 (2011): 170–184.

In the well-known Christian village of Pingyang in Wenzhou that had been put forward as a model for the elimination of Protestantism in 1958,[20] the party secretary of Huli Brigade even turned his home into a gathering spot for church activities.[21] The authorities accused Christian churches of attempting to infiltrate the government's grassroots organizations to usurp their leadership.

Though allegations like these were couched in loaded language, accounts from local Christians confirm that the church did at times benefit from the involvement of local cadres. For instance, Zhushan Brigade in Huling District, Rui'an, had only twenty-some Christians in the early 1970s. The constant harassment of local cadres prevented local Christians from finding a stable meeting place. However, the brigade eventually became a new center of church activities in the district, in part because, as Christians described it, the wife of a town cadre who had been possessed for years converted to Christianity in 1974. She became an activist for the church and on one occasion even housed a Christian family gathering in her home.[22]

Church Diversification and the Convergence of Denominations

When massive factional conflicts died down, some Protestants started congregating again, while others were too intimidated to do so. Those who resumed gatherings had to adapt to new circumstances. After 1958, worship meetings were entirely held in private homes in areas near former churches or meeting places, but political campaigns in the first few years of the Cultural Revolution meant that many of these gathering spots were no longer viable. Though factional conflicts were concentrated in urban areas, rural Protestants periodically had to face "Red Typhoons" (hongse taifeng)—local campaigns targeting class enemies and social issues.

For Christians, the political atmosphere had changed, with the effective criminalization of religious activities. Before the Cultural Revolution, Christians could cite the principle of "religious freedom" in the 1954 constitution to shield church activities from interference, and they were sometimes successful. In the early 1960s, Christians assembled in front of the county government of Rui'an

---

[20] Chen Cunfu, "Zhejiang diqu Tianzhujiao he Xinjiao diaocha yanjiu," Ding/Tripod 131 (2004): 13–20; "Wenzhou diwei guanyu quanqu zongjiao gongzuo xianchanghui qingkuang baogao he Pingyang Huqian Xiang dui zongjiao douzheng shidian zongjie baogao" (Wenzhou Party Committee's report on the regional on-the-spot religious affairs meeting and summary of the experiment on the struggle against religion at Huqian Township, Pingyang County), November 1, 1958, Longquan City Archives, 1-5-172: 76–89.

[21] Rui'an City Archives, 1-21-60: 15.

[22] Shu, Wushi nian jiaohui shenghuo huiyi, Chapter 16.

to ask for a church building to be returned. As late as 1965, when the Xincheng Commune Party Committee attempted to put down the re-emergence of church activities, the cadres had to engage Protestants in public debates about the Bible.

However, the Cultural Revolution consigned the principle of "religious freedom" to irrelevance. Christianity was stigmatized in political slogans and the rhetoric of class struggle. Derogatory terms like "underdogs of imperialism" came to permeate the discourse about Christianity, fostering a pervasive hostility toward Christian followers.

To evade unwanted attention, Protestants further spread out their gathering spots. Fengtagang Brigade was a so-called Adventist gospel village (*fuyincun*) where villagers were predominantly Adventists. Church leaders decided to distribute gatherings to eight locations in surrounding villages to ensure that worship could continue during the Cultural Revolution. Their affairs were "centrally arranged and regulated,"[23] and preachers took turns leading services in each of the eight locations. Even so, they "had to constantly change bases" to navigate the hostile environment.[24]

During one of the most militant anti-religion periods of the Mao era, this cautious, flexible approach allowed some Christian communities to grow, like Zhuyuan Brigade in the mountainous Huling District, which had been a Protestant stronghold since the early 1950s. When deacons Du Zhulai and Du Chongchang re-established Adventist home gatherings in Zhuyuan in 1958, only three people attended the meetings. Nevertheless, the group reportedly expanded to more than a hundred members in the winter of 1961.[25] To avoid the interference of local cadres after the start of the Cultural Revolution, the gatherings were relocated to an Adventist family home in the hills bordering the townships of Jinchuan and Fangzhuang. Adventists from surrounding villages who used to attend meetings in Zhuyuan started to organize congregations in their own villages. Adventists in nearby Dongkeng Brigade formed their own house gathering, which eventually developed into an independent Church.[26]

Many of the new house gatherings that formed in this period were offshoots of old gatherings that started out as prayer meetings (*daogaohui*).[27] Most of the people who led and organized meetings were church elders or deacons, but a few were simply ardent Christians without a formal role in the church. Meeting leaders did not always have the expertise needed to preach or discuss the

[23] Shu, *Wushi nian jiaohui shenghuo huiyi*, Chapter 14.
[24] Ibid.
[25] Rui'an City Archives 1-4-207: 172.
[26] Shu, *Wushi nian jiaohui shenghuo huiyi*, Chapter 15.
[27] Qingquan, "Huishou yiwang de Wenzhou tese xiaozu—daogaohui" (A retrospect of prayer meetings—groups with Wenzhou church characteristics), *Maizhong*, September issue, 2007, http://www.wheatseeds.org/wheatseeds/2007-07.09/wz/25.html (accessed on May 4, 2018).

Bible. It would have been difficult for groups to hold rituals of various kinds, as church elders or deacons were not supposed to perform rituals such as baptism or ordination. The increase in gatherings was beyond the capacity of existing preachers, who typically had two or more gatherings to oversee. Many of the young preachers who emerged during this period were either self-appointed or appointed by church elders, and lacked formal ordination.[28]

There was a great deal of variation in the number of preachers, teachers, and pastors in different rural churches. Before 1958, the Methodist Church's county headquarters in the town of Tangxia had seven preachers, but most of its other twenty churches had only one to three preachers. Several churches even had deacons serving as preachers.[29] Though many local preachers remained active, their geographical distribution was uneven, due in part to the varying impact of political campaigns in different areas, and more importantly, the differing histories of various Protestant communities.

Under these circumstances, "ardent adherents communicated with neighboring gathering places, [and participated in their] Sunday prayer meetings and hymn singing. They also exchanged preachers with neighboring gathering places."[30] Ordained church leaders joined different communities, sometimes bridging the gap between denominations. For instance, Huang Xinrong first served as a pastor in Dongtou, Yuhuan County, Zhejiang, in 1958, then returned to his home area of Hekoutang Brigade in the town of Xianyan. In the winter of 1966, he agreed to serve as a pastor for four Methodist gathering places in the town of Tangxia. He then managed to connect with two other Methodist gatherings and two China Inland Mission (CIM) gatherings in Tangxia District, and subsequently extended his network to several gatherings in Xincheng and in the county seat of Rui'an in 1967. By 1970, similar collaborative systems had likely been established in the county's five other districts.[31]

Given the political circumstances, these collaborative efforts linking congregations and denominations seem to have formed on an ad hoc basis, without

[28] The late Miao Zhitong, for instance, was a self-styled preacher. Yang Duojia (Dorcas) of Oubei, Yongjia, never went through any formal training but claimed to be suddenly enlightened in one day. At the age of twenty, she was asked by her uncle, who was in charge of a Protestant gathering spot in her village, to preach in Protestant meetings. See Yang Duojia, "Benzou rongyao de tianlu" (Running on the heavenly road of glory), ca.2000. http://blog.sina.com.cn/s/blog_52dfd841010152ng.html (accessed on May 4, 2018).

[29] "Zhonghua Jidujiao Xundao gonghui Wenzhou jiaoqu Rui'an lianqu ge zhihui fuzeren ji xintu mingce" (List of division leaders and followers in the Rui'an affiliated district of the Wenzhou ecclesiastical district of the Chinese Christian Methodist Church), 1958, Rui'an City Archives 4-10-75: 29–40.

[30] "Yongjia Xian Jidujiao shiliao" (Historical materials of Christianity in Yongjia), unpublished. Cited by Chen Fengsheng, "Wenzhou jiaohui yigong fazhan lichen" (The development course of volunteers in Wenzhou church), Jinling shengxue zhi 3 (2010): 34.

[31] Rui'an jiaohui, Rui'an jiaohui shi, 20–21.

a coordinated plan. Nevertheless, they marked a critical change in Wenzhou Christianity. Western missionaries had not only brought Protestantism to Wenzhou, they had also brought with them the denominational traditions dividing Protestantism into splintered groups. Now, different denominations were pushed to work together. It was a critical shift which had been unsuccessfully promoted by the Communist state itself through the Three-Self Church.

In the winter of 1971, a meeting was held in Nanchen Brigade, Xincheng, with representatives from all eight districts and from every Protestant denomination barring the Seventh Day Adventists and the Assembly (for reasons described below). Participants in the meeting agreed to found a countywide general council of communication, electing Du Zhixin as general manager (*zongfuze*) and Huang Longcong, Miao Zhitong and several others as council representatives.

According to a history of Christianity in Rui'an,

> The county general council insisted on not distinguishing between denominations but stressed the unification (*heyi*) of the church. In particular, the Methodist church, the China Inland Mission, and the China Jesus Independent Church no longer differentiated themselves by denomination but instead only established churches on the basis of their location. While each denomination still followed its own form of baptism, all other matters were unified.[32]

Denominations began to collaborate on a range of initiatives. "After the creation of the county general council, there were seasonal co-worker (*tonggong*) communication meetings and annual meetings [held to] properly arrange administrative work, co-worker training, evangelism, the cultivation of spirituality as well as Sunday worship for churches throughout the county."[33] From 1972 onward, the county general council of communication established connections with the Protestant Churches in other counties of Wenzhou as well as in several counties of Taizhou and Lishui (such as Yuhuan, Huangyan, and Qingtian). In 1974, the Rui'an county council decided to join the general council of the Wenzhou region (*Wenzhou diqu zonghui*).

The council did not seem to have any great power over local churches. It was not a centralized structure resembling pre-1949 Protestant denominations, but rather an unconsolidated alliance formed to help members survive adverse

---

[32] Rui'an jiaohui, *Rui'an jiaohui shi*, 21. Similar processes took place in other counties of the Wenzhou region as well. The integration of churches in Wenzhou municipality, it was said, occurred even earlier. Local preachers had built up a relatively developed network by the end of the 1960s. In 1970, a unified church had been grounded in Wenzhou municipality. For the unification of churches in Cangnan and Yongjia, see Chen, "Wenzhou jiaohui yigong fazhan lichen," 33–34.

[33] Rui'an jiaohui, *Rui'an jiaohui shi*, 21.

times. Yet with the formation of the council, scattered rural Protestant communities, which were otherwise relatively isolated, formed a network to share resources and preachers across locations and denominational groups. Eventually, a unique system for arranging preacher assignments took shape: *paidan*, literally meaning "tract distribution." It became the most important method of managing Protestant churches in contemporary Wenzhou.[34]

The *paidan* system was not entirely new. According to one church leader's account,[35] it originated as early as the mid-1960s. Protestant communities in the Oubei area of Yongjia started a coordinated "preacher assignment" system in 1965, but it was interrupted for three years by the start of the Cultural Revolution.

Before 1949, Protestant churches in Wenzhou had systems in place to share preachers between congregations, but these systems were different from *paidan* in several ways. First, they were centralized, with each regional (not county) congregation headquarters planning and controlling the dispatch of preachers. Second, each denomination had its own system. Preachers were not sent to each other's denominations.

In the *paidan* system, on the other hand, loosely organized upper-level church organizations were in charge of dispatching preachers. These organizations were coalitions of Protestant gatherings in a certain area, roughly the equivalent of an administrative district or several districts, regardless of their former denominational affiliation. Upper-level church organizations that had established contacts with each other coordinated the dispatch of co-workers to each other's gatherings for Sunday worship or other meetings.[36]

The system greatly facilitated the work of local preachers, opening up new territories for their work and providing a liaison system for Protestant communities all over the Wenzhou region (even parts of Taizhou, Lishui, and northern Fujian). There were frequent exchanges of pastoral visits. Yu Dubing of Yueqing, who later became the president of Yueqing Three-Self Patriotic Association, was invited to preach in Xincheng, Tangxia, and the Rui'an county seat. He also visited the suburban areas of Wenzhou municipality. Miao Zhitong and Ni Guangdao of Rui'an were invited to host services and co-worker training camps in Yueqing

[34] Materials are lacking on the origins of the *paidan* system. It is possible that it originated from the preacher system in the local Protestant church in the pre-1949 period, where preachers were sent by their denominations to different places to preach.

[35] Chen Fengsheng, "Daonian zhu de zhongpu Yang Baoli zhanglao" (In memory of the Lord's loyal servant, church elderly Yang Baoli), http://blog.sina.com.cn/s/blog_4e7519ed0102e59o.html (accessed on May 4, 2018).

[36] For the *paidan* system, see Shehe, "Wenzhou jiaohui guanli moshi qiantan" (A preliminary research of management patterns in Wenzhou church), *Shengming jikan*, June issue, 2011, http://www.cclife.org/View/Article/2566 (accessed on May 4, 2018), and Zhang Zhongcheng, "Cong Wenzhou jiaohui de muqu xianxiang kan jiaohui de muyang guanli" (Pasturage and administration of church through the phenomenon of pastoral district in Wenzhou church), *Jingling shengxue zhi* 1 (2011): 53–85.

and Pingyang.[37] Many preachers expanded the scope of their work across the region. Yang Duojia (Dorcas) initially preached only in areas near her home base of Oubei, Yongjia, but when the *paidan* system appeared in the early 1970s, she started to travel beyond Yongjia, and in subsequent years, rarely stayed at home longer than a single night. On preaching duty, she visited all eight counties of the Wenzhou region as well as Yuhuang County in Taizhou. She was once even stationed in Rui'an for more than two years.[38]

With the *paidan* system allowing preachers to reach a much broader audience, a group of young preachers who emerged after 1958 found an opportunity to build up their influence and reputations in the church. Many later became leading figures in the explosive growth of the Protestant Church in Wenzhou and in some cases nationwide.

Miao Zhitong was one of these self-styled traveling preachers who later became one of the most prominent leaders of house churches in China. Miao was born in Tongxi Village, Taoshan, in Rui'an. His mother's family had a Protestant background for generations. His parents both passed way when he was still young. After graduating from middle school, he worked briefly in a state-owned dairy factory and as a middle school teacher before returning to his home village. In 1966, the first year of the Cultural Revolution, his friend Jiang's wife was allegedly possessed by demons. The family sought help from numerous local deities, to no avail. This was when Jiang went to Miao for help. Miao, his uncle, and another Christian sung hymns before Jiang's wife. According to Miao, this unexpectedly drove the demons away. And only a few days later, Miao witnessed another miracle when he prayed to God to cure his daughter's acute pneumonia. His daughter recovered, and Miao considered these events as signs that God was calling him to service. Along with Jiang and several others, he established a gathering in his village.[39]

Miao was one of those elected to the Rui'an Protestant council in the 1971 meeting, which he helped to convene. According to his account, he traveled extensively in the Wenzhou region in the 1970s, especially in Rui'an, Yueqing, and Pingyang, and probably traveled to other areas of eastern Zhejiang. Though he was still based in Rui'an, his charismatic preaching and theological messages earned him a large following over the years. The county council split in 1982 because of disagreement over whether they should participate in the Three-Self

---

[37] Miao, *Wenzhou qu jiaohui shi*, 153–163.

[38] Yang Duojia, "Benzou rongyao de tianlu."

[39] Zhang Xiaomin, "Ta zaishi de rizi—jinian zhupu Miao Zhitong" (When he was in the world—in memory of God's servant Miao Zhitong), http://wzbxcc.blogspot.de/2013/08/blog-post.html (accessed on May 4, 2018). See also David Aikman's portrayal of Miao, *Jesus in Beijing: How Christianity Is Transforming China and Changing the Global Balance of Power* (Washington, DC: Regnery, 2006), 184–186.

organization, but by then Miao had already established his own church group. In the mid-1980s, Miao permanently moved from his remote home village in the mountainous Huling District to Li'ao Village in Tangxia, where his followers were concentrated. By 1990, his church group was reported to have a total of eleven churches and fifty-two gathering places.[40]

Church Competition and the Adventist Church's Lone Quest for Survival and Revival

The adversity of the Cultural Revolution did not just lead to greater unification among different Protestant communities. Unsurprisingly, it also generated competition between Protestant groups in Rui'an, but this competition led to the multiplication of Protestant house gatherings, ultimately contributing to the church's growth.

For different reasons, neither the Adventist Church nor a number of groups belonging to the Assembly took part in the general council. Assembly churches insisted on maintaining their distinctive practice of "head-covering" (*mengtou*), requiring female attendees to cover their heads with a black hat or kerchief during meetings.[41] Conversely, the Adventist Church clung to its practice of holding worship on Saturdays, not Sundays. However, during the later stage of the Cultural Revolution, both Adventists and members of the Assembly did make efforts to establish connections and integrate their respective communities across the region. They also tried to win over adherents from churches affiliated with other denominations.

Adventist preacher Shu Chengqian, whose story is told in Chapter 4, moved back from Rui'an to Wenzhou in 1968 to ensure better care for his sick wife, and probably also to distance himself from heated factional conflicts within the church. By that time, the Adventists had set up several groups in Wenzhou municipality. When Shu's wife passed away the following year, he devoted himself to visiting Adventist communities throughout southern Zhejiang.

As the smallest Protestant denomination and one of the last to be established in Wenzhou, the Adventist Church likely faced the most severe scarcity of preachers. The southern Zhejiang mission of the Adventist Church was divided into seven independent units in the early 1950s. This system became unviable when the Cultural Revolution came, as many gatherings needed preachers

---

[40] "Guanyu Rui'an Shi zongjiao wenti diaocha qingkuang de huibao" (Comprehensive report on the investigation of religious situation in Rui'an City), December 22, 1990, Rui'an City Archives 1-38-6: 34–35.

[41] The underground "Wenzhou regional church" (*Wenzhou diqu jiaohui*) ruled "head-covering" as a heresy in 1974. See Qingquan, "Wenzhou jiaohui dashi niandaibiao xia."

and other meeting groups were waiting for a preacher before they could establish a regular congregation. Shu, along with other preachers and church members, visited almost every Adventist community belonging to the former southern Zhejiang mission, including Adventist churches in Taizhou and Lishui.

The borders of Zhejiang and Fujian being close to Taiwan, the political atmosphere was tense, but in the early 1970s Shu and other Adventists traveled to Adventist communities there at least two to three times a year. Hu Yuming, Shu's brother-in-law, visited Jinhua in central Zhejiang, Ningbo in eastern Zhejiang, and even Fuzhou and Quanzhou in Fujian during the later years of the Cultural Revolution. They were not welcome everywhere. Besides risking arrest, they sometimes found that local Adventists resisted their presence. Adventist gatherings in the Rui'an county seat had a little more than twenty participants at most during the entire period of the Cultural Revolution. Moreover, Shu and his colleagues were never able to reach Adventists in most parts of Lishui region and Taishun County in Wenzhou, despite their attempts to do so. In other areas, though, they successfully persuaded Adventists to start gathering for worship again. In some villages where Adventist gatherings had already been re-established, they acted as guest preachers, helped with Bible studies, or led prayer meetings.[42]

Shu recalled that they were also invited on visits to villages that only had adherents or gathering spots affiliated with other denominations. Their visits sometimes resulted in villages switching their affiliation to the Adventists. For instance, in Wenzhou municipality, Adventists established several gathering places amid the political chaos of 1967–1968. After being contacted by the Adventist Church, some adherents of the CJIC chose to join Adventist meetings, as their own churches remained in a state of disarray.[43]

The Adventists' contact with churches belonging to other denominations also led to the formation of new gatherings. Such was the case with the establishment of Adventist gatherings in Taoshan. The CIM church in the town of Taoshan (capital of Taoshan District) was established in the early Republican era. It was one of only a few CIM bases in the mountainous areas of Rui'an. Adventists historically did not have a presence there. Huang Longcong and his family had managed the church closely since the early 1950s, but after Huang's younger brother, Huang Longbiao, and some other members of the Taoshan Church came into contact with Shu Chengqian in the late 1960s, they adopted Seventh-Day Adventism. They decided to turn their gathering into an Adventist group that would adhere to Adventist practices and receive only Adventist preachers, but they met with vehement opposition from Longcong, who tried to prevent his

---

[42] Shu, *Wushi nian jiaohui shenghuo huiyi*, Chapters 7–9, 13–21, 22–24.
[43] Ibid., Chapter 6 (section 3).

brother from holding Adventist gatherings in any house belonging to a member of their family.

This led to a split in the Taoshan Church. Huang Longbiao began organizing his own Adventist gatherings in Pichaitan outside of the town of Taoshan.[44] After three to four years, attendees of the Pichaitan gathering from Jinggu Township in Mayu set up a new meeting spot in Shamenshan Brigade, Jinggu, in 1975. A year later, converts from Chen'ao and Shibu villages, Jinggu, which had seen a rapid growth in Adventist church membership, formed another gathering near Chen'ao Brigade.[45]

The Landscape of Protestant Gatherings by the End of the Cultural Revolution

The dissemination and increase of Protestant house gatherings had the same effects as "seeder" (*bozhongji*) and "propaganda team" (*xuanchuandui*)—two terms that Mao Zedong used to evaluate the historical significance of the Long March—though there is no direct evidence to suggest that Protestants deliberately modeled their operations on the Communists before 1949. In any case, the political environment during the Cultural Revolution left them with little choice if they wished to pursue religious work.

After 1958, there were two clear trends in the development of Protestant home gatherings. First, they went from being concentrated to being dispersed. Second, they moved out of densely populated areas and into less populated ones, such as remote villages and mountain areas. Both tendencies, as a comparison of Maps 5.1 and 5.2 clearly shows, intensified as Protestants struggled to adapt to the Cultural Revolution.[46]

For instance, in 1957, over 13 percent of Rui'an's Protestant population was located in Xincheng District. The Xincheng Protestant community had only four churches and gathering spots, three of which were located in the district capital, Xincheng Town itself. From autumn 1961 onward, Protestants established underground gatherings in several locations in the townships of Dongtian and Shangwang, with a few meetings in the county seat.[47] After being briefly interrupted by the Red Guard movement and its armed factional conflicts, gatherings continued to expand. By 1978, forty-four Protestant meeting spots had been

---

[44] Rui'an jiaohui, *Rui'an jiaohui shi*, 18–19.

[45] Shu, *Wushi nian jiaohui shenghuo huiyi*, Chapter 9.

[46] Roughly speaking, Chengguan (the county seat), Xincheng, Tangxia, Xianjiang, and the main part of Mayu belong to the plains. Taoshan, Huling, Gaolou, and other parts of Mayu are mountainous areas.

[47] Rui'an City Archives 1-4-207: 180.

established in all eleven towns and townships in Xincheng District. Similarly, in Huling District, the number of Protestant house gatherings grew from twenty-eight in 1957 to ninety-four in 1978.[48]

Protestantism began to reach new territories, many of which did not historically have a Protestant community, or in some cases had only a small number of Protestant adherents who had to participate in congregations elsewhere. For instance, according to one interviewee, Dadianxia Township had only a few families with Christian members up to the 1960s.[49] By the end of the Cultural Revolution, however, Protestants had set up two gathering places in the township. In 1991, the community had grown into Dadianxia church with 550 members.[50]

Throughout the county, the Protestant Church operated ninety-eight churches and gathering places before 1958 (see Map 5.1). By 1978, 276 gathering places had been created, three times their 1957 numbers (see Map 5.2). At the prefectural level, according to estimates by church members, 1,954 gathering places were established in the entire Wenzhou region between 1971 and 1980.[51]

The vast majority of the growth in Rui'an came from rural areas. Excluding the county seat, Protestant congregations covered forty of a total of sixty-one towns and townships in 1957. By 1978, however, they had expanded to seventy-one of a total of seventy-three towns and townships. Villages experienced an even stronger growth: in 1957, eighty-four villages had Protestant churches or gathering places, but by 1978, there were Protestant gathering places in 227 villages (see Figure 5.1). Conversely, Protestant congregations in the county seat only grew from five to seven in the two decades after 1957 (see Figure 5.2).

The disparity between rural and urban areas could be related to political control, as the county seat tended to be more tightly regulated than other areas. But a lack of leadership could also have slowed down growth. There were further disparities between the plains (Xincheng, Tangxia, Xianjiang, and most parts of Mayu) and the mountainous areas (Taoshan, Huling, and Gaolou), as well as between different districts. Generally speaking, the number of Protestant house gatherings tended to increase faster in mountainous areas than in the plains. However, within mountainous areas and even in the entire county, the growth rate in Huling was exceptionally high and the growth rate in Mayu was relatively low. These differences invite further study.

[48] Rui'an jiaohui, *Rui'an jiaohui shi*, 18–19.
[49] Yu Jixiang, interview by author. Dadianxia, Xincheng, July 25, 2012.
[50] "Xincheng Qu zongjiao qingkuang diaocha tongjibiao" (Investigational chart of religious situation in Xincheng District), 1991, Rui'an City Archives 72-24-10: 56–57.
[51] Qingquan, "Wenzhou jiaohui dashi niandaibiao xia" (Chronicle of events in Wenzhou church). Maizhong, April issue, 2007. http://www.wheatseeds.org/wheatseeds/2007-04.08/wz/08.html (accessed on May 4, 2018).

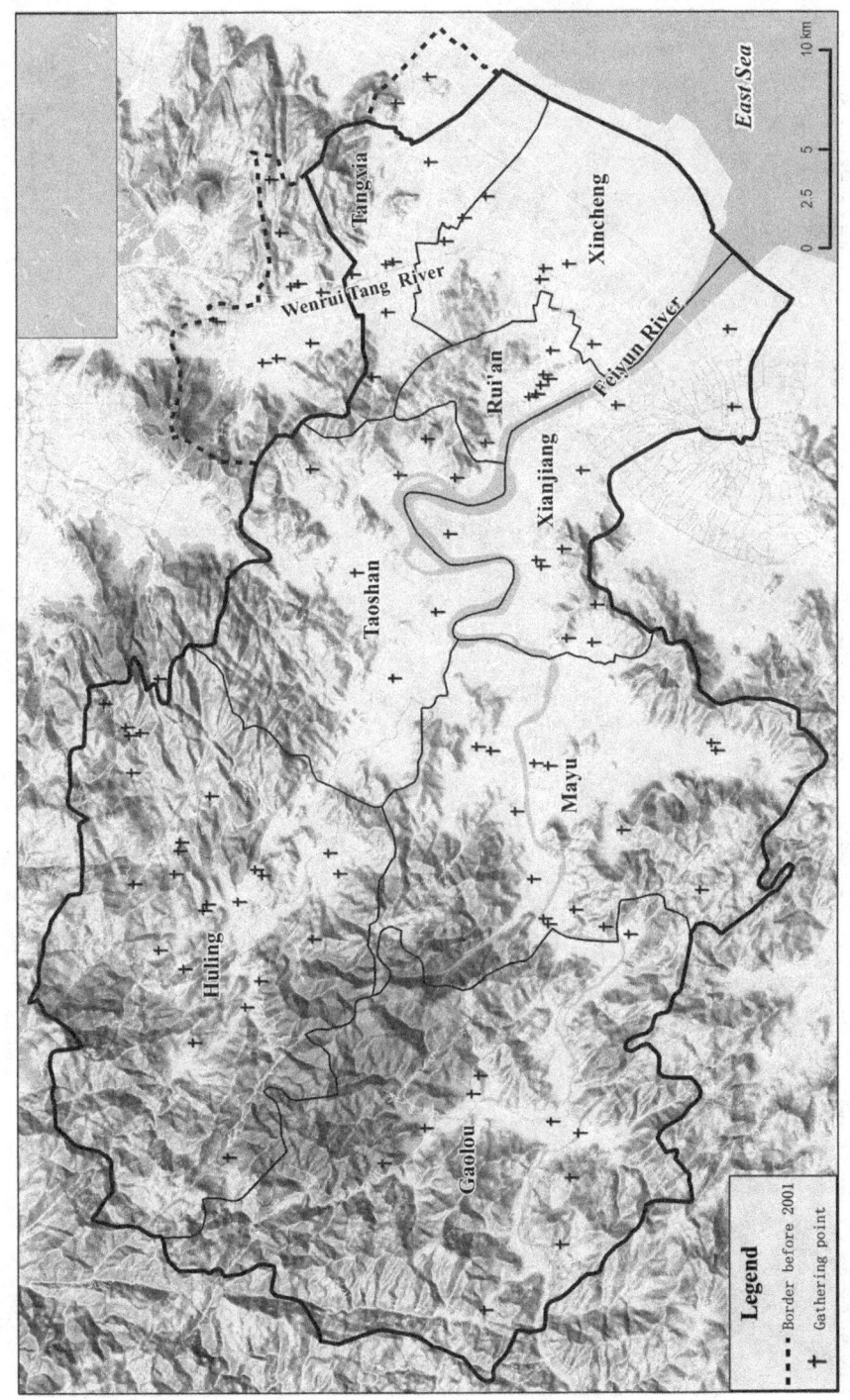

Map 5.1. Protestant churches and gathering places in 1957.

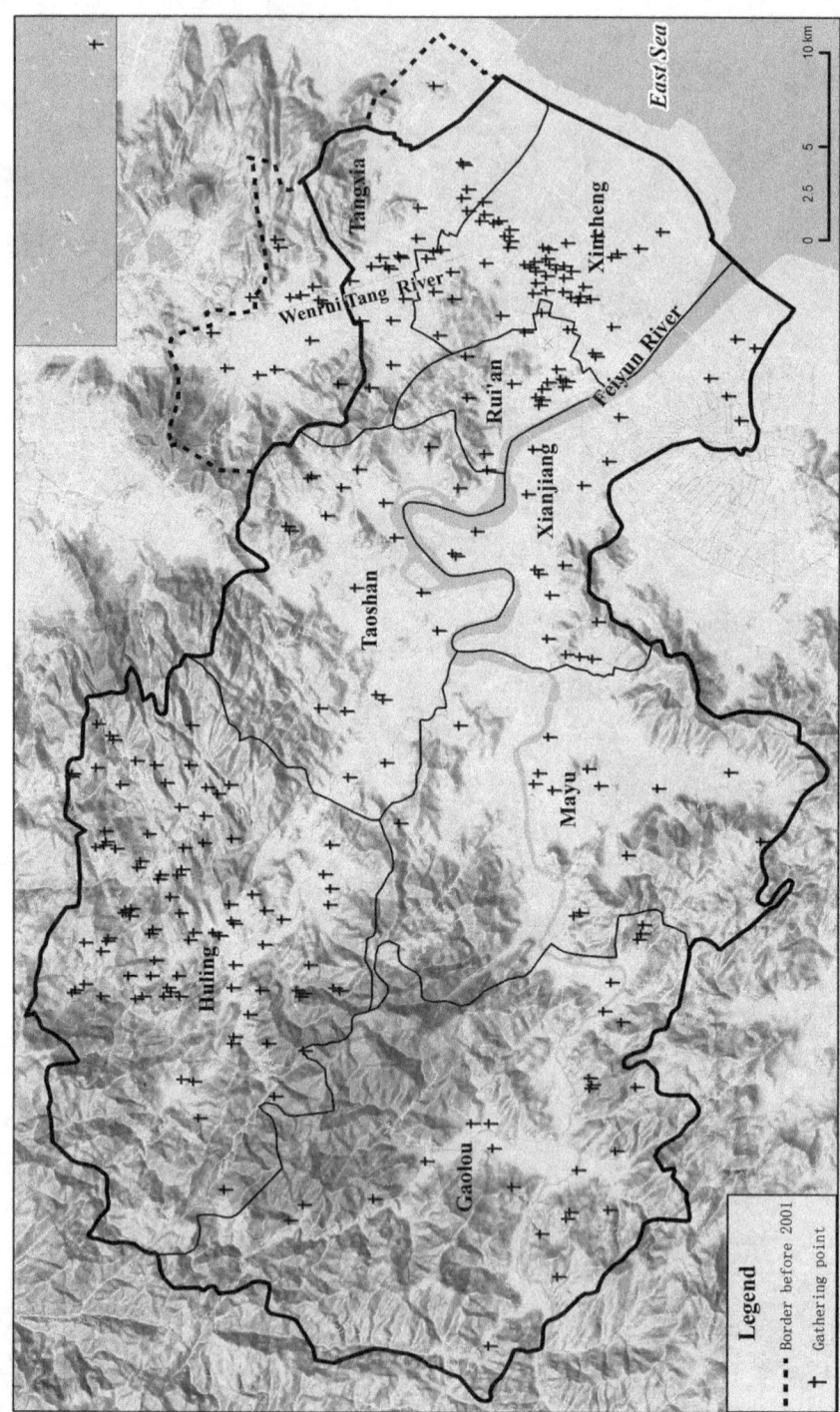

East Sea

Tangxia

Xincheng

Wenzhu Tang River

Rui'an

Feiyun River

Xianjiang

Taoshan

Mayu

Huling

Gaolou

Legend
- - - Border before 2001
✝ Gathering point

10 km

5

2.5

0

Map 5.2. Protestant gathering places in 1978.

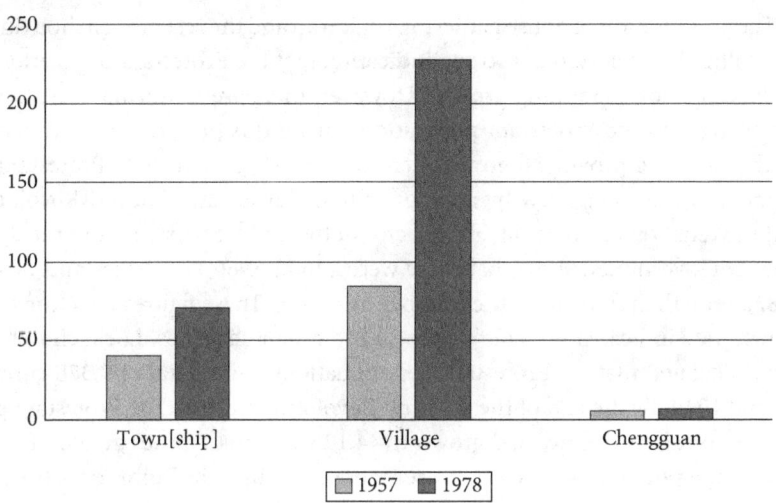

Figure 5.1. The distribution of Protestant congregations in 1957 and 1978.

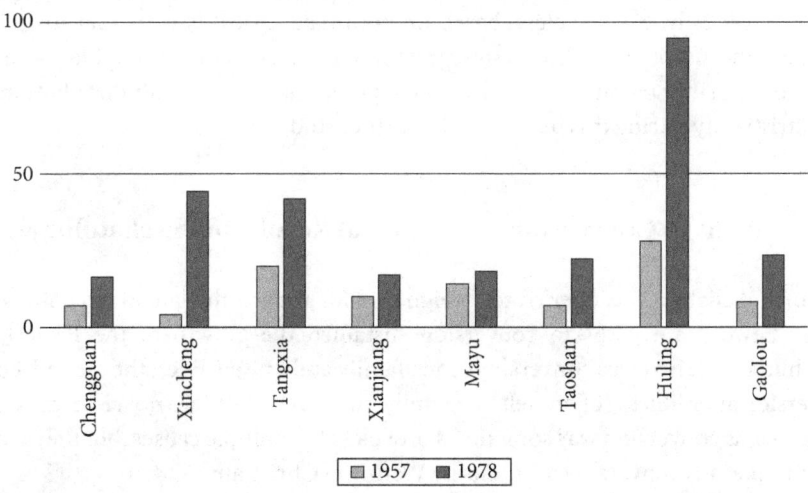

Figure 5.2. The regional distribution of churches and gathering places in 1957 and 1978.

Roughly speaking, Chengguan (the county seat), Xincheng, Tangxia, Xianjiang, and the main part of Mayu belong to the plains. Taoshan, Huling, Gaolou, and other parts of Mayu are mountainous areas.

The proliferation of house gatherings in Rui'an and the rest of Wenzhou during the Cultural Revolution is a strong indication that the Protestant population experienced a corresponding growth. However, there are no formal statistics for the changes to the Protestant population during this period. An investigation by the Zhejiang provincial government in 1981 suggested that "Protestants in Rui'an and Pingyang grew by a factor of four during the Cultural Revolution, and in Wenzhou municipality, by a factor of twenty."[52] Statistics from the Rui'an County Government show that there were a total of 60,185 Protestants around 1982, more than four times the number in 1956.[53] These figures are close to the growth rate indicated in data from local Protestant churches. Local church history calculated that six Protestant denominations had a total of 9,370 converts around 1949. By the end of the Cultural Revolution in 1978, the Protestant population in Rui'an County had grown to 44,125, about 4.7 times greater. For reference, the population as a whole grew about 2.2 times in Rui'an over the same period.[54]

In the preceding data, neither the government nor local churches specified their method for calculating the number of churches or their definition of "Protestant," such as whether this includes "inquirers" or baptized church members only. Nevertheless, based on both data sets, it is clear that in 1958–1978, the number of Protestants grew much faster than the population as a whole. Further parameters, such as the regional, age, and gender distribution of Christianity during this period, invite further study.

Paths to Conversion and Cultural Revolution Eschatology

Since Wenzhou was opened to foreign missionaries in the late nineteenth century, two main paths to conversion sustained the growth of the Protestant Church. The first was conversion along family and lineage lines; the second, conversion after illness (of oneself or a family member). These are not clear-cut categories, as conversion was sometimes provoked by multiple causes, but they recur in numerous conversion accounts by Wenzhou Christians.

---

[52] "Guanyu Wenzhou zongjiao wenti huibao tigang" (Outline report on religious questions in Wenzhou), May 15, 1981, Rui'an City Archives 7-29-46: 31.

[53] "Guanyu Rui'an Shi zongjiao wenti diaocha qingkuang de huibao" (Comprehensive report on the investigation of religious situation in Rui'an City), December 22, 1990, Rui'an City Archives 1-38-6: 32.

[54] Population in Rui'an increased from 456,900 of 1949 to 1,007,393 of 1982. "Zhejiang Sheng renkou pucha bangongshi et al., eds., Zhejiang Sheng renkou tongji ziliao huibian 1949–1985" (Census data collection in Zhejiang province, 1949–1985) (Zhejiang Sheng renkou pucha bangongshi, 1986), 457–458.

The first category consists of people who were descendants of Christians or joined the church through family or matrimonial ties. Christian faith was commonly passed from generation to generation. Among Protestants in Rui'an, family-led conversions clearly grew after 1949, though further study would be needed to reveal the extent of this phenomenon.

The case of Preacher Shu Chengqian's family illustrates the transmission of Christianity along family lines. Shu and his father-in-law were both first-generation Adventists. His father-in-law had been the doorman of a church school in Wenzhou for many years. Shu's daughter, Xiaorong, was baptized at a young age, and later married Adventist preacher Zhao Dianren in the mid-1960s. Preacher Shu's brother-in-law Hu Yuming had been known as a rebellious man, but under family influence, he also became an Adventist in the late 1960s. Hu Yuming's wife was not a Christian when they got married, but she converted to Christianity after an episode where she was believed to be possessed by demons, and was cured through an exorcism using prayer. Hu and his wife's children all grew up Protestant, and their son Hu Fulin became a well-known Protestant entrepreneur in Wenzhou.

These conversions through parents, siblings, husbands, wives, and in-laws were common in Christian communities. The Adventist church leaders whom Shu Chengqian knew shared a similar transmission of Christian faith. Most church leaders in non-Adventist communities, like Miao Zhitong, Yu Dubin, and Yang Duojia, likewise came from Protestant family backgrounds.

A study in the town of Tangxia in 1981 showed similar results. "The [total] Christian population naturally increased with the growth of Christian family members and Christian household numbers. . . . Some converted to Christianity due to the influence of family members and relatives."[55] The investigation also discovered that Christians tended to marry other Christians, and when they did marry someone who did not belong to the church, the union might take place only on the condition that the non-Christian would convert.

One of the church members I interviewed fell into this category. Pou Zuilen of Shang'anchi Village, Xincheng Town, belonged to a family who practiced Buddhism and territorial religion. However, when he got married in 1968, his family could not find a marriage partner from a *xinfode* family (literally, believers of Buddhism and local deities, broadly referencing all non-Christians in local dialect) whose *bazi* (four pillars of destiny in Chinese astrology) matched Zuilen's. Eventually they found Wu Kuoli, a third-generation Protestant, but a condition of the marriage was that Zuilen had to convert to Christianity. Thus after they got married, Zuilen started to attend local Protestant gatherings on and off.[56]

---

[55] Rui'an City Archives 49-33-18: 10.
[56] Pou Zuilen, interview by author. Xianqiao, Xincheng, May 7, 2013.

The second major path to conversion occurred through faith healing. These converts joined the church after Christians healed a physical or mental illness in themselves or in a relative. In such cases, Christian prayers and exorcism were typically the last resort after they had tried other unsuccessful treatments. Once they or their relatives had recovered, they converted to obtain permanent blessings and protection.

Recoveries through faith and exorcism had been the most common motive for conversion in Rui'an since the early Republican era.[57] Most of the charismatic preachers active during the Cultural Revolution, like Miao Zhitong and Yang Duojia, claimed to have gifts of healing and exorcism, which they believed were given to them to help spread the gospel and glorify God. Many of them first developed their reputations as preachers by performing exorcisms and miracles.[58] Local residents, especially the families of sick people, got to know these preachers first as exorcists and Christianity as a healing method before becoming familiar with their spiritual or ideological dimension. Preachers first approached sick people and their families offering to provide free healing rituals for illnesses that the families had no other means to treat. There are no available statistics that would allow us to track the evolution of spiritual healing and exorcism during the Cultural Revolution, but the use of these techniques is widely reported in both state and church records of the period, just as it had been in the earlier history of the church.

Next to family and faith healing, the spiritual message of Christianity was likely a powerful means of attracting interest from new and potential converts. The Cultural Revolution did not "subdue the eschatological fire" of the church.[59] This period of conflict and upheaval saw charismatic preachers, many of whom lacked formal ordination, emerging in communities where the old leadership had fallen for various reasons. They often claimed to have witnessed miracles or to be directly inspired by God. A history of Christianity in Wenzhou recounts, "God often personally summoned preachers either through intense emotions [triggered] during prayers or through marvelous dreams and visions. Someone called upon by God would directly devote [himself] to service upon receiving God's affirmation. He did not need to receive the approval of any organization or

---

[57] Kao Chen-yang specifically suggests the connection between the popularity and transformation of Pentecostal practices and the rise of Protestantism in Fujian during the Cultural Revolution. But the Rui'an case shows neither a rise in nor a significant transformation of evangelization techniques in the county during the Cultural Revolution. See Chen-yang Kao, "The Cultural Revolution and the Emergence of Pentecostal-style Protestantism in China," *Journal of Contemporary Religion* 24, no. 2 (2009): 171–188.

[58] According to Shu Chengqian, many Adventist preachers also had the gift of healing; see Shu, *Wushi nian jiaohui shenghuo huiyi*, Chapter 6 (section 7).

[59] Xi Lian, *Redeemed by Fire: The Rise of Popular Christianity in Modern China* (New Haven, CT: Yale University Press, 2010), 203.

take a vow to anyone. The only subject he needed to be loyal to was God. . . . This was a period when God ruled directly."[60]

Traveling to spread the gospel, preachers also carried with them messages of imminent salvation. While Rui'an was consumed by armed conflicts between Red Guard factions, Methodist preacher Zhang Shidan of Xihu Brigade, Shilong Commune, Gaolou, together with a devout follower, Zhang Zhengcha, went around the county, preaching and performing faith healing to attract new members to the church. Within a few years, Zhang Shidan is said to have attracted 114 new converts in three communes, including cadres and Youth League members. These evangelical activities brought him to the attention of state authorities. In a letter to the Wenzhou Regional Revolutionary Committee dated July 15, 1970, the Rui'an Revolutionary Committee asked for his arrest and described some of his eschatological messages. The letter referred to him as an "imperialist spy" and accused him of several crimes, the first of which was "fabricating rumors to mislead people." He was charged with "speaking nonsense, such as 'if you want to be saved, you should come to believe in God.'" He was also quoted as saying that "Chairman Mao rules the body; God rules the soul. The body is temporary, the soul is eternal . . . [now] the people (min) are fighting the people; soldiers (bing) are fighting soldiers; countries are fighting countries . . . if war breaks out, the world is going to end."[61] In addition to asking for his arrest, the letter recommended a twenty-year jail sentence as punishment for his crimes. Yet the church's records show that he remained active throughout the Cultural Revolution. It appears that his arrest never took place, perhaps because of the chaotic situation at the time.

On July 15, 1970, the same day as the letter concerning Zhang Shidan, the Rui'an Revolutionary Committee wrote another letter to the Wenzhou Regional Revolutionary Committee asking for the arrest of "counterrevolutionary" Zhang Liquan, a Methodist preacher from Tangxia. This letter described similar eschatological messages:

Criminal Zhang took advantage of the social wave of anarchism in 1967 and returned to preaching in family gatherings. [He] zealously visited [the town of] Tangxia, Tangkou, Zhaozhai, Qianzhuang, Shangjin, etc. to mobilize and propagandize, vociferously spreading rumors to slander [our government] and speaking nonsense: "The current situation matches the situation [which will occur in] the end times." "Now one country (guo) is fighting another and the

---

[60] Shehe, "Wenzhou jiaohui guanli moshi qiantan."

[61] "Dui diguozhuyi tewu Zhang Shidan pizhe zongjiao waiyi jinxing pohuai huodong de diaocha he chuli yijian" (Report on the investigation of imperialist spy Zhang Shidan conducting destructive activities in the guise of religion and handling opinions), July 15, 1970, Rui'an City Archives 4-21-27: 118.

people are fighting the people. Many have been killed." "The end of the world is nigh! You should make haste and believe in Jesus. Faith in Jesus will save your soul. Life in this world is short but salvation of the soul is eternal."[62]

The eschatological messages of Protestant preachers during this period are different from those common in the 1950s and early 1960s. They make unambiguous references to the social chaos of the Cultural Revolution in phrases like "the people fighting the people," "soldiers fighting soldiers" and "countries fighting countries," apparently referring to armed fights and other political conflicts between individuals and factions. What these messages attempt to convey is a total collapse of order and morality. The chaos and violence of the Cultural Revolution are reinterpreted according to Christian eschatology as a symptom of end times, where the only salvation lies in God.

Messages like these were not only heard among Methodist preachers in Rui'an, but circulated broadly across denominational lines. For instance, Jin Chengzhou of Shankeng Brigade, a leader of the CJIC in Huling, was officially accused of "publicly spread[ing] poisonous information, speak[ing] nonsense [such as saying] that it has been almost two millennia since Jesus descended into the world. The world is going to end. Those who believe in Jesus will not be affected. Their souls will ascend to heaven. Once the trumpet of Jesus sounds, those who follow [his] way will be reborn after death."[63]

Similarly in Wenling, a county bordering Wenzhou in the south, local authorities reported "rumors" manufactured by Protestant Ye Entu in 1972: "The world right now is in chaos. Countries are fighting countries. Armies are fighting civilians. The people are fighting the people. Everything under Heaven [tianxia, referring to the realm of ordinary existence in Chinese cosmology] will be pacified. Our patriarch [jiaozhu] hopes to rule all under heaven [zuo tianxia]. " "Countries are fighting countries. The people are fighting the people. There will be hunger and earthquakes. All humans in the world will die. Those who believe in Jesus will be saved. [By then] Jesus [himself] will preach. All things will become dung and earth and [will] be useless. You should get closer to Christ, who will bring you to Heaven."[64] In 1972, when the government delivered and implemented central guidelines to expose the Lin Biao anti-party clique, there

[62] "Guanyu dui fangemin Zhang Liquan de shencha he chuli yijian de baogao" (Report on the investigation of counterrevolutionary Zhang Liquan and handling opinions), July 15, 1970, Rui'an City Archives 4-21-27: 110.

[63] "Qingkuang jiaoliu jianbao (di qi qi)" (Bulletin on the current situation, volume 7), January 28, 1970, Rui'an City Archives 4-21-88: 105–106.

[64] "Guanyu dangqian zongjiao huodong de qingkuang yu jinhou yijian de baogao" (Report on current religious activities and opinions for the future), September 20, 1972, Wenling City Archives J1-1-1120: 29–30.

were rumors in Rui'an and Lanxi (a county in central Zhejiang) that the church was going to revive, Jesus was going to descend, and there would be a "change of dynasty."[65]

These eschatological messages are curiously absent in the memoirs of church leaders describing the Mao era. Instead, they celebrate the piousness and religious passion of those who attended church meetings at the time:

> [We] often convened spirit cultivation gatherings that would continue for three days and nights. [No one] felt tired or was afraid of the winds or snow or cold weather. [People] were so thirsty to hear the preaching that they would not leave at midnight and [instead] asked to continue. Those who had no bench to sit on would sit on the floor. Even the stairs and woodsheds were full of people . . . they described prayer meetings at the time as being so quiet you could hear a pin drop. Everyone was filled with the holy spirit. No one waved fans in spite of [enduring] the stench of sweat and mosquito bites. No one tried to swat mosquitoes with their palms. Nothing could deter the sisters' and brothers' passion or reduce their eagerness to participate in prayer meetings. The spirit of God seized people's minds![66]

Official reports documented the same religious passion in an entirely different tone: "Criminal activities such as revival meetings (*fenxinhui*) and spirit dances (*tiao lingwu*) to repel demons and cure illness are gaining pace, which damage public morality, destroy social customs and end lives, and have long been prohibited. Lianzhong Brigade of Yongjia County went to the riverside, dancing spirit dances like lunatics without sleeping for three days and nights. They also spoke nonsense [saying] that they would go to heaven."[67]

The religious passion described in both Christian memoirs and official reports can easily be compared with the feverish cult of Mao in the same period, though Christian worship had none of the violence of the Red Guard movement. But what was the source of this religious enthusiasm? If we turn back to the eschatological messages of Christian preachers, the picture becomes much clearer. What was driving them was a deep insecurity and anxiety about the chaos of the Cultural Revolution, pushing them to seek redemption in Christ.

---

[65] "Guanyu daji liyong zongjiao jinxing pohuai huodong de fangeming fenzi de qingshi baogao" (Report and request about a crackdown on counterrevolutionaries exploiting religion to conduct destructive activities), February 2, 1973, Rui'an City Archives 1-21-60: 14–15.

[66] Shu, *Wushi nian jiaohui shenghuo huiyi*, Chapter 6 (section 3).

[67] Rui'an City Archives 1-21-60: 15.

Conclusion

During the early Cultural Revolution, Christian churches ran into a second wave of repression, more violent than the Great Leap, yet with less severe consequences for the church. Indeed, the political chaos of the time, particularly the factional conflicts crippling the management of and oversight by the state, dramatically increased the space for religious activities.

Faced with the state's intense hostility toward religion, Christian preachers adopted tactics to evade the attention of the state. They implanted new Protestant communities in numerous villages in the form of small house gatherings and used these as a base to spread the gospel further to yet more (new) communities. These tactics ensured not just the survival of the church, but its rapid and dramatic expansion, with a massive growth of Christian communities documented from 1958 to 1978.

The Cultural Revolution saw both diversification and unification in the church. There was competition between different churches, even as new collaborative networks started to reduce the importance of denominational lines. The territorial expansion of the church led to a fundamental transformation in the institutions of Protestant Christianity in Wenzhou, with the establishment of regional networks and the extensive *paidan* system for sharing pastoral resources.

These new collaborative efforts allowed the church to spread its message far and wide across Wenzhou. Yet the growing number of converts and inquirers likely also had to do with the violent upheaval of the Cultural Revolution. The church's millenarian messages tapped into a spiritual crisis, offering redemption in the midst of chaos. Protestant preachers, similar to leaders of salvationist groups, heavily resorted to eschatological messages in order to appeal to villagers and therefore broaden their bases. As they came from different theological traditions, their depictions of the end of the world were different in many respects. But they all interpreted the social disorders and political chaos of the Mao years as signs of the end of the world and predicted various scenes of the last day. They similarly warned people of the need to join their religion in order to be saved in the trial of doomsday and find ultimate redemption.

Some scholars believed that contemporary religious revitalization is a collective response to spiritual crisis of the post-Mao era.[68] Yet the Rui'an case suggests that such a crisis had existed all along throughout the twentieth century. The Cultural Revolution saw an overt display of such a crisis when Protestantism

---

[68] Alan Hunter and Chan Kim-Kwong, eds., *Protestantism in Contemporary China* (Cambridge: Cambridge University Press, 1993), 170; Richard Madsen, *China's Catholics: Tragedy and Hope in an Emerging Civil Society* (Berkeley: University of California Press, 1998), 8–9; David Ownby, *Falun Gong and the Future of China* (Oxford: Oxford University Press, 2008), 4–5.

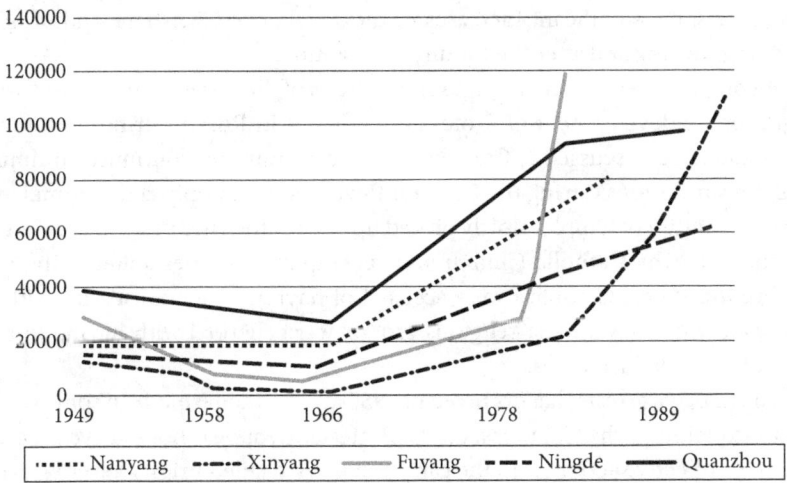

Figure 5.3. The trend of Protestant populations in certain other regions since 1949.
Nanyang Diqu difangshizhi bianzuan weiyuanhui, ed., *Nanyang Diqu zhi* (Nanyang Region
gazetteer) (Zhengzhou Shi: Henan renmin chubanshe, 1994), 457–458; Xinyang Diqu difangshizhi
bianzuan weiyuanhui, ed., *Xinyang Diquzhi* (Xinyang Region gazetteer) (Beijing: Sanlianshudian,
1992), 915–917; Zhang Benle, ed., *Hui huang shi wu nian—Xinyang Diqu juan* (Glorious fifteen
years—Xinyang Region volume) (Beijing: Guangming ribao chubanshe, 1995), 322; Fuyang
Shi difangzhi bangongshi, ed., *Fuyang Diqu zhi* (Fuyang Region gazetteer) (Beijing: Fangzhi
chubanshe, 1996), 1055–1045; Tang Jinhua et al., eds., *Ningde Diqu zhi* (Ningde Region gazetteer)
(Beijing: Fangzhi chubanshe, 1998), 1667; Quanzhou Shi difangzhi bianzuan weiyuanhui,
ed., *Quanzhou shizhi* (Quanzhou City gazetteer) (Beijing: Zhongguo shehuikexue chubanshe,
2000), 3558.

offered an alternative to frantic Maoist ideology. Viewed from this perspective,
if Wenzhou is China's Jerusalem, then this Jerusalem has its roots in the Cultural
Revolution.

The phenomenon of rapid growth and expansion in Protestant communities
was not limited to Rui'an or Wenzhou, but was also evident in some other regions
across China. In Wenling County in the Taizhou region of Zhejiang, church
records show that four of the 116 churches in the county in 2006 originated in
1960–1963, and eighteen were formed during the Cultural Revolution.[69]

As Figure 5.3 shows, Xinyang and Nanyang regions of Henan Province,
Fuyang region of Anhui Province, and Ningde and Quanzhou regions of Fujian

[69] See historical records of local church website "Wenling fuyin zhijia" (Wenling Home of
Gospel):   http://www.wlfyzj.com/content.asp?parent=root3%40%D0%D6%B5%DC%BD%CC%B
B%E1%40 (accessed on April 29, 2015). The Protestant population in Wenling also saw significant
growth under Mao. In 1949, there were 16,079 Protestants in Wenling, but according to government
estimates there may have been as many as 50,000 by the end of the Cultural Revolution (Wenling
Xian zhi bianzuan weiyuanhui, *Wenling Xian zhi*, 831–832).

Province show significant increases in the number of Christians and of house meetings during and after the Cultural Revolution.[70]

A comparison with other religious traditions of the same county sheds further light on the development of Protestant churches in Rui'an during the Cultural Revolution. As discussed in Chapter 3, local communities continued communal religious traditions during the Cultural Revolution, but only at a minimal level. The restoration of temples slowly picked up only in the later years of the Cultural Revolution. The Catholic Church and redemptive societies suffered the most before the 1960s. Catholics were accused of having "imperialist" ties with the Vatican, while salvationist religious groups were charged with having links to Nationalist residual forces.

The massive arrests that occurred in 1955 and their aftermath go some way toward explaining why Catholics, unlike Protestants, appear not to have seen a revival in collective activities in the early 1960s. Two jailed priests never returned. Catholics seem to have established some house gatherings toward the end of the Cultural Revolution, but these were largely concentrated in Mayu under the leadership of Chen Nailiang,[71] a former student of Ningbo Saint Vincent Seminary who was released from prison in 1965, and catechist Jiang Lianghui. These Catholic house gatherings were never as diversified as the Protestant ones, and by 1981, there were only twenty-three gathering places in Rui'an.[72] Similarly, Catholics in Jinbao Mountain of Wenzhou suburb, and Yishan Town and Linjiayuan Village of Pingyang County set up bases from around the late 1960s when some jailed clergymen were released.[73] Chen Nailiang organized gatherings to observe holy dates in Pingyang and Wenzhou, but a networked Catholic community never developed during the Cultural Revolution, at least partly due to the lack of leadership and local preachers. Most clergymen remained in prison for almost the entire duration of the Cultural Revolution.

[70] Nanyang Diqu difangshizhi bianzuan weiyuanhui, ed., *Nanyang Diqu zhi* (Nanyang Region gazetteer) (Zhengzhou Shi: Henan renmin chubanshe, 1994), 457–458; Xinyang Diqu difangshizhi bianzuan weiyuanhui, ed., *Xinyang Diquzhi* (Xinyang Region gazetteer) (Beijing: Sanlianshudian, 1992), 915–917; Zhang Benle, ed., *Hui huang shi wu nian— Xinyang Diqu juan* (Glorious fifteen years—Xinyang Region volume) (Beijing: Guangming ribao chubanshe, 1995), 322; Fuyang Shi difangzhi bangongshi, ed., *Fuyang Diqu zhi* (Fuyang Region gazetteer) (Beijing: Fangzhi chubanshe, 1996), 1055–1045; Tang Jinhua et al., eds., *Ningde Diqu zhi* (Ningde Region gazetteer) (Beijing: Fangzhi chubanshe, 1998), 1667; Quanzhou Shi difangzhi bianzuan weiyuanhui, ed., *Quanzhou shizhi* (Quanzhou City gazetteer) (Beijing: Zhongguo shehuikexue chubanshe, 2000), 3558.

[71] "Chengong jinduo sanshi zhounian shiji jianjie" (A brief introduction to the deeds of priest Chen at the thirtieth anniversary of his ordination), http://www.tianren.org/life/show.asp?id=15836 (accessed on May 4, 2018).

[72] "Yijiubaer nian zongjiao gongzuo qingkuang he jinhou yijian" (Religious work in 1982 and opinions for the future), January 27, 1983, Rui'an City Archives 1-31-45: 147.

[73] Rui'an City Archives 7-29-46: 31; Wang Jingmin, "Jinbao Shan huiyilu" (A memoir on Jinbao Mountain), *Wenzhou tangqu bao*, http://www.tianren.org/life/show.asp?id=17689 (accessed on May 4, 2018).

Protestants in Rui'an remember the Cultural Revolution as an ordeal, but also as a time of renaissance in the church. The church, as it stood in 1978, sought to consolidate its expansion during the Cultural Revolution rather than starting from scratch. Yet the Cultural Revolution also left wounds and rifts, and local churches had to face these as well when they dealt with the aftermath of the years of conflict, asking whether or not they should move meetings from private homes to churches.

6

Mixed Blessings

Growth and Schisms among Protestant Churches, 1978–2014

By 1978, when the Chinese government officially declared the end of the Cultural Revolution, Protestants in Rui'an had established a network of house meeting sites across the county, though churches (both Protestant and Catholic)—as well as most Buddhist monasteries and village temples—were still closed.[1] The home gathering network consisted of 270 sites where families and small groups met for worship, more than twice the number of Protestant gathering sites in 1949.[2] Protestants had grown fourfold and their numbers were still increasing.[3] A history of local Protestant churches claimed that "every year several thousand people were baptized, more than eighty percent of them young or middle-aged."[4]

Mao's death in 1976 and the subsequent government reshuffling led to a dramatic shift in state policy regarding religion, concurrent with a fundamental restructuring of the state's role in rural areas. After 1978, the government set off to "reinstate religious policy" (*luoshi zongjiao zhengce*), adopting a milder approach that had been strongly criticized within the party since 1957.[5] New guidelines reinstated the principle of religious freedom prescribed in the 1954 Constitution and authorized churches to reopen.

This policy shift appeared to be an opportunity for the return of church buildings and the legalization of local Protestant organizations. Yet as before, the guidelines stipulated loyalty to the party-state as a condition for churches to operate. From the central to the local level, religious communities were required to

---

[1] Rui'an jiaohui, *Rui'an jiaohui shi* (A history of Rui'an Church), internal document, 1998, 18–20.

[2] A comparison of locations of gatherings spots and churches shows that many gathering spots had no church in proximity before the 1960s—a clear sign that Protestant churches had extended to new territory during the Cultural Revolution.

[3] "Guanyu Rui'an Shi zongjiao wenti diaocha qingkuang de huibao" (Collective investigational report on the issue of religion in Rui'an City), December 22, 1990, Rui'an City Archives 1-38-6: 31–54. There were 16,853 Christians (Catholics and Protestants) in Rui'an in 1956. See "Guanyu dangqian zongjiao huodong qingkuang de baogao" (Report on current religious activities), April 4, 1957, Rui'an City Archives 1-9-85: 65–68.

[4] Rui'an jiaohui, *Rui'an jiaohui shi*, 18.

[5] Zhang Zhiyi, *Zhang Zhiyi wenji* (The works of Zhang Zhiyi) (Huawen chubanshe, 2006), 351. Zhang was the vice director of the Communist Party's United Front Work Department in the early to mid-1950s and the early 1980s.

Maoism and Grassroots Religion. Xiaoxuan Wang, Oxford University Press (2020). © Oxford University Press.
DOI: 10.1093/oso/9780190069384.001.0001

register and organize themselves within the framework of religious associations that the government had first attempted to implement in the 1950s, essentially a proxy for state control of religion.

At this crucial historical moment, Protestant communities in Rui'an faced both opportunities and challenges. They could leave behind house meetings, with all the secrecy and instability that might entail, join government-recognized churches, and pursue the expansion of the church through officially sanctioned means. Yet many church leaders could not accept the new rules and institutions set up to keep the church under the firm grip of the state. After thirty years of conflict and attacks on religion under Mao, some Protestants were simply unwilling or unable to trust the state.

This chapter explores the ways that Protestants navigated the political and institutional shifts of the early reform period and their consequences for Protestantism in Wenzhou and beyond. The Maoist legacy played a crucial role in the formation of today's flourishing yet deeply divided Protestant church in Wenzhou. While focusing on Protestant communities, I compare them with other religious communities as well, Catholic ones in particular, to better understand why Protestantism has become such a strong force in Wenzhou's contemporary religious revival.

The Reinstatement of Religious Policy and "Regulatory Priority"

In the early 1980s, the Chinese government initiated a series of critical policy changes affecting the regulation of religious affairs. The central government passed its first new rule concerning religious properties in July 1980, when the State Council approved a proposal to return occupied properties that historically belonged to religious organizations and settle issues related to their ownership.[6] This regulation would become the official policy most often cited in the restitution of churches, but in many areas it does not seem to have been implemented right away. Local communities like those in Rui'an were probably unaware of its content or even its existence.[7]

---

[6] "Guowuyuan pi zhuan zongjiao shiwuju guojia jianwei deng danwei guanyu luoshi zongjiao tuanti fangchan zhengce deng wenti de baogao" (The State Council's approval and transmission of the report by Religious Affairs Bureau, National Development Committee, and others concerning implementation of policies on properties of religious organizations), July 16, 1980, Rui'an City Archives 4-31-34: 16–19.

[7] Buddhist leader Po Yiha told me that he did not know the policy until he wrote a letter to ask the national Buddhist association regarding the restoration of Sagely Longevity Temple of Xianyan in 1981. "At that time Shanghai government did implement the policy. But [government] in other places put aside the policy." He explained: "[speaking from] the local government side, you asked schools

In March 1982, the central government issued new guidelines for religious affairs, the "Basic Viewpoints and Policies on the Religious Question during Our Nation's Socialist Period" (*Guanyu woguo shehuizhuyi shiqi zongjiao wenti de jiben guandian he jiben zhengce*), commonly known as Document No. 19. It renounced the use of coercive measures to stamp out "religion" and reiterated the party's policy of "religious freedom." It also stipulated the "selective" and "gradual" reopening of some sites for legal religious activities.

Both the reinstatement of institutionalized religion and the central government's new religious concerns necessitated an adjustment in religious policy. In the early reform period, starting in the late 1970s, economic development became the government's first priority. The state initiated a policy of *boluan fanzheng* (correcting wrongs and returning to normality), with an agenda of settling historical issues, reaffirming policies "distorted" during the Cultural Revolution, and resurrecting the apparatus of state. Religious affairs were attached to United Front work with its own policy restitution intended to strengthen solidarity and clean up leftist influence. The return to a more accommodating policy on religion, somewhat similar to the policy that had reigned before 1957, matched the direction of United Front work.[8]

The most immediate motive for the formulation of the new religious policy was the government's concern about being unable to control religious communities at a critical moment when the country was "opening up." Thirty years of Maoist rule had not eliminated religion, but only pushed it underground, making it difficult for the government to grasp the real scope of religious communities. What the government found even more worrisome was the antagonism against it, which had accumulated during the Mao era. United Front officials pointed out that it might "push religious followers to the side of the enemy," especially "overseas hostile forces."[9]

The peril was real and imminent in their eyes. Foreign churches, as well as churches led by overseas Chinese, particularly those based in Hong Kong and Taiwan, were taking steps to establish a presence in the PRC. With the

and factories to move out, where did you want them to move? Therefore the policy was put aside." Interview with Po Yiha, May 15, 2013.

[8] Zhang, *Zhang Ziyi wenji*, 351, 397–398, 413–414. It was actually not a return. Even before 1957, there was never a stable policy line on religion. The religious policy in the period 1949–1957 fluctuated between marginalizing and eliminating by coercive measures, and fostering unity with religious communities (Fuk-Tsang Ying, "The CPC's Policy on Protestant Christianity, 1949–1957: An Overview and Assessment," *Journal of Contemporary China* 23, no. 89 (2014): 884–901). The guidelines of new religious policies in the early 1980s were closer to the more lenient end of the spectrum.

[9] "Guanyu dangqian zongjiao gongzuo zhong jixu jiejue de liang ge zhengce xing wenti qingshi baogao" (Request for instructions on two policy questions in current religious affairs urgently needing to be resolved), October 21, 1978, Rui'an City Archives, 1-27-670: 101–110.

assistance of local Chinese Christians, they smuggled tens of thousands of Bibles, pamphlets, and other religious materials into Guangzhou and other coastal cities. Overseas churches reconnected with churches in China, often in the name of visiting family or making investments.[10] All these developments urgently demanded changes in the regulation of religion to allow the government to contain religious communities and the political threats they might pose. After coercion and blunt repression under Mao had failed to eliminate religion, the government turned to a more permissive stance.

In principle, the new religious policy applied to all legal religions. In practice, the central government perceived religions differently depending on factors such as their history in different regions. There were differences in how the national policy was applied, particularly by local administrations.

Buddhism, Catholicism, and Protestantism all represented different issues in party ideology under Mao. In the 1950s and 1960s, Buddhist temples had been stripped of their estates. Land reform had eliminated the wealthy class who made up their customary patrons.[11] There were no Buddhist ordinations for almost two decades, and very few regular active Buddhist communities. Provincial authorities estimated that more than 70 percent of the population of Zhejiang Province had been Buddhist in 1940,[12] but by the end of the Cultural Revolution, the religion had fallen into a slump. Moreover, the threat of "feudalism" was no longer a pressing ideological concern.

By contrast, the state associated Catholicism and Protestantism with the threat of imperialism. The state intended to force Christians to sever their connections to overseas churches and to nurture the Three-Self organizations to ensure compliance and loyalty to the state.[13] Isolating Chinese Christians from foreign influence and keeping them under the control of the government became all the more important when China reopened to the world in the 1980s.

Wenzhou was a particularly crucial site in the government's battle against foreign influence because of its position as an entryway into China and its large

[10] "Zhongyang guanyu dizhi waiguo jiaohui dui wo jinxing zongjiao shentou wenti de qingshi baogao" (Report and request by the Central Committee on the issue of resisting infiltration by foreign churches), March 4, 1982, Rui'an City Archives, 1-28-47: 1–12. See also Zheng Datong (*Mengfu zhi lu—Jidu li shiyi de rensheng* (The path of blessing—poetic life in Christ) (Hong Kong: Xundao weili zhongxin, 2010), chapter 22) for the account of a church leader on their contacts with the outside world during this period.

[11] Goossaert and Palmer, *The Religious Question in Modern China*, 159–160.

[12] The Republican government had continued to track the changes to the number of both Christians and Buddhists, as well as followers of other legal religions. According to the Zhejiang Department of Civil Affairs, by 1940, Buddhists occupied 70.47 percent whereas Christians (Protestants and Catholics) only occupied 10.65 percent of the total of 663,231 religious believers in the province. See Zhejiang minzhengting (Zhejiang Department of Civil Affairs), *Zhejiang minzheng yuekan* 4 (1940): 149.

[13] Vincent Goossaert and David A. Palmer, *The Religious Question in Modern China* (Chicago: University of Chicago Press, 2011), 158–159.

share of Christians compared to the country as a whole. In 1949, Zhejiang Province had 17 percent of the total Protestant population in the country, which represented the largest share of Protestants among all the provinces.[14] Zhejiang also had numerous Catholics at the time. A historical study estimated that there were nearly 95,000 Catholics in Zhejiang in 1949.[15]

Unlike Buddhist temples, Christian churches in Zhejiang success-fully endured Maoism. The government estimated that the total number of Christians (both Protestants and Catholics) in 1983 was more than 600,000, twice the number in 1949.[16] However, the pro-government Three-Self organization established at various levels in the early 1950s was virtually disbanded after the Great Leap. Starting in the early 1970s when China normalized its relations with the United States, local authorities in Zhejiang began to raise concerns about growing links between local and foreign Christian organizations: local Christians attempting to reconnect with foreign churches, as well as foreign churches penetrating Chinese Christian communities.[17] After 1978, the rapid increase in China's communication with the outside world made this a more pressing concern.

Therefore, in the early reform period, local authorities in Zhejiang treated Christianity as a priority in the regulation of religious affairs. Zhejiang Party Secretary Wang Fang made this clear in a 1983 provincial religious affairs meeting: "[Zhejiang] is one of the key provinces in terms of religious work. We have 700,000 religious followers. Protestants and Catholics are the majority. Other religious groups are the minority."[18] In another provincial religious af-fairs meeting in 1991, Zhejiang Governor Liu Feng said, "religions of faith are concentrated [in our province]. Number one is Protestantism, which has 960,000 followers, and number two is Catholicism, which has 130,000 followers. Therefore we have to prioritize focal regions (*zhongdian diqu*) and focal religions

---

[14] Fuk-Tsang Ying, "Zhongguo Jidujiao de quyu fazhan: 1918, 1949, 2004" (The regional devel-opment of Protestant Christianity in China: 1918, 1949 and 2004), *Hanyu Jidujiao xueshu lunping* (Sino-Christian Studies) 3 (2007): 171.

[15] Zhejiang Sheng zongjiaozhi bianjizu, ed., *Zhejiang Sheng zongjiaozhi ziliao huibian yi: Tianzhujiao* (Documents on history of religion in Zhejiang, volume one: Catholicism), internal document, 1993, 47.

[16] See "Guanyu Wenzhou zongjiao wenti huibao tigang" (Outline report on religious questions in Wenzhou), May 15, 1981, Rui'an City Archives 7-29-46: 31.

[17] "Guanyu daji liyong zongjiao jinxing pohuai huodong de fangeming fenzi de qingshi baogao" (Report and request about a crackdown on counterrevolutionaries exploiting religion to conduct de-structive activities), February 2, 1973, Rui'an City Archives 1-21-60: 14–17.

[18] "Wang Fang shuji zai quansheng zongjiao gongzhuo huiyishang de jianghua" (The speech of Secretary Wang Fang at the provincial religious work meeting), June 22, 1983, Rui'an City Archives 1-31-63: 36. One wonders how the Zhejiang government came up with this figure. Zhejiang had about 600,000 Christians in 1983. Therefore, it is very likely that either the government did not add the data of lay Buddhists, or the number of people self-identified as lay Buddhist was extremely low at the time.

(*zhongdian zongjiao*)."[19] Liu's message was clear: Buddhism and other legal religions in Zhejiang were in the minority, while Christianity should be the focus of their regulatory efforts.

In the context of religious policy and the government's focus on Christianity, the remainder of this chapter explores different Christian communities' experiences of the new religious policy, as well as the dramatic, far-reaching effects these had on the development of Christianity in Rui'an and Wenzhou today.

The Legalization and Proliferation of Protestant Churches

When the Cultural Revolution gave way to reform, the most urgent issue for Protestant communities in Rui'an and elsewhere in China was the restitution of churches. The vast majority of these had been occupied, demolished, or shut down in the 1950s and 1960s. For different reasons, the Chinese government shared a similar concern. Document No. 19 considered "appropriately arranging religious activity sites" a "crucial material condition of religious normalization" and made this one of two priorities for officials engaged in works on religion.[20]

In Rui'an, the number of religious sites whose restitution was planned (*ying luoshi*, literally meaning it "ought to be implemented") was significantly different for Buddhism and Christianity. Christianity was allocated disproportionate government resources in the restitution of religious sites.[21] The government set out quotas allowing a maximum number of sites to be restored. Seventeen Catholic churches and fifty-nine Protestant churches were included in the quota, including each of the permanent Protestant churches that had been in operation before 1949.[22] Buddhism was allocated a quota of fifty-six temples, less than 15 percent of the total number of Buddhist temples that had been active in the early 1950s.[23]

By 1990 two Catholic churches and thirty-two Protestant churches had been returned and reopened "with the approval of the [county] government" (*zhengfu pizhun*),[24] which in fact meant "after direct intervention by the county

---

[19] "Liu Feng tongzhi zai quansheng zongjiao gongzhuo huiyishang de jianghua" (Comrade Liu Feng's speech at the provincial religious work meeting), November 24, 1991, Rui'an City Archives 49-43-5: 63.

[20] The other task was to "let patriotic organizations fully play their roles."

[21] The difference in political arrangement, which was a critical instrument of United Front work, was also pronounced. In the 1980s, six Protestant leaders and two Catholic leaders were selected as people's political consultative committee members, whereas only one Buddhist leader was assigned as a committee member.

[22] Rui'an City Archives 1-38-6: 32–33. Thirty-seven temporary meeting spots established before 1949 were not included.

[23] It is unclear how the county government selected and decided the number of Buddhist temples to be restored in Rui'an.

[24] Rui'an City Archives 1-38-6: 33.

government." Christian communities salvaged five Catholic churches and eighteen Protestant churches after negotiations with the occupying entities, in some cases employing the mediation of town, district, or other lower-level branches of government. In contrast, there were extremely few government interventions to aid the restitution of Buddhist temples in the 1980s. Buddhists managed to obtain the return of fifty-two of the fifty-four monasteries in the quota; none of them was returned with the "approval" (meaning assistance) of the county government.[25] In seeking the restitution of temples, Buddhists were largely left to fend for themselves.

Equally striking was, within Christianity, the difference between Catholics and Protestants in their attitudes toward the government, which significantly influenced the extent to which each benefited from the status of Christianity as a "regulatory priority." The conditions for Catholic communities in Rui'an were certainly not as good as for Protestants, though both had to operate without a formal church. In 1982, none of the seventeen Catholic churches had been restored. Only four Catholic communities were reported to be active. In one of these four communities, Li'ao of Tangxia District, a joint investigation by provincial, city, and county officials in July 1981 found that only a fraction of Catholics regularly attended meetings.[26] The number of Catholics in 1982 had increased about two and half times since 1949, only slightly faster than the growth rate of the population as a whole.

Catholics in Wenzhou adamantly refused to cooperate with the authorities. As a result, they benefited much less from "regulatory priority" status. Soon after the end of the Cultural Revolution, Catholic clergymen were released from prison and re-established the Roman Catholic diocese of Wenzhou. The diocese reconnected with the Vatican and insisted on two "no contacts": no contact

[25] Ibid. Lack of approval from the county government does not mean there weren't interventions on the temples' behalf from lower level officials. Most temples were occupied by state institutions. The overall progress of the return of Buddhist temples was not necessarily smoother and quicker than that of Christian churches. *A Concise History of Buddhism in Rui'an* written by Pan Yiheng listed 489 monasteries that were still active in the late 1940s (Pan Yiheng, *Zhe'nan Rui'an Fojiaozhi* [History of Buddhism in Rui'an of Southern Zhejiang], internal document, ca. 1992). Only 119 of them were returned or rebuilt between 1978 and 1991. For the county seat and the suburb, the ratio is 23.81 percent. Ten of forty-two Buddhist temples were restored by 1991. Seventy-six among 178 temples (42.7 percent) were returned or rebuilt in Xincheng and Tangxia of Tang River basin. Yet in sharp contrast, only ten of 119 Buddhist temples (0.08 percent) were returned or rebuilt in the western mountains, including Huling, Taoshan, and Gaolou. For Mayu and Xianjiang in the plain areas to the south of Feiyun River, the ratio is, respectively, six out of ninety two (0.06 percent) and thirteen out of sixty-one (21.31 percent).

[26] "Guanyu Tangxia Gongshe zongjiao qingkuang ji Li'ao Gongshe xinyang zongjiao qingkuang" (A preliminary investigation of the religious situation in Tangxia Commune and Li'ao Commune), July 2, 1981, Rui'an City Archives 49-33-18: 18. It is unclear how "Catholic" was defined in this report. Local Catholics seemed to report all of their nuclear family members as Catholics, including newborns, to local authorities in the 1950s, whereas no such case is found among the surveys of Protestant population.

with the government and no contact with patriotic associations.[27] The Wenzhou Patriotic Catholic Association established in 1980 was virtually inactive for at least ten years. The Rui'an Patriotic Catholic Association was only established in 1999, though the city government had planned it since 1982.[28]

The Roman Catholic church established twenty-one gathering spots by the end of the 1980s. By then, Catholics had restored seven churches, but only one had set up a "church affairs regulation team" (tangwu guanli xiaozu), a sign of official recognition. In 1990, in the entire Wenzhou region, local authorities believed that more than 90 percent of Catholics were still under the influence of "underground forces" (dixia shili), that is, Catholic churches loyal to the Vatican.[29]

By contrast, Protestant responses to the new religious policy were polarized, but in the early reform period, most Protestants did not refuse to build links with the government. The Meeting of the Rui'an County Council of Communications, a countywide network of five Protestant congregations (still excluding the Seventh-Day Adventist Church and some communities belonging to the Assembly), reassembled in June 1980. The position of general manager was abolished and managers of each section (pianqu) were given seats on the council.[30]

After the reshuffling, those who supported the establishment of the Three-Self Church of Rui'an were in the majority, and the council formally voted in favor of joining the Three-Self Church.[31] Some Protestant leaders left the council in protest, but the majority of the board members, plus a number of leaders in the Seventh-Day Adventist Church, remained. In 1981 they established a Three-Self Church incorporating the Rui'an County Protestant Three-Self Patriotic Committee (Rui'an Jidujiao Sanzi Aiguo Weiyuanhui) and the Rui'an Protestant Council (Rui'an Jidujiao Xiehui).[32]

Christians and church observers have long characterized the Three-Self Church as merely a puppet set up to serve government aims. This is not entirely fair. The re-establishment of the Three-Self Church created a platform for

---

[27] Rui'an City Archives 49-43-5: 36–37.

[28] Rui'an Buddhist Association was not formed until the end of 1988. One reason, I learned in an interview with Po Yiha, is that monks were traumatized and did not want to take the responsibility. Master Daofa, the first head of the Buddhist Association, hesitated to take the position for years until he was finally persuaded by Master Yuanche, a friend and the general secretary of the National Buddhist Association at the time.

[29] Rui'an City Archives 49-43-5: 36.

[30] A section roughly corresponded to an administrative district. Tangxia was the only exception. It has two sections.

[31] Rui'an jiaohui, Rui'an jiaohui shi, 22–24.

[32] The Protestant council was a new setup created within the Three-Self (self-governance, self-support, and self-propagation) Church and implemented nationwide since the 1980s. The division of labor between the committee and the council, according to the Three-Self Church itself, was that the former aims at promoting unity of Protestants and the Three-Self movement, whereas the latter is in charge of internal affairs of the church, such as theological education and publication.

Protestants (that other religions did not enjoy at the time), allowing them to reach out to the government during a crucial period of religious development.

The Three-Self Church played a pivotal role in the restitution of churches in the early reform period. In 1980, the central government mandated the return of religious properties to religious organizations only.[33] Moreover, the church restitution procedures issued by the Rui'an County Government in 1982 stipulated that only religious organizations were qualified to apply for the return of church buildings. Before the establishment of the Three-Self Church, it was difficult for local officials to identify legal religious organizations. Because no law recognized local Christian communities as legitimate organizations, the return of churches could only be negotiated in an informal way between relevant parties, such as local Christian communities and occupiers of church buildings. Even after successfully negotiating an agreement, Christian groups could not be certain that a church would actually be returned. The county government was even less willing to condone informal negotiations of this kind: being left out of the negotiation process meant they lacked effective control over local churches, which was an essential purpose of church reopening per the central government's directives. The problem was the same for every county government in the Wenzhou region before the establishment of a local branch of the Three-Self Church.[34]

After the Rui'an Three-Self Church was established in July 1982, the Three-Self Committee suggested to the county government: "some district and commune leaders proposed that . . . it ought to be the patriotic organization that files the petition [to reopen a church]. Once the county government approves, local [government] leaders should do their work to carry it out."[35] Making the Three-Self Committee the proxy in church reopening, they believed, "is conducive to building up the authority of the Three-Self patriotic organization."[36] The suggestion was accepted.[37]

That same year, the Three-Self Committee intervened in its first case of church recovery, filing a request to reopen Lower Village Church in Xinmin Commune, Xincheng. This request was immediately approved. The following year, the county government formally issued a notification requesting the establishment of a church affairs committee within Lower Village Church. The main

33 Rui'an City Archives 4-31-34: 16–19.
34 "There was no church that was reopened at the initiation of the government. . . . Yet by March of the year (1981), in the entire [Wenzhou] region, the number of religious activity sites, whose reopening were spontaneously resolved, has reached nearly one hundred." See Rui'an City Archives 7-29-46: 31.
35 "Guanyu kaifang Xinmin Xia Cun jiaotang de baogao" (Report on reopening the Lower Village church at Xinmin Commune), November 20, 1983, Rui'an City Archives 4-3-50: 58–59.
36 Rui'an City Archives 4-3-50: 58–59.
37 In the subsequent registrations of religious properties, all churches had to be nominally registered in name of the Three-Self Church since they are considered the legal organization of Christianity.

hall and some of the annexes were returned. In 1986, the remaining property issues were settled between Lower Village Government and the county Three-Self
Committee with the mediation of the county government.[38]

Once this pattern proved viable, the committee rapidly expanded its work. In
November 1984, the county government authorized at once a total of "seventeen
Protestant churches to be Protestant activity sites (*Jidujiao huodong changsuo*)....
The applicable church properties . . . should be returned to religious organizations."[39] Property issues regarding major churches in eight districts were eventually settled pursuant to this notification. Among the earliest of major churches
to be returned was Yahou Protestant Church in the county seat, formerly the
headquarters of the Methodist Church in Rui'an (Photo 6.1). By early 1995, fifty-
four of fifty-nine churches had been returned, that is, nearly 92 percent of the
churches that Protestants possessed in 1949, with only a few cases remaining to
be settled. At least thirty-seven of those fifty-four churches were re-established
through the Three-Self Church's collaboration with the county government.[40]

In addition to the quota of fifty-nine former church buildings which could be
reclaimed, local authorities in some areas granted Protestant communities permission to build new churches. One of these was the Xincheng Assembly, the
largest of all the Assembly congregations in Rui'an. Before 1949, the community
did not have a formal church building, and thus it was not on the list of churches
to be reopened, though its membership had significantly grown during the Mao
era. Thanks to a petition by the Three-Self Church, the Xincheng congregation
was allocated a parcel of land to build a permanent church.[41] The petition argued
that the nearby Lower Village Church, historically the China Inland Mission's
headquarters in Rui'an, was already overcrowded during Sunday meetings and
could not possibly hold the more than two thousand members of the Xincheng
Assembly (who therefore would have had to congregate in private homes instead). This would have been a problem for county officials, as the central government required that they channel Christians into sanctioned church meetings
rather than family assemblies. The Xincheng Assembly later built the Qianbu
Church on the parcel of land allocated by the government.

The Three-Self Church intervened in cases of official restitution and new construction. Yet most of the newly erected churches in the 1980s and early 1990s
were neither on the first official list of Protestant churches to be restored, nor

---

[38] "Guanyu jiejue Xincheng Xia Cun jidujiaotang fangchan yiliu wenti de qingshi" (Request of settling the remaining property issues in the Protestant church at Lower Village, Xincheng), March 26,
1986, Rui'an City Archives 72-19-6: 42–46.

[39] "Guanyu huifu shiqi zuo jidujiaotang de tongzhi" (Notification on restoring seventeen
Protestant churches), November 10, 1984, Rui'an City Archives 4-35-16: 17–18.

[40] Rui'an jiaohui, *Rui'an jiaohui shi*, 29.

[41] Ibid., 30.

Photo 6.1. Yahou Protestant Church in Rui'an county seat, 2013. Formerly the headquarters of the Methodist Church in Rui'an, it is among the first of the churches to be restituted, in the 1980s.

Source: Author.

was their construction officially sanctioned by the government. For instance, the Seventh-Day Adventist Church was the smallest of the six Protestant denominations in 1949, with only three churches and a few temporary gathering spots, but by 1992, not only had those three churches been restored, six new churches had been built, leaving only two Adventist communities without church buildings.[42] None of the six new churches had been built with the official permission of the county government.

The construction of new churches was motivated by the hope of securing and furthering the development of the church through the creation of permanent gathering places. Moreover, it was greatly encouraged by the accommodating attitude of local authorities. Most of the churches built without official permission,

---

[42] Shu Chengqian, *Wushi nian jiaohui shenghuo huiyi* (Memoirs of fifty years' life in the church), internal reference materials ("neibu cankao ziliao"), 2002.

as well as the church organizations attached to them, were allowed to register with the government as long as the church communities joined or recognized the leadership of the Three-Self Church. Occasionally the communities were asked to pay a fine.[43] Because Preacher Shu Chengqian and several other Adventist leaders participated in the Three-Self Church, the government sanctioned the new Adventist churches soon after their construction.[44]

Thus, amid the "church-building fever" (*jiantangre*) that swept all of Wenzhou in the 1980s and early 1990s, the number of "patriotic associations" soared (*aiguo hui*, an alternative name for Three-Self churches). By 1990, the number of Three-Self churches in Rui'an rose rapidly to 126, including sixty-seven of the eighty-nine newly built churches.[45] In 1995, the total number of Three-Self churches reached 185, including 131 newly constructed church buildings.[46]

The local authorities' accommodating stance toward newly erected churches was above all grounded in local realities. Though the central government had requested the selective reopening of a small number of churches, the high number of Protestants in Rui'an after the end of the Mao era made this an unrealistic goal. Protestants had not only greatly increased in number since 1949, they had also become more widely distributed throughout the county. It would have been impractical, perhaps impossible, to squeeze the large Protestant population into the fifty-nine churches initially permitted to reopen.

The political imperative to bring religious communities under centralized control may have played an even more important role in facilitating the establishment of new and restored churches. The central government's new religious policy in the 1980s was to channel Christians from underground (*dixia*) to above ground (*dishang*), and from family gatherings to meetings in government-sanctioned church buildings. In this context, allowing the construction and recognition of new churches was in accord with the principle of channeling Christians into formally recognized churches.

Schisms among Protestant Churches

As Protestant leaders sought to exploit the new religious policy to retrieve, rebuild, and legalize church buildings, rifts already present within the church

---

[43] Zhu Yujing, "Guojia tongzhi, difang zhengzhi yu Wenzhou de Jidujiao" (State rule, local politics and Christianity in Wenzhou) (PhD dissertation, Chinese University of Hong Kong, 2011), 158.

[44] In contrast, a sect led by Chen Dengyong, which separated itself from other Adventist groups, did not recognize or join the Three-Self Church. They (and the churches they built) could not be legally recognized as the heir of old Adventist churches.

[45] Rui'an City Archives 1-38-6: 32.

[46] Five of fifty-nine old churches were still not restituted.

became more pronounced. The Three-Self Church became a pervasive presence in church life, bringing tensions to the fore. Recent alliances forged during the Cultural Revolution fell apart, shattering the delicate unity among Protestant communities.

Preexisting Discord

The unity among Protestant churches in Rui'an and throughout Wenzhou which took shape before 1978 was doomed to be fragile due to its weak institutional underpinnings. For Protestant communities in Wenzhou, one of the most important consequences of Mao-era policy was probably the flattening of hierarchies within the church (which probably also occurred in Buddhist and territorial temples and monastic institutions). With the departure of missionaries, the discontinuation of foreign aid, and the persecution of Chinese clergy in the 1950s, Protestant communities survived by temporarily forging bonds across denominational divides.

Protestant networks established during the Cultural Revolution were not formal organizations with a coherent internal structure, but rather a loose cooperative network set up under exceptional circumstances to weather the political storms of the Cultural Revolution. There were no hierarchical relationships or financial ties between different member communities, or between member communities and regional or county councils.[47] Consequently, even as the Cultural Revolution elicited cooperation between church groups across villages, towns and denominations, it also pushed church groups to become more independent of each other and of umbrella organizations. Thus, at the start of the reform period, these networks of Protestant communities lacked the means to prevent a schism.

Moreover, sources of discord existed within Protestant churches, sometimes even dating back to before 1949.[48] The political campaigns of the 1950s and 1960s and the interference of the Three-Self patriotic movement deepened old rifts and caused new cracks to appear between Protestant groups.

During the Mao era, many Protestants gave in to political pressure and publicly renounced their Christian faith.[49] Some were pushed to attack and denounce fellow Protestants and church organizations for their own survival, while others exploited the political currents for their private interests. Many of those

---

[47] There were mutual financial aids, but in no case did a gathering place entirely live through the financial support of others.

[48] Shu, *Wushi nian jiaohui shenghuo huiyi*, Chapter 12 (section 2).

[49] See also Zhu, "Guojia tongzhi," 105–106.

who fought back were tortured, imprisoned, or even killed for refusing to renounce their faith, suffering the verbal and physical attacks of those who had
been their fellows in the church.

Religious persecution provoked a strong antagonism toward the government,
but it also ripped apart the church, creating an atmosphere of distrust, disdain,
and even resentment between Protestants. These feelings were so pervasive
that they could only be put aside temporarily when the need to endure severe
attacks on religion surpassed all other concerns. Yet while contained, the affec-
tive burden of the Mao era never went away.

Other sources of friction in the church were less personal, but no less divisive.
The political attacks of the Mao era and particularly the Cultural Revolution had
pushed Protestant denominations to set aside their differences, but these came
back in force during the early reform period. Before 1949 the different Protestant
denominations in Wenzhou had distinctive theological beliefs, ritual practices,
and even different versions of hymns, which they transmitted to their followers.
There were sometimes differences in the theological interpretations and practices
of preachers belonging to the same denomination. While these differences were
mostly set aside during the Cultural Revolution, they did not disappear. With reform and the legalization of Christian practices came the opportunity to act on
theological differences. Miao Zhitong, a preacher from Rui'an, recalls that when he
traveled through the Wenzhou region to preach in the early 1970s, he had heated
debates with several other preachers on the question of who qualified for salvation,
in particular with Preacher Yu Dubin of Yueqing County.[50] Their disagreements
eventually led to Yu leaving to join the Three-Self Church in the early 1980s.[51]

Protestants in the early years of reform did take steps to patch over denominational differences, such as sharing preachers and unifying different versions
of hymns.[52] But not everything could be the subject of tolerance or compromise.
The Wenzhou Meeting of the Regional Council of Communications (*Wenzhou
Qu jiaotong zonghui*), a loose intraregional alliance of all pre-1949 denominations
forged in 1971 (excluding Seventh-Day Adventism), ruled that the "head-
covering" (*mengtou*) custom of the Assembly was a heresy.[53] The causes for

---

[50] Miao Zhitong, *Wenzhou qu jiaohui shi* (Church history in Wenzhou), internal document, 2005–
2006(?), 153–163.

[51] Yu stayed only briefly and then left after losing in the power struggle in the Three-Self Church,
according to Miao.

[52] Chen Fengsheng, "Wenzhou jiaohui yigong fazhan lichen" (The development course of
volunteers in Wenzhou church), *Jinling shengxue zhi* 3 (2010): 33–36, and "Wenzhou Jidujiao
shengshi fazhan lichen" (The making of hymns in Wenzhou Christianity), *Jinling shengxue zhi* 1
(2009): 69.

[53] Qingquan, "Wenzhou jiaohui dashi niandaibiao xia" (Chronicle of events in Wenzhou church).
Maizhong, April issue, 2007. http://www.wheatseeds.org/wheatseeds/2007-04.08/wz/08.html
(accessed on May 4, 2018).

the decision are uncertain, but the implications were clear. Communities who insisted on maintaining this custom would not be accepted into the alliance. The Adventist church was also labeled a heresy and even an evil cult for proselytizing among followers of other denominations.[54]

Around the same time, the southern Zhejiang network of the Adventist Church faced similar accusations. Jiang Xinghua of Hushang'ao Village of Yueqing was a senior Adventist preacher and was very influential among Adventists in surrounding communities. It was said that he attached great importance to the practice of the Ten Commandments but placed much less emphasis on the saving grace (*jiu'en*) of Jesus Christ. Because he considered the use of the cross as a form of idol worship, his gatherings prohibited the display of crosses in any form. Water baptism was also abolished, as were the dietary rules of the traditional Adventist church. These unorthodox practices worried other Adventist leaders in the region. After attempts to sway him proved futile, Jiang and his gatherings were declared heretic and were cut off from all connections with other Adventists in 1975.[55]

All these internal issues—disagreements and feuds, theological and ritual differences—resurfaced after the end of the Cultural Revolution, a few years before the re-establishment of the Three-Self Church in the Wenzhou region. The network of Adventist communities in southern Zhejiang experienced its first major split in May 1978. The split seems to have been provoked by reform measures concerning hymns and Saturday worship instituted by Shu Chengqian and other church leaders. The reform of Saturday worship included the addition of a procedure for worshipping the Holy Spirit and the Holy Father, which allowed multiple people to lead prayers individually (rather than just one or two people, as in the traditional practice). Wu Buxun, a young preacher in the Wenzhou municipality, maintained that the Father must be worshipped before the Holy Spirit because the Father, he believed, is greater than the Holy Spirit. He also disagreed with the revision of the number of hymns, as well as the content of some of the hymns. After realizing he could not persuade other leaders to adopt his suggestions, Wu asked to take a share of the common fund for his gatherings and no longer accepted visits from preachers belonging to other Adventist groups.[56]

Initially the split was limited to a small number of gathering spots in Wenzhou municipality and its suburbs that were under the influence of Wu and Zhao Dianhua, another young preacher. Yet the schism soon took on catastrophic proportions as it spread to member churches throughout the Adventist network

---

[54] Shu, *Wushi nian jiaohui shenghuo huiyi*, Chapter 9.
[55] Ibid., Chapter 24.
[56] Ibid., Chapter 12 (section 1).

in southern Zhejiang, including the Wenzhou region, neighboring Taizhou, Lishui, and Fuding in northern Fujian.

In his memoir, Preacher Shu Chengqian blamed older pastors and preachers who stood behind Wu and Zhao for aggravating the schism. According to Shu, these older church colleagues had been absent when the church was suffering, hiding and not daring to participate in gatherings, certainly not preaching or serving the church. When they suddenly re-emerged after the end of the Cultural Revolution, Shu believed they stirred up conflict so they could seize leadership of the church.[57]

The separatists referred to themselves as the "old sect" (*laopai*), emphasizing the authenticity of their path and their connections to the pre-1949 church. These characterizations, argued Shu, were a matter of expedience and did not reflect the truth. Many older colleagues who had suffered for the church during the Cultural Revolution chose not to join the "old sect."

These schisms in the Adventist Church foreshadowed the difficulties that all other Protestant churches would have to face sooner or later. The lifting of political constraints boosted the church's growth as more people, old and new converts alike, could be encouraged to publicly join church activities. Yet the lifting of constraints also made internal differences rise to the surface, eroding the fragile unity among Protestant communities.[58]

Tensions Generated by the Three-Self Church

If the loosening political environment had the effect of reopening schisms in Protestant churches in Rui'an and Wenzhou, the government's plan to re-establish the Three-Self Church made further rifts almost unavoidable.

In 1979, the government set out to restore religious work offices as well as "patriotic religious associations" at all levels. In December of that year, twelve former members of the Three-Self Church in the 1950s were convened to re-establish the Wenzhou Three-Self Protestant Patriotic Association. With the assistance of the Wenzhou Three-Self Association, the government sought to re-establish the Three-Self Church at the county (prefecture) level.

---

[57]   Ibid., Chapter 12 (section 2).

[58]   The Unified Church in 1978 had not yet had to deal with the great split that the Adventist Church experienced at the time. The Unified Church was not without signs of discord, though. Some perennial issues, such as the form of water baptism, the issue of communion cup (one cup or many cups), and the issue of salvation were frequently brought up for debate among rival groups in the meetings of Wenzhou Regional Communication Meeting, suggesting that the unity within the Unified Church was fragile (Miao, *Wenzhou qu jiaohui shi*, 167–168).

This almost immediately sparked off controversies among Christians throughout Wenzhou. The Three-Self movement engendered both support and opposition in the Meetings of the Wenzhou Regional and Rui'an County Councils of Communication. Many of those who were petitioning the government for church restitution[59] felt that the Three-Self Church acting as a liaison could help them take back church properties and allow Christians to meet again in church halls (as opposed to temporary house gatherings). Endorsing the establishment of a Three-Self Church organization matched their goal of furthering the overall interests of the church. Yet their opponents argued that "church hall meetings would allow the government to control the church. The government is atheistic and wants to eliminate us. Therefore we should not congregate in church halls."[60] Opposition to formal church meetings turned to antipathy toward the Three-Self Church, which the government had tasked with ending home gatherings and replacing them with approved church hall meetings.

The strongest opposition to the Three-Self Church came from the accumulated distrust and resentment against the government and the former Three-Self Church under Mao. Having suffered decades of religious persecution, many church leaders felt a strong hostility toward the government. They likely felt an even greater antipathy toward those working for the Three-Self Church, considering them not to be true believers, perhaps even traitors to the church.

Twelve founding members of the new Wenzhou Three-Self Church in 1979 all belonged to its former incarnation in the 1950s. Most former leaders in the Three-Self Church were members of the clergy who seemed to have given up Christian activities for decades, as no evidence shows any of them actively engaging in church activities during the Cultural Revolution. Miao Zhitong, a church leader who was opposed to the Three-Self movement, accused the Three-Self Church leaders of having "either betrayed God and friends or committed blasphemy [in the past], and denied their Christian faith."[61] A few of them, Miao believed, were in fact Communist Party members. Their return therefore only served to increase hostility toward the Three-Self Church.[62]

The self-styled unified churches in Wenzhou faced the first major split around 1981 due to the polarization in attitudes toward the Three-Self Church. Members of the Wenzhou Regional Council had attempted to reach a basic consensus in

---

[59] Zhu, "Guojia tongzhi," 115.

[60] Zheng, *Mengfu zhi lu—Jidu li shiyi de rensheng*, prologue of Chapter 5.

[61] Miao, *Wenzhou qu jiaohui shi*, 179.

[62] The re-emergence of former church leaders, from the perspective of power, could be a challenge to regional and county Communication Meetings and church leaders at the time. Council members of Communication Meetings, that is, those who were leading Protestant churches in Wenzhou in 1978, including preachers and church elders, were all non-clerical church co-workers. In this case, there was understandably unrest among incumbent church leaders over the return of former clergies and the Three-Self Church they attempted to reorganize.

dealing with shifting social and political conditions in March 1980, but what transpired is unclear. Some claimed that the council came to an agreement that it would oppose the Three-Self movement, while others denied the existence of such an agreement.[63] The following year, Lin Naimei and Jin Daoxing,[64] two of the three standing committee members, decided to participate in the activities of the Three-Self Church and left the council. The Meeting of the Wenzhou Regional Council of Communications virtually fell apart, with only Miao and his colleagues remaining.

After the reshuffling of the Meeting of the County Council of Communications in Rui'an in June 1980, Miao, the most vocal opponent of the Three-Self movement, was marginalized. In July, the General Council formally voted to support the Three-Self Church. The Meeting of the Rui'an County Council of Communication dissolved, with most council members joining the Three-Self Church formed in September 1981, though Miao and his colleagues in Rui'an continued to operate under the name of the Communications Council.

In 1987, Miao and his colleagues organized a new Meeting of the Wenzhou Regional Council of Communications, with Miao elected to be one of the co-directors.[65] Miao's leadership, however, never went unchallenged. In 1986, member churches belonging to the Meeting of Communications in Rui'an split into two sects: the Zhitong sect (*Zhitong pai*, named after leader Miao Zhitong) and the *yuehan* sect (*yuehan pai*, Yuehan being a transliteration of "John"). These two sects controlled fourteen churches and developed seventy-six gathering spots with a total of 7,880 followers.[66]

In the 1980s, opposition to the Three-Self movement became a nearly universal mobilization strategy for any individual or group who wished to initiate a separation from their own or other Protestant communities. The strategy was so effective that some anti-Three-Self sects would set themselves apart by questioning and attacking the motivations of other sects opposed to the Three-Self Church. In this climate of maneuvering and opposition, the Yingling sect (named after its founder), which wanted to be the dominant organization among non-Three-Self churches, went so far as to criticize Miao's sect because some of its leaders maintained personal communications with members of the Three-Self Church, accusing them of being "polluted" (*dianwu*).[67]

---

[63] Zheng, *Mengfu zhi lu—Jidu li shiyi de rensheng*, Chapter 5 (section 2).

[64] Both soon stopped engaging in the activities of the Three-Self Church.

[65] "Zhuanfa shiwei tongzhanbu 'guanyu Yueqing Xian Jidujiao "Jiaotonghui" huodong qingkuang ji chuli yijian de baogao'" (Transmitting "the report on activities of Protestant 'communication meeting' in Yueqing County and handling opinions" by the United Front Department of the Wenzhou Party Committee), June 31, 1987, Rui'an City Archives 1-35-41: 46–47.

[66] Rui'an City Archives 1-38-6: 34–35. See also Miao, *Wenzhou qu jiaohui shi*, 189–191.

[67] Ibid., 192–193.

At the same time as the split in the regional and county meetings, the Shouters (*huhan pai*) were making discreet steps to infiltrate Protestant churches in the Wenzhou region. The Shouters were named for their distinctive practice of shouting the name of the Lord during worship. Organizationally, the sect was a direct offshoot of the Assembly and mainly carried out evangelical activities among communities affiliated with the former Assembly.

Apart from their distinctive practices and theological positions,[68] the most significant way in which the Shouters appealed to Protestants was none other than their determined opposition to the Three-Self Church. In their propaganda, like other groups opposed to the Three-Self Church, they compared it to an "adulterous woman" (a biblical metaphor), and "a tool that the Communist Party used to eliminate Christianity."[69] They said that they "would defeat and bring down Three-Self [organizations]," and "occupy church territory and keep a firm grip over the power of the church."[70] The strategy was effective: twenty-seven churches and gatherings, the majority of the former Assembly communities opposed to the Three-Self Church, joined the Shouters in early 1983.

Within the Adventist Church, the initial split in 1978 did not have much to do with the Three-Self Church: some of the major leaders in the "old sect" also participated in Three-Self activities. In 1984, however, an Adventist Church leader, Wu Huanwen, approved the ordination of pastors in the Three-Self Church. This provoked a severe disagreement between Wu and Chen Dengyong, an Adventist Church leader from Rui'an. They consequently split from each other and formed their own sects. Chen renamed his sect the "Church in the Wild" (*kuangye jiaohui*), a biblical reference implying that it was the one left to endure persecution and glorify God in the wild.

Objecting to the Three-Self Church was made into the core appeal of the "Church in the Wild." The sect refused to register under the name of the Three-Self Patriotic Church. Comparing the Three-Self Church to an "adulterous woman" (like the Shouters), they described the act of registering with the government as a Three-Self Church with the phrase "worshipping the beast," another biblical metaphor, drawing an analogy between Satan and the socialist state.[71]

As schisms grew rapidly among Protestant churches in the 1980s, church leaders leaned into theological disagreements to justify their opposition to the Three-Self Church. Many of the theological trends that appeared in Wenzhou

---

[68] Theologically they stressed rediscovering the true meaning of the Lord and using a recovery version of the Bible that was heavily annotated by their founder Lee Changshou. The Shouters' theological stands are controversial even among Christians. Many church leaders consider the Shouters a heresy even today.

[69] Rui'an City Archives 1-35-41: 47.

[70] Ibid.

[71] Shu, *Wushi nian jiaohui shenghuo huiyi*, Chapter 21 (section 3).

during the reform period came from abroad, from the Shouters in the 1980s to Arminianism and Evangelicalism in the 1990s and Reformed theology in the first decade of the 2000s. These imported theological stances were intentionally emphasized and even exaggerated in order to justify opposing the Three-Self Church. The result was often another split in the church.

For instance, in 1995, the issue of salvation provoked a great debate within the network of the Meeting of Wenzhou Regional Communications. Several Yueqing churches had adopted Reformed theology and advocated the idea that those who had taken refuge in Christ were "once saved, always saved." Conversely, under the leadership of Miao Zhitong, several churches in Rui'an had chosen to follow Arminian theology.[72] These churches proclaimed that being saved was a lifelong process, and that a follower should "always believe, [to] always be saved." The disagreement could not be resolved, and the western Liushi section of Yueqing churches split from the rest of the Meeting. While some churches formed their own alliance, many member churches were still allied with the Arminian churches in Rui'an.

In Wenzhou, after the 1980s, theological disagreements also played an important role in splits within the Adventist Church. Some members of the "new sect" (*xinpai*) were strongly influenced by Evangelicalism and eventually formed their own splinter group, which they dubbed the "new-new sect" (*xinxinpai*). Today there are at least fourteen sects in the Adventist Church in Wenzhou (Photo 6.2).[73]

Consequences of Schisms

Pervasive schisms in the 1980s had a lasting effect on Protestant churches in Rui'an, Wenzhou, and beyond. Not all of these were detrimental to the expansion of Protestantism in Wenzhou: in fact, the immediate outcome of internal splits was the proliferation of Protestant communities. In many cases, rival groups within a community would completely cut off ties with each other. Two or more communities then took shape, each with its own followers and place of worship. This type of split was fairly common in the 1980s and for some time thereafter.

Protestant communities that had built or intended to build churches and did not stand in opposition to the Three-Self Church indirectly benefited from the state imperative to suppress dissident groups. Indeed, the appearance of dissident

---

[72] See Nanlai Cao, *Constructing China's Jerusalem: Christians, Power, and Place in Contemporary Wenzhou* (Stanford, CA: Stanford University Press, 2010), 103–104.

[73] See Duan Qi, "Cangnan fuyin dahui yougan" (Comments on the Cangnan evangelical meeting), *Maitian*, Autumn issue, 2010, http://www.mtfy.org/magazine.php?mod=view&id=212 (accessed on May 4, 2018).

Photo 6.2. A house Adventist Church in Rui'an county seat (2019). The sign reads: "Seventh-Day Adventist Church."
Source: Author.

sects—many of whom made their hostility to the Three-Self Church into one of their main rallying points—proved an added incentive for the government to "settle [the issue] of religious activity sites" by acknowledging and aiding Protestant groups willing to recognize the leadership of the Three-Self Church.

In 1983 the central government launched a nationwide campaign against the Shouters, whose rapid dissemination, overseas connections, and nonconforming political stance deeply worried central leaders.[74] In Wenzhou, a crucial measure to counter the influence of the Shouters was to open more churches and legalize house meetings. As Wenzhou Party Secretary Yuan Fanglie said in a meeting on the handling of the Shouters sect:

> one of the means [they] employ to expand their power is to force people to comply by occupying churches. We should fully utilize church space as a front to fight the Shouters. Different places should draft internal plans for opening churches and (re)open some churches accordingly . . . based on their own

[74] "Guanyu chuli Huhanpai wenti de baogao" (Report on the handling of the Shouters), May 26, 1983, Rui'an City Archives 1-31-63: 18–25.

conditions. . . . Family gatherings . . . are not permitted in principle and we should actively induce them to come to churches for gatherings. In places where people have no church or where churches have been destroyed . . . [we should] merge dispersed "family gathering spots" into joint gathering spots and implement the regime of fixed members, fixed locations, and fixed times [of worship] in order to reinforce the regulation of believers.[75]

Schisms sped up the outward expansion of Wenzhou churches. Starting in the 1980s, Wenzhou Christians—businessmen in particular—strove to spread the gospel to other parts of China and even directly established a number of new churches throughout the country. The internal splits in Wenzhou churches significantly contributed to this movement as they pushed some preachers to seek new territory for expansion outside of Wenzhou.

In the process of creating his own organization, Adventist leader Chen Dengyong adamantly refused to register his "Church in the Wild" as a Three-Self Church. But Chen did not enjoy strong support among local Adventists. He had to rely on the endorsement of pastors from the Adventist churches in Shanghai and Hangzhou. Today, the Church in the Wild still has only a very limited presence in Rui'an and has not even built a church. Since the end of the 1980s, Chen has spent most of his time preaching and ordaining new pastors to build up his personal influence elsewhere in China.

The case of Miao Zhitong is more complex. Miao's organization remains a major sect in Wenzhou. However, competition from other sects drove him to develop his church and organization elsewhere in China. Considered a major separatist in the Wenzhou Protestant church, Miao was under heavy government surveillance from the early 1980s onward. Since then, he has been much more active outside Wenzhou, which in turn has helped him achieve nationwide fame. By his death in 2013, he was widely eulogized within China as a major house church leader.

The repercussions of the schisms for Wenzhou Protestant communities still leave much room for further research. Splits in local churches have likely intensified internal competition, as different sects compete for the same pool of potential converts. As church leaders admit, the rivalry between churches sometimes got very ugly and in extreme cases even went from squabbles to actual fights,[76] which could have harmed the reputation of the church in society at large.

[75] "Yuan Fanglie tongzhi zai chuli Huhanpai wenti baogaohui shang de jianghua" (Comrade Yuan Fanglie's speech at the meeting on the handling of the Shouters issue), May 17, 1983, Rui'an City Archives 1-31-63:15–16.

[76] Zheng, *Mengfu zhi lu—Jidu li shiyi de rensheng*, Chapter 9 (section 2); Shu, *Wushi nian jiaohui shenghuo huiyi*, Chapter 12 (sections 3–5).

A curious phenomenon I learned is that local churches in recent years no longer treat proselytizing native local residents as a priority. When they do carry out evangelism at home, it is more likely to be with migrant workers, not Wenzhou natives. Their focus is on expansion elsewhere in China. As Wenzhou preachers have traveled beyond Wenzhou in part to propagate their own idiosyncratic theological ideas, theological splits in Wenzhou Christianity may have had a significant impact on Christianity throughout China.

Conclusion

After the Cultural Revolution, Protestant communities in Wenzhou transitioned from underground family gathering to meetings in formal church buildings. This shift has not been adequately studied until now. A dramatic passage in the history of Christianity in Rui'an and Wenzhou, it generated both prosperity and chaos, occurring alongside deepening splits in Christian communities.

While Christianity had never been a majority religion in Zhejiang, the expansion of Christianity under Mao made it a "regulatory priority" for the reform-era government. While Buddhism and village temple activities had entered a steep decline during the same period, the number of Christians and churches had grown dramatically. Most Protestant leaders adopted a pragmatic stance toward the re-established Three-Self Church, a state-backed organization that acted as a liaison with the local government, allowing Protestant communities to take full advantage of their status as a regulatory priority. By contrast, Catholic communities could not do so because of their persistent refusal to collaborate with the government and the Three-Self Church.

Yet the loosening political and institutional environment was a mixed blessing for the Protestant Church. The government's accommodating attitude toward formal church meetings (as opposed to family gatherings) considerably accelerated the construction, restitution, and legalization of churches both old and new. But the reappearance of the Three-Self Church tested the fragile unity that churches had achieved during the Cultural Revolution. Protestant communities were torn apart by schisms at every level, from pan-denominational organizations to small village churches, spawning splinter groups and dissident sects. Opposition to the Three-Self Church, mingled with often exaggerated theological disagreements, repeatedly ignited schisms, which appear to have become a new normal in the Christian ecosystem of Wenzhou.

From the perspective of the church's relationship with the community at large, the rapprochement between the government and mainstream Protestant churches also had far-reaching consequences for Wenzhou Christianity. The government's new policy framework and the local dynamics associated with it may have alienated the larger community in which churches were embedded. The restitution of former churches and the legalization of many newly built churches in the 1980s de facto confirmed the church's territorial expansion and penetration of the Wenzhou region. To non-Christian villagers, the state assistance afforded to Christian communities in reopening churches was in striking contrast to the government's attacks on village temples. To them, this contrast revealed a bias toward Christianity among local authorities, provoking strong grievances. Non-Christian villagers found it difficult to understand such favoritism.

The government's new policy on property rights for Christian churches may have been a further source of discontent. Under the new religious policy, only state-sanctioned church organizations could legally claim property rights to occupied churches. Conversely, villagers had no right to do the same for village temples. Christian communities and the Three-Self Church representing them, on the one hand, and the village government, on the other hand, often became adversaries in the struggle for ownership of former church buildings, which was unlikely to occur in the case of former village temples. Most church buildings were eventually returned in one way or another. Yet there was not always a smooth transition, and the settlement of property rights often required the intervention of the county government, sometimes after years of conflict. The Protestant Church in Lower Village, Xincheng, did not obtain the return of its entire church building. Its plan to construct a new church was delayed for decades due to opposition from villagers living nearby. In a few extreme cases, old churches were even demolished by non-Christian villagers after negotiations were unsuccessful.[77]

Do these conflicts signal a deterioration in the relations between Christians and non-Christians? In any case, they seem to represent a hostile current in attitudes toward Christians, echoing tensions in religious life in Wenzhou dating back to before 1949. How non-Christians accommodate the much increased presence of Christians since the 1980s, now legally protected by the state, invites further study. The next chapter discusses the revival of communal religion, and how it relates to resentment against Christian communities.

---

[77] "Guanyu Tangxia Xinhua Qianchi Dadui jiaotang bei chaihui de baogao" (Report on the demolition of the church of Qianchi Brigade, Xinhua [Commune], Tangxia [District]), March 25, 1982, Rui'an City Archives 49-34-22: 28–30; "Renzhen zuohao dang de zongjiao gongzuo wei woshi zhili zhengdun he shenhua gaige fuwu" (Taking the party's religious work seriously to serve rectification and readjustment and the deepening of reform in our city), May 1990, Rui'an City Archives 109-9-15: 77.

7

Déjà Vu?

The Temple Reclamation Movement and the Revitalization of Rural Organizations, 1978–2014

At the end of the Cultural Revolution, most communal temples in Rui'an were shut down or occupied, typically by state-owned institutions. Yet within a few years of the end of the Cultural Revolution, the situation had changed dramatically. In 1979, after being discontinued for more than a decade, the annual ritual of dragon boat racing resurfaced in a number of communes in Xincheng and in the suburban areas around the Rui'an county seat. The following year, local authorities noted that the ritual revival had spread throughout the plains, even to some communes where the tradition did not formerly exist. The number of dragon boats rose sharply from fewer than 40 to 157, more than four times higher than the previous year.[1]

Temples also returned to public life. In Mayu District alone, villagers reopened at least eighty village temples before 1983, seventeen of which were rebuilt and eleven of which were taken over from schools.[2] In some village temples, it was not uncommon for "[workers to] set up seats for deities in the main hall where incense fire burns all day long, but the aisles on both sides are [still] classrooms where [one can hear] students loudly reading the textbook."[3] One might also see that "at one end [of a temple], artisans are carefully carving statues of divinities whereas at the other end, schoolteachers are intently grading student's homework. They are face to face but do not interfere with each other."[4]

The rapid revival of traditional activities in Wenzhou even caught the attention of officials in Beijing. The Policy Research Office of the Central Party Secretariat wrote in an internal report: "almost every village has rebuilt temples

---

[1] "Guanyu hualongzhou de dongtai" (Current situation of dragon boat racing), March 27, 1981, Rui'an City Archives 29-33-5: 45.

[2] "Mayu Qu quanmian shaochu fengjian mixin huodong changsuo" (Thoroughly eliminating feudal superstition activity sites), March 18, 1983, Rui'an City Archives: 1-31-38: 18. Schools of various levels had been a major, if not the largest, occupant of temples and monasteries, most of which were village temples. As statistics indicate, schools were using 270 temples and monasteries in 1970. See Rui'an Shi jiaoyu weiyuanhui jiaoyu zhi bianzhuanzu, ed., *Rui'an jiaoyu zhi* (Rui'an education history) (Nanchang: Jiangxi renmin chubanshe, 1992), 275.

[3] Rui'an City Archives: 1-31-38:18.

[4] Ibid.

Maoism and Grassroots Religion. Xiaoxuan Wang, Oxford University Press (2020). © Oxford University Press.
DOI: 10.1093/oso/9780190069384.001.0001

in six out of seven Wenzhou counties. . . . A large number of temples and ancestral halls, which during land reform had been turned into public facilities such as schools, factories, and hospitals, were forcibly seized back and rebuilt."[5] The same report also mentioned that the wave of ancestral hall reconstruction and genealogy compilation, starting in late 1980, had swept through all seven counties in Wenzhou by the spring of 1982.

These familiar scenes echo the time when schools first started to take over temples in China. The campaign to seize and convert religious properties began at the turn of the twentieth century and reached its climax in the 1950s under Communism. But this time the process was turned on its head. The massive reclamation and restoration of temples in the 1980s and 1990s were perhaps smaller in scale than the requisition of temple properties in the Republican and Maoist periods, but they carried with them a powerful symbolic meaning. The wave of temple reclamation was an ideological movement of sorts, mobilizing group actions and seeking to reshape the social and political order in local society.[6] As communities reclaimed and reopened temples, they ushered in a new era for communal religion.

This chapter explores the significance and consequences of the wave of temple reclamation in Rui'an in the 1980s and 1990s. I begin with the institutional changes at the start of the reform era, including restitution policies, the collapse of the commune system, and the end of the command economy. The material described here reveals that new institutional environments opened up new possibilities, while also posing new challenges for the restitution of communal temples, particularly issues of political legitimacy. The chapter then looks at local communities' attempts to cope with these challenges and the consequent proliferation of Elderly People Associations (*laoren xiehui*; EPAs). I argue that the rise of EPAs not only facilitated the revival of communal religion, but also breathed new life into traditional rural organizations in Rui'an.

Village Temples by the End of the Cultural Revolution

In the late stage of the Cultural Revolution, when local government was preoccupied with factional politics, the loosened social control in rural areas allowed

---

[5] See the report: "Wenzhou nongcun shehui zhian yu dangfeng buzheng de yanzhong qingkuang" (The serious situations of public security and incorrect Party ethos in rural areas of the Wenzhou region). It was published in *Qingkuang jianbao*, January 21, 1983, 2-7. *Qingkuang jianbao* is an internal journal edited by the Policy Research Office of the Central Party Secretariat.

[6] For a study that compares religious revival in China since late 1970s to a social movement, see David Palmer, "Religiosity and Social Movements in China: Divisions and Multiplications," in *Social Movements in China and Hong Kong: The Expansion of Protest Space*, eds. Gilles Guiheux and Khun Eng Kuah-Pearce (Amsterdam: Amsterdam University Press, 2009), 257–282.

some village communities to start renovating or rebuilding communal temples.[7] But as Chapter 3 shows, temple renovation or reconstruction was not a widespread phenomenon at the time. Other communities may have planned to renovate or rebuild their temples but were intimidated by the potential political consequences and the extensive efforts that such an attempt would require. Any attempt to reopen temples, especially reclaiming a temple occupied by state-owned institutions, could easily be construed as a challenge to the political order imposed by the Communist government and could entail punishment.

Though the mass wave of temple reclamation and restoration was yet to come, local society in Rui'an, as elsewhere in the country, was experiencing significant changes at the end of 1970s that prefigured the precipitous dissolution of the collective order. Private business activities began to boom in Wenzhou, which was then still an impoverished region by national standards.[8] "Study classes" (xuexiban)—makeshift centers for temporary detention—were packed with peddlers, smugglers, and profiteers (touji daoba fenzi), but were also frequented by Christian preachers, Buddhists, and other "superstition bosses" (mixin touzi).[9]

Starting in the early 1970s, more and more sojourners from Wenzhou had to travel elsewhere to make a living. Many found ways to leave the collective.[10] They went as far as Yunnan, Xinjiang, and the Northeast, doing all sorts of small trades such as cotton quilting, shoe repairing, beekeeping, or peddling cheap wares. The people who stayed behind also often had their side businesses. They set up private handicraft workshops and small factories, many of which were under the umbrella of collective enterprises, often with the tacit acquiescence of cadres.[11]

In the meantime, the household responsibility system (lianchan chengbao zerenzhi) quickly spread through Rui'an before it was in any way officially sanctioned by the county government. It was in this climate of loosening social control, as the collective order started to fall apart, that village temple reclamation

---

[7] Yu Binghui, "Zhengzhi, jingji, shehui: dui Wenzhou moshi de zaikaocha" (Politics, economy, society: a revisit to the Wenzhou model) Zhongguo nongcun guancha 2 (1988): 11–12.

[8] Average income for rural residents in Wenzhou had never exceeded RMB 60 before 1978, which is far lower than the national average income of RMB 133 as of 1978. See Zhongguo shehuizhuyi yanjiuyuan malie yanjiusuo diaochazu, "Yitiao juyou Zhongguo tese de fazhan shehuizhuyi nongye de xinluzi—Zhejiang Wenzhou nongcun diqu diaocha baogao" (A Chinese-character new way of socialist agricultural development—an investigational report on rural areas in the Wenzhou region of Zhejiang), Makesizhuyi yanjiu 2 (1984): 288.

[9] Interview with Buddhist leader Po Yiha, May 15, 2013. See also Wenzhou Protestant leader Zheng Datong's experience in the study class. See Zheng Datong, Mengfu zhi lu—Jidu li shiyi de rensheng (The path of blessing—poetic life in Christ) (Hong Kong: Xundao weili zhongxin, 2010,) 62–83.

[10] Interview with Zou Zeiyi, May 12, 2013. People would pay a certain amount of money to the collective. The latter then would either buy grains from the black market or hire other people to farm the land of those who left.

[11] Yu, "Zhengzhi, jingji, shehui," 13.

emerged and swept through all of Wenzhou, in a reawakening of traditional community identity.

Property Rights and the Temple Reclamation Wave

When the Cultural Revolution officially ended, in the spirit of "correcting wrongs and returning things to normal" (*boluan fanzheng*), the government issued new policies on private real estate (such as houses belonging to overseas Chinese) and real estate belonging to "religious organizations." None of the *boluan fanzheng* initiatives regarding property or religious policy was devised to benefit sites of "superstition" such as village temples. On the contrary, Document No. 19 even singled out the task of suppressing "superstition." Yet these new policies created a tense atmosphere that motivated villagers to seek the return and restoration of temples.

When villagers saw the government granting churches the right to reopen and intervening in the restitution of church properties occupied by collective institutions, they raised grievances with local cadres about the unequal treatment of different religious groups. One county official complained, "[Christians] were happy that you helped reopen churches. But if you did not allow the reopening of the *niangnianggong* ["palace of the princess," a local term for village temples], people would be mad at you, and [even] act against you. [It was] raucous . . . [we] really don't want to deal with this situation."[12]

Because of the obvious disparity between the government's treatment of churches and village temples, non-Christians frequently challenged local cadres about the unfairness of state policy. The only answer cadres could give was to tie temples to illegal superstition and churches to legal religion. But non-Christians were not convinced.

When the government forcibly demolished a village temple in Mayu Town, villagers raised four "could not understands" (*xiangbutong*). Two of them complained: "Catholics in the brigade wrote reports [to the government] asking for the removal of the rice factory and the restitution of the Catholic Church. The United Front department sent people to comfort them. Yet the village temple is treated as inferior. We could not understand. . . . The constitution stipulates 're-ligious freedom.' Why aren't we allowed to believe in *niangniang*? We could not understand."[13]

---

[12]   Zhu Yujing, "Guojia tongzhi, difang zhengzhi yu Wenzhou de Jidujiao" (State rule, local politics and Christianity in Wenzhou) (PhD dissertation, Chinese University of Hong Kong, 2011), 120.
[13]   Rui'an City Archives 66-35-4: 140.

Even local cadres sometimes questioned the fairness of the religious policy in front of superior officials who asked them to stay away from "superstition" and carry out the directive to destroy temples. Facing direct criticism and pressure from Christians and non-Christians alike, many grassroots cadres were also aggrieved by the new religious policy. "*Yesu* (Protestants) and *tianzhu* (Catholics) are the worst headache. Yet they spread all over the place unchecked. Are *pusa* (local deities) supposed to be demolished only because they are mute? *Yesu* and *tianzhu* clamor all the time. But we cannot do anything to them. People are saying that we, the Communist Party, only bully honest people!"[14] Some cadres complained and questioned why "believing in *fo* (local deities, literally Buddha) is inferior to believing in Jesus?" and why "the homegrown (*guochande*) is inferior to the imported?"[15]

If new policies aroused the ire of villagers and consequently their passion for temple activities, the dissolution of the commune system—followed by a series of other institutional changes—gave villagers what they believed to be legitimate reasons to engage in temple reclamation and restoration.

The dissolution of the commune system began with the proliferation of the household responsibility system. This new system allowed individual households to sign contracts with their villages and become responsible for their own production profits and losses. Official records show that by February 1981, most of the brigades in Rui'an (9,617 of 12,349, or about 77.3 percent) had spontaneously adopted the household responsibility system without the authorization of upper levels of government.[16] The central government formally endorsed the household responsibility system a year later in January 1982, when it issued the "minutes of the national rural work conference" (*quanguo nongcun gongzuo huiyi jiyao*). By then the household responsibility system had already been adopted in 95 percent of brigades in Rui'an.

The widespread adoption of the household responsibility system was followed by the formal abolishment of the commune system. In the new constitution, also in 1982, the central government stipulated the establishment of town and township governments and village committees in rural areas as entities separate from the organs of the collective economy on a local level. This provision ended the people's communes. Deprived of their political function as a grassroots institution crucial to the organization and implementation of communal economic

---

[14] Rui'an City Archives 1-31-38: 25.

[15] "Rui'an Xian Mayu quwei guanche Yaobang tongzhi pishi: xindong xunsu, xiaoguo xianzhu" (Mayu District Government of Rui'an County implemented the instruction of comrade Yaobang: the action was swift and the effect was remarkable), March 22, 1983, Rui'an City Archives 1-31-36: 12–22.

[16] Zhonggong Rui'an shiwei dangwei yanjiushi, ed., *Zhongguo Gongchandang Rui'an lishi dashiji 1949–1999* (A chronicle of the Chinese Communist Party in Rui'an 1949–1999) (Beijing: Zhonggong dangshi chubanshe, 2001), 106.

planning, they could hardly function as they did during the collectivization period.

The breakdown of the commune system provided a framework for the rapidly emerging quest for temple reclamation and restoration to be positioned as a battle to win rights over real estate (*chanquan*) historically belonging to communities. A letter from self-appointed representatives of the Jiuli area,[17] Xincheng nicely encapsulates this reasoning. Villages in Jiuli were historically the joint owners of Jiuli Temple (*jiuli miao*). The temple was occupied by the Shangwang division of the Xincheng Supply-and-Sale Cooperative since the 1950s. In their letter to the Rui'an county headquarters of the sale-and-supply cooperative asking for the temple's return in 1989, the representatives wrote:

> Jiuli Temple has long been a public site collectively owned by several thousands of households in our "area" (*difang*). . . . After liberation, the government uniformly claimed that temples are owned by all the people [of the nation], but this was just rhetoric for the sake of the overall interests [of the country] and the government never went through any [formal] procedures. During the collectivization period, agricultural cooperatives, supply-and-sale cooperatives, and credit cooperatives were integrated into one. [Since supply-and-sale co-ops] became a commune enterprise, we temporarily lent Jiuli Temple to the [Shangwang] supply-and-sale co-op to carry on the business of [managing] agricultural materials and everyday supplies. The nature of the various cooperatives has altered given the current development and situation. In addition, temples elsewhere have been restored to their former appearance. We in the Jiuli area only had one temple and one palace (*yi gong yi miao*). Without exception, we should also get them back and let the people of the whole area share [them].[18]

As the letter makes clear, both the temple's change of ownership after 1949 and the temple's occupation by the supply-and-sale co-op during the collectivization era were state impositions with which the community had no choice but to comply. Since the commune system collapsed, arrangements related to the commune had to be straightened out. In other words, the supply-and-sale co-op's occupation of Jiuli Temple was no longer legitimate.

When people dared to request the return and reopening of temples under Mao, their requests could easily be construed as attempts at "feudal restoration" (*fengjian fubi*) or signs of counterrevolutionary involvement. The same request

---

[17] *Difang* literally means area. A *difang* here refers to a geographical area that is roughly equal to the center of a town[ship] and surrounding villages.

[18] "Guanyu shouhui Xincheng Qu Jiuli miao de baogao" (Report on retrieving Jiuli Temple of Xincheng District), August 15, 1989, Rui'an City Archives 25-24-38: 37–39.

in the 1980s, now couched as a claim to property rights, might still be turned down as a "restoration of feudal superstition." This is precisely how the government and occupying entities opposed a number of such requests. However, it was becoming increasingly impractical to intimidate or punish people simply by using coercive measures, as the government had done during the Mao era, particularly as the rhetoric of class struggle was dissipating and the government made economic development its first priority. Furthermore, disputes over property rights were not sporadic cases, but a ubiquitous phenomenon occurring all over Wenzhou. As the government attempted to defuse the hostility toward it in local society, this, too, made coercive measures impractical.

Confronted with repeated requests and even direct encroachment from local communities, many institutions occupying temple buildings found themselves in a tricky situation. They had gained the right to use village temples under extraordinary circumstances, when political campaigns forced local communities to comply. But their occupation of village temples was most often a temporary measure designed to facilitate the collective economy and commune system under Mao. The government never passed legislation to give them permanent ownership of occupied religious buildings.[19] So when these occupying institutions were faced with the daily presence of protesters and repeated requests for the temples' return, they had trouble justifying their occupancy in legal terms. They could, and often did, simply ignore these requests without demonstrating the legitimacy of their use of temple buildings, but doing so only gave villagers an excuse to forcefully retake them. Indeed, some local residents moved into former temples without negotiating with the occupying institutions, or in some cases even demolished the buildings on temple sites and built build new temples there—scenarios bearing an eerie similarity to the forcible expropriation of religious sites in the 1950s and 1960s, but reversing the roles of defender and attacker.

With the dissolution of the commune system and the decline of the planned economy, the relationship between the government and the collective institutions occupying temples was also changing. Among the most common occupants of village temples, supply-and-sale co-ops faced the most delicate challenge. These

[19] The Land Reform Law did not stipulate to seize and distribute real properties of religious organizations. Temples and churches were not included in what ought to be confiscated (*muoshou*) and expropriated (*zhengshou*) for they "usually belong to public (*gongyou*) properties and shared (*gongyou*) properties of a certain group of people," according to a supplementary explanation by the Zhejiang provincial government in 1953 to the Land Reform Law ("Duonian wuren zhu guan zhi citang miaoyu deng fangwu chuli wenti fu xi zhizhao you" [Reply on the handling of ancestral halls and temples uninhabited and unmanaged for years], July 9, 1953, Yueqing City Archives 30-12-34). Common real properties might be leased, but occupying entities had to pay rent ("Zhejiang Sheng gongyou fangdichan guanli shixing banfa" [Zhejiang Province tentative regulations on common real properties], June 1952, Rui'an City Archives 4-4-91: 76–80). In reality, though, these laws and regulations were a mere scrap of paper at that time. Temples and churches were taken over at no cost.

co-ops bought agricultural products and sold everyday supplies during the collectivization period. But starting in the early 1980s, policy changes and competition from private business meant that the co-ops no longer had a monopoly on agricultural purchase and consumption. Moreover, they had to deal with pressure from the central government to restructure their organization from nominal state-owned enterprises to real collective businesses serving the goal of economic development.

The county grain department was another major occupying presence, and it too was undergoing a structural decline under the new economic regime. While grain remained a key concern for the Chinese government, peasants were becoming less dependent on the grain department due to a series of policy changes in the 1980s. From the start of the reform period in Zhejiang, the government first decreased the grain procurement quota (1979–1981), then fixed it for three years (1981–1984). Then, in 1985, the central government formally abolished the unified purchase-and-sale policy (*tonggou tongxiao*) that had existed for more than thirty years and replaced it with a contracted procurement system.[20] With these changes in place, the government no longer needed the grain department to forcefully enforce agricultural production quotas. Peasants became less dependent on it, and it lost its iron grip on the rural economy.

With their role in rapid decline, occupying entities of the decaying collective economy found that the county government was much less motivated to defending their interests than it had been under Mao. When forced to surrender numerous properties in the 1980s, the supply-and-sale co-op found itself without much government support. A representative of the Rui'an City Supply-and-Sale Co-op even co-drafted a proposal with representatives of the government's grain and education departments for a 1995 meeting of the people's political consultative committee, urging city leaders and relevant departments "to take forceful measures" in dealing with "the loss of state-owned and collective assets."[21] Under Mao, each of these institutions was crucial to local governance. They would not have had to go through the people's political consultative committee—a relatively weak platform in political affairs—to express their grievances. But the economy had changed, and with it the power balance throughout rural Wenzhou.

[20] For the grain marketing system reform, see Yuk-shing Cheng and Tsang Shu-ki, "The Changing Grain Marketing System in China," *The China Quarterly* 140 (1994): 1080–1104.

[21] "Zhou Sifa deng weiyuan guanyu guoying jiti zichan bei feifa qinzhan xuyao zhuajin chuli de ti'an" (Consultative Committee member Zhou Sifa et al's proposal on hurrying up in the handling of state-owned collective assets illegally trespassed), March 4, 1995, Rui'an City Archives 109-14-23: 52.

Temples Restored: A Political Rollercoaster and a Crisis in Legality

As new property legislation came into effect, and as occupying entities retreated from rural life, followers of communal religion were in a fundamentally different position than they had been during the 1950s and 1960s. Yet in spite of these changes, the restitution of village temples never turned out to be an easy affair. Local communities making claims for temple return were dogged by the label of "superstition" and the illegal status of village temples, which forced them into an inferior position in their interactions with the local government.

Due to the complex circumstances surrounding different temples, the restitution of village temples took a variety of forms. In cases where the temples had been left unoccupied or torn down, the task at hand was to renovate or rebuild the temple without needing to evict its occupants, and there were fewer disputes over property rights. However, in many cases, temple buildings or sites were still occupied, and communities first had to seek their return.

The return of an entire temple complex could be a time-consuming affair. When the Universal Salvation Palace (*tongji gong*) in the Rui'an county seat was restored to its religious role in 1993, the occupying entity—a lock factory— initially returned only the third of five rows of buildings in the temple complex. Local communities only obtained the return of the remaining buildings in the first decade of the 2000s, when a great number of collective and state-owned enterprises (like the lock factory) fell apart, and the local government further loosened its policy regarding communal temples.[22]

In some cases, the temples were not returned, but the occupants agreed to pay compensation in the form of cash, land, or both, and the communities concerned were thus able to rebuild their temples in a different location. Ye Pan Hall (*ye pan tang*) in Xingguang Brigade, Xincheng, was given to "five guarantee households" (*wubaohu*) as housing during land reform.[23] Xincheng District Public Health Center then "borrowed" (*jieyong*) the temple in 1962 with the permission of the district and commune governments. In 1980, a group of elderly men attempted to take over the old houses of Ye Pan Hall to use as a "superstition site" (as the government described it), reportedly invoking their rights to "religious freedom." While the health center dismissed the men's claims as an absurd request of uneducated folk, it was more difficult for them to dismiss the Xingguang Brigade government, which by then also claimed ownership rights to Ye Pan Hall. After the health center filed complaints, the Xincheng District Government conducted an

[22] Ying, *Rui'an Shi Daojiao zhi*, 7. I visited the temple in May 2012.
[23] "Five guarantee household" is a special program for those families without the capability to make a living.

investigation and negotiation, and finally recognized the health center's ownership rights to Ye Pan Hall. Nevertheless, the district government asked the health
center to provide Xingguang Brigade with RMB 5,000 in compensation because
the center has expanded to land that did not belong to the original Ye Pan Hall.[24]

In this case, the transition in property rights was comparatively smooth. Yet
government records show that in many other instances, property disputes over
former communal temples resulted in a tense, sometimes even violent process,
with no positive outcome for the claimants. Some temple reclamation efforts ultimately failed after years of stalemate and clashes with occupying institutions and
local officials. Temple buildings or sites were not returned, nor did the claimants
receive compensation to forgo their property rights.

One such case concerns Rock Head Palace (*yantou gong*) in Yantou Brigade,
Mayu. The temple is dedicated to the worship of Princess Chen Jinggu (*Chen
Shisi niangniang* in local dialect), a popular goddess on the southeastern coast
of China. After 1949, the government gave the entire compound to the Mayu
District Elementary School. Then in the spring of 1980, a small group of local
women, led by the mother of brigade head Wu Shoukui, took over parts of the
temple compound,[25] with the backing of village cadres and the assistance of
other locals. The women made renovations and put up new statues of divinities,
turning the Palace back into an active temple.

The Mayu Office of the Rui'an Education Bureau felt that the Mayu Commune
and the Mayu District Government did not provide adequate support to protect the former temple from being partially reclaimed, and took their complaint
to the county government. On October 4, county executive Peng Kexing and
other county and Mayu District officials went to Rock Head Palace and forcefully
destroyed the religious facilities. Then, in an act of retaliation said to have been
instigated by temple leaders and village cadres, some brigade youths smashed up
some of the school's walls, tables, and windows in the name of defending brigade
possessions. The school had to temporarily suspend classes.

The situation only settled down after multiple mediations by the district party
committee. Subsequently, the school avoided direct confrontations with the brigade, and villagers once again set up religious facilities in the temple.[26]

---

[24] "Guanyu dui Xincheng weishengyuan fangwu bei zhan gao mixin huodong wenti de laixin
diaocha chuli qingkuang baogao" (Report on investigation and handling of the question in an in-
coming letter of Xincheng Public Health Center's houses occupied for superstition), March 27, 1981,
Rui'an City Archives 162-2-1: 1–2.
[25] I did not learn this from the government reports, but from Zui Zhanluo, one of ladies who initiated the actions to restore Rock Head Palace. Zhanluo gave up her job at the supply-and-sale co-op
and has served in the temple since the early 1980s.
[26] "Chaichu Mayu jizhen fengjian mixin changsuo—Yantou 'niangniang' gong qingkuang zongjie"
(Demolishing feudal superstition sites in Mayu Town—the summary of the situation of Rock Head
'Princess' Palace), March 17, 1983, Rui'an City Archives 66-35-4: 136–142.

But two years later, the situation changed dramatically once again. On January 22, 1983, after reading an internal report on social and religious issues in Wenzhou, CCP Central Committee Secretary Hu Yaobang sent a special hand-written directive (*pishi*) to the Zhejiang Party Committee asking them to imme-diately investigate conspicuous social issues in Wenzhou. In order to carry out Hu Yaobang's instructions, local authorities launched the biggest anti-superstition campaign since the Cultural Revolution, which shut down hundreds of temples and destroyed hundreds of statues of divinities over the following months.[27]

The Rui'an County Government chose Rock Head Palace as a major target of the campaign. On January 28, the Mayu District Government dispatched a group of fully armed police officers to Rock Head Palace, along with district officials and county court officers. The police worked unceasingly through the night to tear down the temple and immediately erected a two-level house in its place the following day.

Before the action was carried out, the government apparently convened all the brigade cadres and warned them not to support or instigate any counter-actions. The county government later praised and promoted the attack on Rock Head Palace as a model act of anti-superstition action in response to the special direc-tive from Hu Yaobang.

Oddly, villagers told me that on the very day when Rock Head Palace was razed to the ground, people were able to relocate statues of the goddess and some of their other religious items to the Lords of the Two Offices Palace (*erfuye dian*), a smaller temple in the same village that was not targeted for demolition. The statue of Lord Yang in Rock Head Palace was also carried to the Lords of the Two Offices Palace. The goddess Chen Jinggu took over the Lords of the Two Offices Palace, and shortly thereafter the village government sold several houses next to the new Rock Head Palace to accommodate more worshippers. In 1997, the new Rock Head Palace was completely rebuilt, with the village government donating a theatre stage. Immediately after the completion of the new temple, villagers registered it with the city Daoist association. Since then, the temple manager told me when I visited the facilities in 2012, the Daoist association and the city religious bureau have selected Rock Head Palace as a model temple (*mofan gongguan*) almost every year (see Photo 7.1).

Rock Head Palace in many ways exemplifies an issue faced by all local commu-nities in the early 1980s: the issue of legality. The continued existence of temples that had been returned or rebuilt could not be assured because it went against the juridical framework set out by the central government. Framing the quest for

[27] "Guanyu guanche Yaobang tongzhi pishi jingshen de qingkuang baogao" (Report on implementing the spirit of comrade Yaobang's special directive), March 5, 1983, Rui'an City Archives, 1-31-63: 48.

Photo 7.1. The meeting room of the Rock Head Palace displays many prizes from the authorities and the city's Daoist Association (2012).
Source: Author.

temple restitution within the rhetoric of property rights imbued it with a certain level of legitimacy, but the use of temple sites for communal religious activities remained illegal. Village temples were still attacked as a form of "superstition," though the propaganda was not at the same high pitch as it had been under Mao.[28] The continued stigmatization of communal temple activities, along with periodic crackdowns, significantly affected the recovery of communal temple activities. Villagers certainly could and did rebuild shrines and temples, but they could not set aside concerns about the future of their temples until they found a legitimate way to shield everyday religious life from interference.

The temple revival movement was shaped by these legal ambiguities. Temple reclamation and restoration were typically initiated in the name of elderly villagers. The high status of elderly people in traditional Chinese patriarchy

---

[28] Besides the 1983 actions, there was an anti-superstition campaign in May 1986, with hundreds of temples shut down and thousands of statues of divinities destroyed in Rui'an. See "Jiji caiqu cuoshi ba hualongzhou huodong yin shang jiankang guidao" (Take active measures to channel dragon boating race into a healthy track), May 21, 1986, Rui'an City Archives 1-34-8: 101–105.

may have lent them greater authority and made such actions less subversive in the eyes of local officials, to ward off the threat of political retaliation. Senior village groups in Rui'an and Wenzhou dated back at least as far as the Mao era,[29] but they could only operate in a loose form due to the difficult political environment at the time. Any attempts to further institutionalize and formalize these societies without government authorization could be labeled as a politically motivated action and therefore could face serious consequences. Thus, however they portrayed themselves, societies and ad hoc organizations created to fight for temple restitution were all caught up in the issue of legitimacy, and the problem came up again and again when they represented villages in negotiations with the government and the collective organizations occupying temples.

Groups fighting for temple restitution could easily be dismissed as a small handful of people (*yixiaocuo ren*)—in the rhetoric of the Chinese government—who were engaged in a deliberate subterfuge to restore feudal superstition.[30] Local communities therefore urgently needed a legal institutional framework for temple restitution. In this context, the EPAs suddenly emerged in the villages of Rui'an and the wider Wenzhou region beginning in the mid-1980s. In the decades that followed, it was EPAs that sustained the existence and development of village temples.

The Rise of the Elderly People Associations and Village Religion

The EPAs were originally established to encourage self-government and self-support among the elderly after the breakdown of collective institutions. During the Mao era, collectives were responsible for providing support for elderly villagers, but when these disintegrated in the late 1970s and early 1980s, many senior village residents could no longer adequately provide for themselves,

[29] In Yuecheng Town, Yueqing County of Wenzhou, during the Mao years, for instance, there were organizations of elderly people who frequented tea pavilions (*chating*), which provided tea for passengers in transportation juncture points. Its history can be traced back to the pre-1949 period. See Gao Yideng and Nan Xian, eds., *Yuecheng Zhen zhi* (Yuecheng Town gazetteer) (Beijing: Dangdai Zhongguo chubanshe, 1990), 301–302. See also Wang Ximing, "Zuzhi wangluo, jingji shiti yu laoren fuli—Zhejiang Rui'an Zhaozhai laonian xiehui diaocha" (Organizational networks, economic entities and elderly people welfare—an investigation of senior resident association in Zhaozhai Village, Rui'an, Zhejiang), *Wenzhou Luntan* 3 (2009): 48–55.

[30] "Tangxia Fengshan Gongshe yaoqiu dui qinzhan gongyou sufo zaodian mixin zuo'an de chuli baogao" (Investigational report on the request of Fengshan Commune, Tangxia, to handle the criminal case of encroaching public [properties] to build temples and set up statues of divinities), September 23, 1981, Rui'an City Archives 49-33-9: 33–34.

especially those who were too old to farm. Some reportedly sued their children for failing to support them.[31]

Thus, starting in the early reform era, the central government promoted organizations for the elderly in the countryside as one measure to address the problem of an aging rural population lacking adequate support. Other measures included the introduction of the pension system and the construction of nursing homes.[32] Following China's participation in the International Conference on Aging in 1982, the government also created a permanent national committee on aging issues. From then on, provincial and lower levels of government throughout China started to set up institutions for the elderly at a local level.[33] The state planned the EPAs to create a sense of community and to allow elderly people to take care of each other. To show its support, the central government also asked local governments, from provincial to village governments, to provide space and funding for EPAs.[34]

The timely appearance of the EPAs provided a convenient platform for the temple restitution movement, equipped with new narratives and a sustainable organizational form that could justify actions to retrieve and restore village temples. In temple restitution claims, villagers soon replaced abstract self-descriptions such as "the elderly people of our village/place" (*ben cun/difang laoren*) or "the entire village" (*quancun*) with "the village EPA" (*cun laoren xiehui*, also abbreviated as *cun laoxie*). They repackaged the mission of resurrecting traditional ritual sites as an effort to find space for elderly people's activities.

In a petition for the return of a Lord Chen Temple, representatives of Zhupaitou, a semi-urban neighborhood, wrote: "That we want our temple to be returned is not so we can carry out the superstitious activities of burning incense and worshipping deities but to have a place for elderly people's activities. This is indisputable and should be supported by all of society."[35] The new narrative framed the call for temple restitution into a harmless request for space to

---

[31] Liu Shuhe, "Lun b018ge zhong de nongcun yanglao shiye" (On transforming old-age support enterprise in rural areas), *Renkou yu jingji* 4 (1988): 23–28.

[32] Liu Shuhe, "Yingjie nongcun renkou laolinghua de yixiang zhongda juece—lun fazhan nongcun laonian xiehui" (A major measure for the aging problem in rural areas—on developing old-age associations), *Renkou xuekan* 5 (1993): 61–64.

[33] Deng Yanhua and Ruan Hengfu, "Nongcun yinse liliang heyi keneng? Yi Zhejiang laonian xiehui weili" (How is gray power in rural China possible? A case study of elderly people associations in Zhejiang), *Shehuixue yanjiu* 8 (2008): 136.

[34] Instead of giving money periodically, most villages in Wenzhou chose a one-time solution by giving a piece of land or houses to EPAs, which turned out to be more sustainable, as the latter could make profit from them and provide for old villagers.

[35] "Guanyu yaoqiu luoshi Zhupaitou Chenfu miao fangchan zhengce de baogao" (Report on implementing real estate policies in the case of Lord Chen Temple in Zhupaitou), June 7, 1993, Rui'an City Archives 32-N/A-13: 85–86.

house the apolitical activities of the elderly, drawing on state rhetoric to forestall accusations of a revival of "superstition."

These claims did not invent the concept of the temple as a public recreational space, but rather revived it from previous eras. Village temples historically were and still are the most important place for senior villagers to rest and drink tea. The long-standing label of "superstition" imposed on village temples since the turn of the twentieth century had overshadowed their use as a multifunctional public space, but the appearance of the EPAs allowed the concept to resurface in public narratives, as it was appropriated to give a legitimate cover for their main function as a ritual space.

The narrative of providing space and support for elderly residents added a crucial element to the existing ideas that local communities could legitimately invoke in dealing with occupying institutions. Previously, two main ideas had dominated the quest for the return or reconstruction of temples. One was the discourse of property rights, which, though viable in some cases, encountered significant government interference and resistance from occupying institutions. The other set was the idea of temples as monuments of sorts, such as "historical relics" (lishi wenwu) or "revolutionary sites" (geming yizhi), that needed to be preserved. Getting them recognized as historical sites, however, meant dealing with time-consuming procedures at various levels of government.

The rhetoric of the EPAs provided a narrative that was more compelling and more legitimate in the eyes of the state than either historical preservation or the tenuous claim to religious property rights. Every village was eligible to create its own EPA and thereby demand space for its activities. To register an EPA, moreover, was an easy process. Because the central government considered the EPA to be part of the "old-age enterprise" (laoling shiye), the registration of a local EPA was placed under the jurisdiction of the local old-age commission (laolingwei). Thus, communities could avoid the rather complex procedures required for the approval of other types of civil associations, which were attached to the local civil affairs bureau. As the old-age commission's only purpose was to promote support for the elderly, it lacked administrative oversight and had no incentives to regulate or control the boom in local EPAs.[36]

A major difference between the EPAs and the elderly people's organizations that came before them lay in their legal status. From the time when the EPAs first appeared in the early 1980s, they had the status of a state-sanctioned civic association. Local communities engaged in temple restitution could not entirely avoid the suspicion that they planned to conduct superstitious activities, but no

[36] Deng and Ruan, "Nongcun yinse liliang heyi keneng?"; Chen Xun, "Xiangcun shehui liliang heyi keneng? Jiyu Wenzhou laonian xiehui de yanjiu" (How is rural social power possible? Research on elderly people association in Wenzhou), *Zhongguo nongcun guancha* 1 (2012): 80–88.

one could deny the legitimacy of the EPA, which was endorsed and promoted by the central government itself. The EPA absorbed most, if not all, preexisting elderly people's organizations, such as those attached to tea pavilions, elderly people's pavilions, and those providing ritual and burial services for the elderly. It supplied a convenient yet sustainable organizational form that fundamentally altered and accelerated village temple revival.

Did local officials believe in the EPAs' co-option by villagers engaged in temple reclamation efforts? For a time, they did. County officials and rural and urban cadres had been supportive of the organization and encouraged villages to create local EPAs. Indeed, assigning former temples to the EPA allowed local officials to get around a tiresome and commonplace occurrence which they called "demolish today, rebuild tomorrow" (*jintian chaimiao, mingtian jianmiao*).[37] That is, immediately after officials damaged or demolished temples facilities, these would be rebuilt or repaired by locals. The same cycle could be repeated every time local officials were ordered to destroy sites of superstition.

Local officials were constantly questioned about the fairness of religious policies, and the questions were sometimes mixed with insults and even physical attacks. Urban and rural cadres whose family members worshipped local deities could face family pressure to allow temples to be reclaimed. In some cases, cadres themselves feared divine retaliation and respected religious taboos.

The emergence of the EPAs gave grassroots cadres a legitimate way of dealing with temples without incurring retaliation from upper levels of government or the wrath of local communities. Instead of destroying and shutting down temples, they could "remodel [them] into Elderly People's Pavilions (*laorenting*), carry out normal recreational activities, and enrich the latter years of the elderly."[38] Cadres were certainly aware that Elderly People's Pavilions and Old-Age Palaces would soon house the worship of local deities. Yet the coexistence of religious sites and EPA activities gave them room to accommodate government directives while avoiding the "demolish today, rebuild tomorrow" phenomenon and other conflicts with local communities.

Because the leadership of EPAs consisted mainly of veterans and retired cadres,[39] local officials hoped to use them as intermediaries in dealing with village issues such as controlling and curbing the spread of village temples and

[37] "Guanyu qingli miaoyu jianjue shazhu fengjian mixin he fengjian zongzu waifeng de tongzhi" (Notification on suppressing village temples and decisively stopping the bad ethos of feudal superstition and feudal lineages), January 20, 1981, Rui'an City Archives 1-7-20: 21.

[38] "*Daomiao gantan pochu mixin*" (Demolishing temples and driving away fortune tellers to eliminate superstition), May 21, 1986, Rui'an City Archives 1-35-40: 41.

[39] To give one example, when in 1987 villages in Tangxia Town established their EPA, their registrations were submitted to a Tangxia Retired Cadres and Retired Factory Worker Association (*Tangxia li tui xiu ganbu zhigong xiehui*) because the town did not yet have an old-age commission (*laolingwei*). This arrangement suggests strong connections between retired cadres and EPAs.

communal rituals. A report by the Rui'an Cultural Bureau in 1982 depicted the EPA of Xiyi Village, Meitou, as the defender of, and contributor to, a "socialist spiritual civilization."[40] The Xiyi EPA, it was said, helped destroy the village's dragon boat by sawing it into pieces, citing the fact that villagers rowing in this dragon boat had previously had fights with dragon boat teams from other villages. Not only this, they also persuaded a group of elderly women who had previously collected some funds to restore the Great Yin Palace not to spend the money on re-erecting statues of divinities but to instead set up the palace site as a "cultural activity room" (*wenhua huodongshi*) for young people. In a 1986 document, the county government explicitly stressed that "letting elderly people fully exert their special influence" should be a central strategy in regulating that year's dragon boat racing.[41]

EPAs were certainly not just tools of the government, as these official reports seemed to suggest—and local officials were aware of this. The elderly people who assisted the government by sawing up dragon boats or destroying temples and shrines were often the same people who initiated ritual and temple activities. Actions like destroying dragon boats or ritual sites are better interpreted as a strategic retreat or a temporary compromise. Once an anti-superstition initiative drew to a close, it was quite common for the same group of people to build new dragon boats or sites of worship. However, given the importance of EPA leaders in temple and ritual activities, local cadres had to rely on them to perform a double game that seemed designed to fool only superior levels of government.

Since the mid-1980s, EPAs have proliferated in Rui'an and the Wenzhou region.[42] In Rui'an, local communities started to establish and register their EPAs with the government around 1985. Within a few years, EPAs became popular throughout the region. In the Tangxia District alone, more than 85 percent of all villages (115 out of 135) had established and registered local EPAs by the end of 1987.[43] There are numerous records of the construction of "latter-year palaces" (*wannian gong*) in government publications after 1985, some of which were built on former village temple sites. In 1990, the Taoshan District Government granted permission for the construction of a latter-year palace in Xitu Village on

---

[40] The group head and two vice heads were retired cadres and old party members. Two former village party secretaries were among fifteen council members elected.

[41] Rui'an City Archives 1-34-8: 2.

[42] For EPA in other provinces, see Gan Mantang, "Cunmin zizhi, zuzhi fazhan yu cunji zhili—yi Fujian Sheng xiangcun diaocha weili" (Village autonomy, organizational development and village governance—a case study based on the investigation in rural Fujian), *Fuzhou daxue xuebao* 3 (2007): 98–106, and "Xiangcun caogen zuzhi yu shequ gonggong shenghuo: Yi Fujian xiangcun laonian xiehui wei kaocha zhongxin" (Rural grassroots organizations and communal life: a case study of elderly people associations in rural Fujian), *Fujian xingzheng xueyuan xuebao* 107 (2008): 17–21; Mette Halskov Hansen, "Organising the Old: Senior Authority and the Political Significance of a Rural Chinese 'Non-governmental Organisation.'" *Modern Asian Studies* 42, no. 5 (2007): 1057–1078.

[43] *Rui'an nianjian (1988)* (Rui'an yearbook 1988), internal document, 249.

the site of the village's Xidian Palace (*xidian gong*), which had previously been demolished or abandoned.

The term "latter-year palace" refers to a type of cultural center for elderly people that is omnipresent throughout rural and urban China. Similar centers go by different names such as "old-age palace" (*laoniangong*), "activity room for the elderly" (*laoren huodongshi*), or "activity center for the elderly" (*laonian huodong zhongxin*), and so on. These old-age centers were not created merely as a disguise for village temples. Rather, they allowed people to embed ritual space within recreational space and therefore secure its continued existence. In most instances, old-age centers serve a dual purpose as recreational and ritual sites. Sometimes a temple and old-age center are housed on different floors of the same building. In other instances, they are located in separate buildings close by. In Rui'an and Wenzhou today, old-age centers are practically a synonym for village temples.

Elderly People Associations in Contemporary Village Politics

Three decades on, the EPA has firmly established itself in the villages of Rui'an and Wenzhou. Local EPAs have taken on their mandated responsibility of providing old-age support, turning themselves into financial caregivers through sustained economic planning. In Rui'an, almost every village EPA initially received some financial support from the village government. This came in various forms, such as a share of management fees for local markets, a plot of farmland, or a house. Later, as the village economy flourished, many village EPAs—especially those in Xincheng and Tangxia, two of the wealthiest districts in the semi-urban areas around the county seat—were allocated more properties or privileges as a source of income.[44]

Some EPAs have actively expanded their scope of business to maximize revenue or acquire more assets. The EPA of Yantou Village, for instance, owns a plot of land that was provided by the village. The EPA later helped take back the building that served as a movie theatre for the town, which had previously been a temple, and persuaded the village government to give it to them. They redecorated the building to host commercial song and dance performances, which became an important source of revenue for their association. They also

---

[44] Economic activities, in spite of differences among mountainous, plain, and urban areas, are the major source of income for most village EPAs in Rui'an. Though an annual membership fee is required in some villages, membership fees are almost never the main source of income of EPAs. The temple is not the main source of income for EPAs neither. In places where village temples have a stable income, as far as I was told, EPAs and temples always keep separate finance systems. Sometimes when the latter does not have a stable income, they tend to need financial help from the former.

revived a festival fair held on the twenty-third of the first lunar month in the town center of Mayu, which is now mainly for the sale of merchandise. They receive the organizing fees from the fair. Each year Yantou Village EPA has more than 200,000 RMB total income.[45]

Financially independent EPAs are more and more frequently involved in village affairs other than old-age support and religion, in part due to the weakening of the two most powerful village institutions: the village party committee and the village residents committee. Following the disintegration of collectives and the widespread adoption of the household responsibility system, the central government abolished the agricultural tax (*nongyeshui*) in rural China in 2003. Thus, the village residents committee is no longer in charge of regulating agricultural production and collecting taxes on behalf of the government, and its power has inevitably waned.

In Rui'an, the high mobility of some villagers no longer engaged in agricultural production makes it difficult for the village residents committee to convene a village meeting or even a meeting of village representatives. The corruption of village cadres, especially in construction, land issues, and village elections since the mid-1990s, has aggravated the relationship between village leaders and civilians, further damaging the legitimacy of village government.

The village party committee has also lost its former importance. In recent years, it has barely been active in some villages, and the same goes for its offshoot organizations, the youth league and the women's association.[46]

Amid the changing power dynamics of village life, the EPA has further inserted itself into village affairs. Local EPAs in Rui'an are commonly involved in charity and public works. Projects such as the cleaning and maintenance of rivers, roads, and public facilities were often entrusted to them. During natural disasters or other difficult events, the EPA in the Rui'an area and beyond would respond to government calls for action by mobilizing its members to donate funds to the affected families.

EPAs also served as a liaison between village cadres and residents, facilitating the implementation of administrative matters such as birth control and funeral reform. Village cadres needed the assistance of EPAs in mediating domestic issues or inter-village disputes. Also, it is not rare for EPAs, village residents committees and village party committees to be housed in the same building, suggesting EPAs' proximity to the village's power center (Photo 7.2).

[45] Interview with Ou Zhanwu, May 12, 2013.

[46] Hu Qiting, "Zhuanxing shiqi cunzhuang quanli jiegou bianhua de shizheng fenxi—Wenzhou Shi Dingtian Zhen X Cun ge'an yanjiu" (Empirical analysis of village power structure in transitional period—a case study of X village in Dingtian Town, Wenzhou). *Liaoning xinzheng xueyuan xuebao* 4 (2006): 9–12.

Photo 7.2. The Elderly People Association in Hushi Village, near the center of Gaolou District, is set in a village temple (2012). The signs on the door indicate that the temple is also the offices of the village's government and party committee.
Source: Author.

The greater presence of EPAs in village affairs manifests in their interactions with incumbent village cadres. Because many EPA leaders are party members, they still attend village party committee meetings. Being embedded in the committee affords the EPA a measure of participation in village governance, such as providing consultation on the village economy and infrastructure projects, or handling some village affairs—though this sometimes results in tension between EPA leaders and incumbent cadres.[47] The EPA has even allegedly interfered in elections in a handful of villages in Shacheng and Tianhe, Longwan District, in Wenzhou municipality. A 2007 proposal to the Chinese People's Political Consultative Conference in Wenzhou to strengthen the regulation of the EPAs described tensions and conflicts between local EPAs and two village committees (the village party committee and the village residents committee) as the most prominent problem regarding the EPAs.[48] Statistical data reveal that more than

---

[47] Chen Xun, "Xiangcun shehui liliang heyi keneng?"

[48] Chen, Weiwen, "Woshi nongcun laoren xiehui guanli queshi yinfa zhuduo shehui wenti, jidai zhongshi guifang" (The lack of regulation over elderly people associations in our city has caused many social issues, urgently needing attention and regulation), a proposal to the Wenzhou the

one-quarter of EPAs in Rui'an, Yueqing, Ouhai, and Longwan in Wenzhou municipality are on bad terms with their local village party committee and village residents committee. Though these figures may or may not be accurate, they reveal a difficult dimension of the relationship between the EPAs and village authorities.[49]

In recent decades, EPAs have taken on an increasingly prominent role as grassroots political pioneers, whether fighting the corruption of village cadres or encroachments on village land by outside parties.[50] The rapid urbanization of China since the mid-1990s has exacerbated corruption in Wenzhou and elsewhere. Across the country, village cadres have sought to profit from land acquisition and construction projects to benefit themselves, allies, family, and friends. As the EPA is the most important organization in village life apart from the village party committee and the village residents committee, villagers often rely on it to defend their rights. For instance, since 2009, the EPA in Zhuangquan Village, Longwan District, repeatedly filed reports with various relevant offices about village cadres who embezzled compensation fees for land requisition until the cadres were prosecuted.[51]

In other cases, EPAs served as a channel through which villagers expressed discontent with the government, especially when village cadres, due to their position, are reluctant to appear in person. There are a growing number of cases where EPAs are involved in organizing collective petitions and protests over land-related disputes. In one recent incident, the EPA in Zhongxing Village, Haicheng Street (formerly Meitou Town, Rui'an), in the Longwan District of Wenzhou municipality, sent several dozens of elderly people to hold a protest about issues related to land acquisition. The protest occurred in front of the Wenzhou municipal government during the first world Wenzhounese diaspora symposium of 2013. In November of that same year, they sent twenty-eight elderly people to Beijing to make a petition.[52]

People's Political Consultation Assembly in 2007, http://220.191.204.205/taya/new2007/showzx.asp?CASE_NO=555 (accessed on May 4, 2018).

[49] Ibid.
[50] Deng Yanhua and Ruan Hengfu, "Nongcun yinse liliang heyi keneng?"; Gan Mantang and Xiaoting Zhang, "Chuantong shequ ziyuan dongyuan yu nongmin de you zuzhi kangzheng" (Mobilization of traditional community resources and organized peasant resistance), *Liaodong xueyuan xuebao* 12, no. 5 (2010): 58–65; Deng Yanhua and Kevin J. O'Brien, "The Society of Senior Citizens and Popular Protest in Rural Zhejiang," *China Journal* 71 (2014): 172–188.
[51] Chen, "Xiangcun shehui liliang heyi keneng?" 84; see a petition letter from the Zhuangquan Village EPA: http://blog.sina.com.cn/s/blog_6074b7d40100e2ng.html (accessed on May 4, 2018).
[52] Zhonggong Rui'an shiwei dangwei yanjiushi, *Zhongguo Gongchandang Rui'an lishi dashiji*, 91.

Conclusion

The temple restitution movement of the 1980s was a highly symbolic moment in several ways. Since 1898, the Qing, Nationalist, and Communist governments had been engaged in the destruction and expropriation of communal temples. Now, local communities were able to seek the return of traditional ritual sites on a massive scale.

The movement for temple return capitalized on the disintegration of collective institutions and the weakening of the planned economy to reclaim sites that had been expropriated by public enterprises and organizations. Reversing the expropriation of ritual space, urban and rural residents taking over temple sites ushered in a new era for communal religion.

This was also a time of reinvention in the social life of villages. The wave of temple reclamation in the 1980s was not just about religion. It occurred as a social response to a larger issue: the instability of property rights during decollectivization. In the post-Mao era, because land was not privatized, the debate about property rights has mainly centered on land reallocation, usufruct, and agricultural and economic development under a regime of common property rights.[53] Beyond agriculture and the economy, unstable property rights have prompted a crucial transformation in the politics and organization of village life.

The co-option and repackaging of EPAs as a proxy for temple reclamation allowed local residents in Rui'an to reinvent communal religion, circumventing the problem of legality and securing a stable existence for territorial temples. However, local EPAs have grown beyond their early role as a cover for religious activities. As they grow socially and economically, drawing retired cadres and other village elites, they are moving toward the center of village politics. There are echos of imperial times, as ritual organizations once more take on a pivotal role in village life.

---

[53] James Kai-sing Kung and Shouying Liu, "Farmers' Preferences Regarding Ownership and Land Tenure in Post-Mao China: Unexpected Evidence from Eight Counties," *The China Journal* 38 (July 1997): 33–63; Jonathan Unger, "The Decollectivization of the Chinese Countryside: A Survey of Twenty-eight Villages," *Pacific Affairs* 58, no. 4 (Winter, 1985–1986): 585–606; Jean Oi and Andrew Walder, eds., *Property Rights and Economic Reform in China* (Stanford, CA: Stanford University Press, 1999).

Conclusion

The Transformation of Chinese Religion under Mao

When travelers today go from downtown Wenzhou to Rui'an, the first things they see along the newly built Yong-Tai-Wen highway are stretches of paddy fields; small, winding rivers, and lush, low hills in the distance. Next to appear are traditional Chinese buildings dotting hillsides and fields, too bright to miss. Some of them have yellow-painted walls and grey tile roofs. Others are adorned with colorful motifs, statuettes of various kinds displayed in cornices, and occasionally flags of various colors on the rooftops. The yellow buildings are easily recognizable as Buddhist temples, while the colorful buildings are temples for territorial religion. Most of them look fairly new. Careful observers will also notice many newly built Christian churches in a variety of styles, some recognizable, others harder to identify, dispersed in the plains along the highway. These are views the northern soldiers would not have seen on their way to Rui'an in the summer of 1949, when the Communist Party's Eastern China Field Army came south to Wenzhou to take over the region from local Communist guerrillas.

Revolution and Religious Life

Much of the local religious landscape in Rui'an today, from newly erected Christian churches to rebuilt territorial and Buddhist temples, has been profoundly shaped by China's Maoist past. Looking back at the region's history since 1949, there is a strong continuity in religious life, echoing recent studies that demonstrate the resilience of religious traditions under Mao; yet the landscape of religion in Rui'an today has been forged through a series of attacks and radical policy shifts that have left rifts as well as revivals in their wake.[1]

The Mao era engendered a double crisis for followers and communities of every religion in Rui'an. The first was the removal of traditional leadership. Land

---

[1] Edward Friedman, Paul G. Pickowicz, Mark Selden, and Kay Ann Johnson, *Chinese Village, Socialist State* (New Haven, CT: Yale University Press, 1991); Gregory A. Ruf, *Cadres and Kin: Making a Socialist Village in West China, 1921–1991* (Stanford, CA: Stanford University Press, 1998); Jeremy Brown and Matthew Johnson, eds., *Maoism at the Grassroots: Everyday Life in China's Era of High Socialism* (Cambridge, MA: Harvard University Press, 2015).

Maoism and Grassroots Religion. Xiaoxuan Wang, Oxford University Press (2020). © Oxford University Press.
DOI: 10.1093/oso/9780190069384.001.0001

reform toppled the local elites who had been the patrons and leaders of communal religion. Many of the leaders of salvationist religions were executed in the "Campaign to Suppress Counterrevolutionaries"; others were sent to prison. Foreign clergy in the Catholic and Protestant churches were sent home, while Chinese clergy were ousted, imprisoned, or even killed. The second crisis was the massive suppression of established ritual space and the obliteration of the economic foundations of religious communities, two issues that followers of communal religion in particular had to wrestle with from the very beginning of the Mao era.

Despite these adversities, local residents carried on with religious life, on and off, overtly or covertly, throughout the Mao era. The Dragon Boat Festival persisted until the eve of the Cultural Revolution and was revived again immediately after the Cultural Revolution. Public rainmaking ceremonies took place at the height of Red Guard conflicts, the most chaotic time during the Cultural Revolution. Even the most violently repressed local salvationist groups had their voices heard during the Cultural Revolution. The large scale of disruption in public religious life as a whole lasted for a much shorter time than previously assumed. The most severe attacks on religion during the Cultural Revolution were concentrated in cities during the first few years of the movement. In its later stages, the chaos of the Cultural Revolution even created opportunities for the expansion of religious groups.

The continuation of religious life benefited from the porous nature of state control. From the very beginning, the evolution of the local religious landscape in Rui'an after 1949 unfolded in the context of the government's revolutionary agendas to restructure Chinese society. By extending state bureaucracy into rural and remote areas, the Communist government created a new political system with unprecedented possibilities of social control.

But this extensive system came with built-in weaknesses. There were broad inconsistencies between different arms of government and policies in different political periods. As religious policy constantly fluctuated with the ebb and flow of political campaigns, grassroots cadres appointed as agents of the state were faced with the conflicting demands of locals and superior officials, making it impossible for them to provide the unwavering support that the government needed to implement its sweeping agenda. Local cadres sometimes even resisted religious directives from their superiors, and some even actively participated in or sheltered religious activities. Thus, in spite of state attacks on religion, there was always a space for religious activities at the margins of political campaigns.

Moreover, the agenda to control social life while suppressing religious life generated widespread uncertainty, which in turn created a fertile environment for the continuation of religious practices. Under Mao, religious explanations remained a crucial way for local residents to come to terms with social changes and natural and manmade disasters, as well as the recurrent uncertainty and violence of the times.

The strategies that local residents adopted to cope with capricious political environments played a crucial role in the survival of religion. To cope with financial scarcity, people would knock door to door to ask for donations or stage ritual performances to collect funds. Age-old tools such as divine revelation (in the dreams of spirit mediums) or eschatological messages foreshadowing end times were used to mobilize religious followers and sometimes led to successful movements to defend traditional ritual space.

Difficult political situations demanded new strategies alongside the old. Christians used the discourse of religious freedom in the Chinese constitution to defend churches from occupation and expropriation. Even adherents of territorial cults, which the government did not recognize as a religion, cited religious freedom as a defense. Villagers even used Maoist struggle meetings to attack the cadres and school principals who destroyed temple facilities.

When it was impossible to preserve temples or churches, religious followers found numerous ways to recreate religious space. In many villages, people were able to retain a small space within their temples for religious practices. Lighting incense on former temple sites was the most common way to pursue worship when the environment was at its most hostile. Some religious followers created new spaces of worship, as the Great Leap Forward and the Cultural Revolution prompted Christians to shift entirely to home gatherings, divide big meetings into many smaller ones, and spread them out over a wide range of locations to avoid attracting the attention of the state. Non-Christian villagers moved statues of deities to small shrines in remote locations or in their homes to continue worship.

Religious life could only persist at a minimal level for most of the Mao years. The political pressure on religious groups and their leaders made it nearly impossible to restore and stably operate temples and churches, especially during major nationwide campaigns. The suppression of religious activities, however, did not mean villages were isolated from each other in religious life. Far from being "highly self-contained units"[2] or "cellularized communities,"[3] different locales frequently communicated with one another. Protestant communities spread outward from their original gathering places to weather the political storms. Preachers often traveled far and wide to lead house gatherings in other villages, counties, or regions. These visits occurred not just in Rui'an or Wenzhou but all over southern Zhejiang.

---

[2] Vivienne Shue, *The Reach of the State: Sketches of the Chinese Body Politic* (Stanford, CA: Stanford University Press, 1988), 134.

[3] Helen Siu, *Agents and Victims in South China: Accomplices in Rural Revolution* (New Haven, CT: Yale University Press, 1992).

To some extent, the hostile political environment actually reinforced communications and connections between Protestants in different places, pushing them to cooperate in order to ensure the survival of their communities. Followers of communal religion also sometimes acted together. The "superstition riots" in the summer of 1953 and the massive "feudal superstition restoration" of the early 1960s appeared almost spontaneously in numerous villages across Rui'an. People continued to visit certain important religious sites like East Hall Palace in Xincheng for worship and communal rituals. Some remote sacred sites, such as the Daluo Mountains of Tangxia and the Baiyan Mountain of Taoshan, likely never stopped receiving pilgrims throughout the Mao era.

Yet the survival of religious life in Rui'an under Mao is full of remarkable variance and unevenness across many dimensions, which we may characterize as *uneven continuities*. These variances existed in both time and space, within and across religious traditions. During land reform, the Great Leap Forward, and the early Cultural Revolution, public religious life in Wenzhou seems to have completely ceased. However, after each of these nationwide political campaigns lost momentum or drew to a close, religious practices surged again, regardless of the type of worship, from local deities, Buddhism, and Christianity to other religious traditions.

The religious resurgence of the early 1960s was in fact observed in many other provinces besides Zhejiang, indicating a widespread phenomenon. In Gaoyao County of Guangdong Province during that time, local residents collectively donated money and devoted labor to help rebuild temples.[4] In Changshu of Jiangsu Province, "many production teams set up altars to chant ritual scrolls (*xianjuan*) in the name of bringing great peace and harvests, [while] others chanted scriptures and performed rituals in the name of making sacrifices to ancestors."[5] Similar revivals were also seen in Hebei and Anhui.[6]

The fluctuation in religious activities often related to variations in social control. During nationwide campaigns, social life was highly politicized. Public religious meetings and rituals entailed enormous political risk. In the intervals between major political campaigns, however, the risks were relatively low. The looser political environment during these calmer times shaped the behavior of

---

[4] "Nongcun mixin huodong de fazhan yingxiang shengchan he shehui zhi'an" (The development of superstitious activities in rural areas affected production and public security), *Neibu cankao*, December 25, 1962, 6–7.

[5] "Youxie Gongshe chuxian mixin huodong" (Superstitious activities appeared in some communes), *Neibu cankao*, January 24, 1962, 13–14.

[6] Stephen Jones, "Chinese Ritual Music under Mao and Deng," *British Journal of Ethnomusicology* 8 (1999): 27–66; Dong Chuanling, "Jianguo liushinian huabei nongcun shehui shenghuo bianqian—yi Shandong Sheng Liangshan Xian wei ge'an" (The evolution of rural social life in the six decades after 1949—the case of Liangshan County, Shangdong Province) (PhD dissertation, Nankai University, 2010), 225–227.

both cadres and religious followers. When local cadres had more space to maneuver on religious issues, they generally did not make it a priority to interfere in religious activities. Religious followers felt the change in atmosphere as well and became more actively engaged in the restoration of temples and churches. During land reform, for instance, local residents did not voice their resentment over the destruction of temples, but instead expressed their grievances in the 1953 rainmaking "riots." Similarly, the religious resurgence of the early 1960s was tied to the relaxation of the commune's direct control over brigades. In a broader perspective, the temporality of religious life can be understood alongside Gail Hershatter's study of "campaign time" and women's memories of collective years as examples of how Maoist campaigns punctuated and constructed everyday life.[7]

The variance in religious life after 1949 is also evident in the divergent paths of different religious traditions. The "counterrevolutionary" label imposed on salvationist groups and the Catholic Church forced these religions to fall into a long silence after the massive crackdown of the early 1950s. Salvationists remained silent in Rui'an even in the post-Mao era. Territorial and Buddhist temples were devastated when land reform took away the landed estates most of them relied on as a primary source of income. Both territorial and Buddhist temples continued to lose ground as political campaigns further squeezed traditional ritual space. Collectivization impeded any lasting efforts to preserve and restore temple activities.

In this context, the successful survival of Protestant Christianity is a striking exception. Despite serious setbacks suffered during the Great Leap and the early stages of the Cultural Revolution, from the early 1970s onward, Protestant communities swelled in numbers and expanded into vast new territories, multiplying and scattering across Rui'an. When the Mao era ended, Protestant communities leveraged this period of growth to rapidly build new churches and restore old ones, turning many house gatherings into churches recognized by the state.

Looking at the broader context of social and political changes since the turn of the twentieth century sheds new light on the historical continuities and discontinuities in local religious life. When viewed against the overall continuity of religious life, the violent attacks on religion during the Mao era can be understood as short-term crises—drastic and sometimes brutal, but ultimately short-lived. In the year 1949, the disruption of religious life was much less severe than has been previously assumed, especially in the case of Protestant churches. By the late stages of the Cultural Revolution, both Christianity and communal religion were already recovering, and the expansion of Protestant churches was well underway.

---

[7] Gail Hershatter, *The Gender of Memory: Rural Women and China's Collective Past* (Berkeley: University of California Press, 2011).

The post-1978 religious revival was a continuation of such developments. In other words, the religious revival in the post-Mao era did not happen overnight and did not begin with reform, but rather got its start during the Cultural Revolution, and appears to have been stimulated in part by the chaos and instability of the Cultural Revolution itself.

Nevertheless, the reinvigoration of religious life in the post-Mao era is far from a return to what it was before 1949. In many ways, the landscape of religion changed irrevocably under Mao. The large-scale religious revival was built on what religious life has become following three decades of Maoist rule.

The experiences of Rui'an religious communities as a whole suggest that a fuller understanding of the vicissitudes of the Mao era must first begin with the dynamics of revolutionary political campaigns. Attempts to control religion through policy and the apparatus of state cannot fully explain the evolution of religious life under Mao.[8] The Communist government, like the Republican government that preceded it, embraced "secular nationalism."[9] Yet unlike the Nationalists, the Communist state aimed beyond religion, at the total transformation of the "old society." Throughout the Mao era, religious policies were highly dependent on the central political and economic agenda enacted through state campaigns. Though they rarely directly targeted religion, major campaigns such as land reform had a profound impact on religious life.

It was the interaction between central directives and grassroots politics, as well as the local landscape of religion, that ultimately determined the effects of the revolution on local religious life and the trajectories of the different religious traditions. This is crucial to understanding what happened to Protestant churches in Rui'an after 1949, and why Protestantism in the Wenzhou region fared so differently than other religions under Mao. Contrary to what religious ecology theorists have suggested, Christianity did in fact suffer harsh repression during various stages of the Mao era.[10] Yet the impact of Maoist campaigns (not

---

[8] Fenggang Yang, for instance, has used changes in religious demand and supply that government regulations caused to explain religious changes in the PRC. See Fenggang Yang, *Religion in China: Survival and Revival under Communist Rule* (Oxford; New York: Oxford University Press, 2012).

[9] Rebecca Nedostup, *Superstitious Regimes: Religion and the Politics of Chinese Modernity* (Cambridge, MA: Harvard University Asian Center, 2010).

[10] Religious ecology theorists argued that the attacks on village temples and lineage organizations in the name of anti-superstition since 1949 have severely damaged the balance of religious ecology and led to the sharp decline in influence of traditional religious activities, making rural society vulnerable to the penetration of Protestantism. For a survey of discussions of "religious ecology" in Chinese academia, see Philip Clart, "'Religious Ecology' as a New Model for the Study of Religious Diversity in China," in *Religious Diversity in Chinese Thought*, eds. Perry Schmidt-Leukel and Joachim Gentz (New York: Palgrave Macmillan, 2013), 187–199. For a study that systemically applies the theory of "religious ecology," see Xiaoyi Chen, *Zhongguoshi zongjiao shengtai: Qingyan zongjiao duoyangxing ge'an yanjiu* (Chinese religious ecology: a case study on religious diversity at Qingyan) (Beijing: Shehui kexue wenxian chubanshe, 2008).

just religious policies), Christian evangelism to a populace living in social chaos and uncertainty, and above all the local history of the church (its focus on house gatherings and its prior indigenization during the Republican era) all meant that Protestant communities had a vastly different experience of Maoism than communal religion or Catholic churches.

In this sense, the dynamics of religion under Mao cannot be boiled down to a dichotomy of state repression and local responses. In spite of the state's profound penetration of local society, local actors—state and non-state—sometimes succeeded in manipulating central campaigns to their own ends. Maoist campaigns diverted the course of local religious history, notably by ending the ascension of salvationist religions. Yet in other ways Maoism reinforced other trends, like the indigenization of Christianity and the reinvention of communal religion.

The history of Wenzhou invites us to revisit the effects of state violence on the history of religion under Mao. At the peak of national campaigns, religious followers and organizations suffered extreme and brutal attacks. At these times, heightened political passions, combined with preexisting tensions, served to push attacks on religion far beyond what central policymakers expected or demanded. The "great leap in religious work" in 1958 is a powerful example of this, when local cadres took advantage of the Great Leap Forward to rapidly subdue religious communities.

The impact of national political campaigns often lasted far beyond these initial, brutal attacks. In the intervals and lulls between the most fervent periods of political activism, cadres and ordinary villagers alike exploited the stigmatization of religion to their own ends in daily life, as in the routine encroachments on temple property after land reform. Local actors navigated the rhythms of political campaigns both to attack and protect religious activities, followers, and organizations. The brutality of Maoism toward religious life is better understood through the local dynamics of social and political life, rather than solely as an expression of central political agendas. In other words, extreme violence against religion is better construed as an unintended consequence of Maoism, rather than its intended aim.

Looking at the transformation of religious life from a perspective encompassing local dynamics invites us to reconsider the Maoist governance of religion. Communist and socialist states, in China and elsewhere, are not "secular" in the classical sense, as they actively promote atheism as an anti-religious doctrine. But the Communist Party in fact did not have immediate plans to eliminate religion, and sometimes even co-opted religion to its own ends. Until the mid-1960s, officials at every level of government, from central and provincial authorities down to the lower levels of the state, made efforts to curb the enthusiastic anti-religious sentiments of local cadres, periodically reiterating the importance of religious freedom.[11] The Cultural Revolution virtually criminalized all religious practices, but this was never a centrally formulated policy. Recent studies have proposed to include communism in some other socialist countries as a type of "atheist secularism" in order to understand how secularism came to be universalized.[12] We should add Maoism to this list.

In this light, the Maoist governance of religion was inherently self-defeating due to the unstable political environment created by mass campaigns. As the temporality of the revolution became intertwined with local politics, it generated numerous unintended consequences, taking over the CCP's project of secularization. The Chinese government has had to continually adapt to these unintended consequences of Maoist politics, as well as the unintended consequences of reform-era campaigns, including the "Three Rectifications and One Demolition" campaign in Zhejiang.

The Legacy of Maoism and the Transformation of the Religious Landscape

Destruction and disruption have tended to be the focus of discussion when it comes to the impact of Maoism on Chinese religion. Yet a closer look reveals that Maoism is both destructive and constructive, or *destructively constructive*, to Chinese religion, as is evident in three aspects of religious history in Rui'an.[13]

The first of these is the wholesale revitalization of sacred spaces, alongside a profound transformation in the geography of religion. Maoism led to the deterritorialization of religious space across all religious traditions on a scale never seen before, but this was accompanied by its reterritorialization as local communities strove to continue religious practices throughout the Mao era. Since the late 1970s in Wenzhou and elsewhere in China, a great number of temples and churches have been rebuilt and built. Never before in Chinese history were so many religious sites built or rebuilt in such a short period. Numerous temples

---

[11] For an example in other provinces, see Qin Heping, "Ershi shiji wuliushi niandai Wazu diqu Jidujiao de tiaoshi ji fazhan zhi renshi" (A discussion on adjustment and development of Protestant Christianity in Wa regions in 1950s and 1960s), in *Zhongguo Bianjiang Minzu Yanjiu* (Studies of China's Frontier Regions and Nationalities) 3: 219–222.

[12] Tam T. T. Ngo and Justine B. Quijada, eds., *Atheist Secularism and Its Discontents: A Comparative Study of Religion and Communism in Eurasia* (New York: Palgrave Macmillan, 2015).

[13] Dan Smyer Yu has suggested that communism has been destructively creative to religion in the history of the PRC. His statement focuses on how Chinese Communism has cleared social spaces for the return of Christianity and how it has lent Buddhism the rhetoric of scientism for the latter's reconstruction of legitimacy in the post-Mao era. His take on Christianity is very similar to those religious ecology theorists in mainland China. See Dan Smyer Yu, "Apologetics of Religion and Science: Conversion Projects in Contemporary China," in *Atheist Secularism and Its Discontents: A Comparative Study of Religion and Communism in Eurasia*, eds. Tam T. T. Ngo and Justine B. Quijada (New York: Palgrave Macmillan, 2015), 155–172.

and churches were rebuilt in new locations because their original sites could not be reclaimed. For the same reason, many of the local deities of communal religion are now housed in temples originally dedicated to other deities. To this day, numerous religious sites, rituals, and organizations still have not been restored and are most likely gone forever. Salvationist religion, which swept through China in the first half of the twentieth century, has been effectively silenced in mainland China since 1949, though it experienced a revival of sorts during the Qigong craze of the 1980s and 1990s. These developments have shifted the relative importance of various religious groups, as well as the sites and buildings used for worship, fundamentally altering the religious landscape.

Maoism and its legacies inadvertently facilitated a rearticulation of communal religion with elites and politics as local communities sought to reinvent communal religion. This is the second transformative effect of Maoism on Chinese religion that the Rui'an case suggests.

Beginning with the anti-superstition campaigns at the turn of the twentieth century, village elites departed from traditional cultural networks, at different times distancing themselves from, or being forced to leave, the religious field, a process Prasenjit Duara has described as a "disarticulat[ion]" of social relations.[14] After 1949, this disarticulation culminated in the purge of traditional elites, who were removed from their role as the patrons of communal religion. This, alongside the loss of landed estates and temple buildings, pushed followers of communal religion to find new ways of embedding traditional religious practices in an altered social landscape.

During the Mao era, communal religion retreated from everyday social life, yet it continued to coexist and compete with the state apparatus and party organizations in rural areas. Thus, as Edward Friedman notes, tradition "has continued even as the traditional elite has not, because newly risen groups from the poor have bound culture to politics."[15] The dissolution of the collective planned economy and the start of reform pushed forward the reinvention of communal religion. The institutionalization and legitimization of temple organizations (relying heavily on the EPAs) allowed followers of communal religion to reverse the process of "disarticulation." In this light, religious transformations in Rui'an after 1949 appear as part of a longer process of renewal and rearticulation in traditional rural organizations that began at the turn of the twentieth century, allowing communal religion to re-engage with the state.[16]

---

[14] Prasenjit Duara, *Culture, Power and the State: Rural Society in North China, 1900–1942* (Stanford, CA: Stanford University Press, 1988), 215.

[15] See Edward Friedman's review of *Culture, Power, and the State: Rural North China, 1900–1942* (Duara, *Culture, Power, and the State*) in *The American Historical Review* 95, no. 3 (1995): 885.

[16] Duara, *Culture, Power, and the State*. In particular, see Chapters 4 and 5 on the decline of lineage and religion.

Finally, the "destructively constructive" effects of Maoism on religious life in Wenzhou are most evident in the ascension of localized Christianity, in particular Protestant Christianity, a trend that continues today and that has greatly transformed the dynamics of Christianity and local religion throughout the region.

Protestant Christianity as it emerged from the Mao era was different from Christianity before 1949 in several important respects. After the Mao era, Christianity was much further integrated into local society. Christianity in Wenzhou today, in its religious practices, its structure, and its self-representation, is deeply permeated with the values, symbols, and ways of thinking of local society. The denominations brought by Western missionaries have largely disappeared, replaced by local articulations of religious practice and belief. From the late 1970s onward, Christian businessmen from Wenzhou started to disseminate "Wenzhou Christianity"—a type of Christianity heavily invested with localized practices and modes of operation unique to this region. Throughout China and even overseas, Wenzhou Christian entrepreneurs spread the gospel among locals and migrant workers through their nationwide network of businesses and factories.[17] Moreover, they have established a large number of what they refer to as "brother churches" across vast parts of China, stretching all the way from the Northeast to the Southwest, and in Wenzhounese communities across the world.[18]

This type of localized Christianity is also characterized by rampant schisms and new denominationalism, which manifest most visibly in the standoff between house meetings and Three-Self churches emerging from the Mao years. Schisms and new denominationalism are partly driven by the legacy of the Mao era: not only deep distrust and antagonism toward the state, but also distrust and division within Christian communities. Throughout China, during the Mao era, Protestant churches became more divided than ever. Paradoxically, the development of schisms and new denominationalism has also contributed to the dissemination and expansion of Protestantism.

A similar and important trend of survival and expansion, as Chapter 5 shows, is also visible in Protestant communities elsewhere in China, such as Wenling County of Zhejiang, Nanyang and Xinyang regions of Henan, Fuyang region

---

[17] Nanlai Cao, *Constructing China's Jerusalem: Christians, Power, and Place in Contemporary Wenzhou* (Stanford, CA: Stanford University Press, 2010), Chapters 4 and 6.

[18] For an example in Henan Province, see David Aikman, *Jesus in Beijing: How Christianity Is Transforming China and Changing the Global Balance of Power* (Washington: Regnery Publishing, 2006), 74–89. For the global expansion of Wenzhou Christianity, see Nanlai Cao, *Wenzhou Jidutu yu Zhongguo caogen quanqiuhua* (Wenzhou Christians and grassroots globalization) (Hong Kong: The Chinese University Press, 2017).

of Anhui, and Ningde and Quanzhou regions of Fujian. Furthermore, as in Wenzhou, this increase in church membership often occurred alongside the dissemination of Protestantism to new areas, laying the foundation for a much bigger revival in the post-Mao era.

The Aura of Revolution and Religion in Urbanizing China

One of the most fundamental aspects of religious change under Mao is the issue of religious property, particularly land. Because the Mao era left behind it numerous disputes over religious property and estates, communities throughout China are still seeking the restitution of religious sites. These efforts are likely to continue in the foreseeable future.

Although the temple and church restitution movement in the 1980s and 1990s reversed the long trend of encroachment on traditional religious space, the national-ization of land after 1949 permanently changed the outlook for religious properties, creating a new long-term threat to the existence of religious sites and organizations. As long as the current land regime remains in place, religious communities will not be entirely secure in their rights to their land and buildings.

The restoration of temples and churches during and after decollectivization gen-erally lacked formal legal status, even though it often took place with the tacit or overt acceptance of local authorities. In cases where restitution efforts failed, some communities and religious organizations built new temples or churches in new locations, also lacking official recognition. Paradoxically, the lack of legal recog-nition gave village temples, monasteries, and house churches a certain freedom to build, rebuild, or expand their buildings as they wished. This gave rise to a creeping gray zone in property issues, which the government came to see as an obstacle to its grand urbanization of rural areas.

Urbanization has been rapidly changing Chinese society. From 2000 to 2017, the urban population jumped from 35.39 percent to 58.5 percent. The govern-ment plans to increase the urban population to around 0.9 billion, or 70 per-cent of the total population, by 2025. The massive urbanization that the Chinese government is forcefully promoting today is conducted through programs like "Three Rectifications and One Demolition" in Zhejiang, seemingly with much less brutality than the transformations in rural and semi-urban society under Mao. It even enjoys popular support to a great extent, as to many people it represents development and progress. Yet the ambition of urbanizing China to such a degree in such a short period equates to another total reordering of so-cial life. Massive urbanization can thus be construed as the manifestation and continuation of "authoritarian high modernism,"[19] as James Scott has described it, which was a prominent aspect of the 1949 revolution.

The vast expansion of urban areas and the reorganization of social space have inevitably made religious sites face another major challenge, if not crisis. The insecure property rights and vulnerable legal status of religious organizations make them particularly susceptible to state crackdowns. In Zhejiang since 2015, the local government has ordered village EPAs to transfer the management of their assets to village governments, creating a further challenge for religious life.

In recent years, alongside urbanization plans, the Chinese government has been promoting the legalization of territorial temples—a radical shift compared with the loss of status these temples have experienced since the early twentieth century. At the same time, the government is also pushing Buddhist temples and Christian churches to register their properties with the government and open their own bank accounts (in the church or temple's name). The state is expanding its bureaucratic machinery, using big data technology in the surveillance of religious sites. These developments foreshadow an increasing legibility of religious communities that would allow the state to exert greater control. Yet, as this book suggests, the state's heavy hand when it comes to religious life has so far left room for maneuver, manipulation, and change. It is likely that as some gray areas disappear, new ones will emerge. And as was the case throughout the radical political movements of the twentieth century, forthcoming changes may not signal the end of religious life, but instead bring about renewal and other unexpected transformations.

---

[19] James C. Scott, *Seeing like a State: How Certain Schemes to Improve the Human Condition Have Failed* (New Haven, CT: Yale University Press, 1998), Chapter 3.

Chinese Term List

aihu tankuan 挨戶攤款
aiguo gongyue 愛國公約
aiguo hui 愛國會
anguo si 安國寺
Anxi (County) 安溪
anxiri hui 安息日會
Anyang (Town, Rui'an) 安陽
Anyang (County, Hunan) 安陽
Aodi (Village) 岙底
Aojiang (River) 鰲江
bao taiping 保太平
baocun wanzhengde 保存完整的
Baotian (Township) 鮑田
baozhang 保長
baozheng 保證
bazi 八字
beifen 輩分
Beishan (District) 北山
ben cun/difang laoren 本村/地方老人
benji si 本寂寺
bing 兵
boluan fanzheng 撥亂反正
bozhongji 播種機
Cai Yuexiang 蔡月祥
Cangnan (County) 蒼南
Cao Yongqi 曹用啟
Caocun (Town) 曹村
Changqiao (Township) 場橋
changqing guan 長青觀
chanquan 產權
chating 茶亭
Chen Changman 陳昌滿
Chen Dengyong 陳登庸
Chen Huimin 陳惠民
Chen Jinggu/Chen Shisi 陳靖姑/陳十四

Chen Liangkui 陳良奎
Chen Libin 陳立斌
Chen Nailiang 陳乃良
Chen Shangsheng 陳上聲
Chen Shicong 陳世聰
Chen Wenzheng 陳文征
Chen Wenzhu 陳文柱
Chen Zhaorao 陳召堯
Chen Zhehai 陳哲海
Chen'ao (Village) 陳岙
chenfu miao 陳府廟
chenghuang 城隍
Chengshanping (Brigade) 呈山坪
Chuanhe (Township) 川和
chujishe/gaojishe 初級社/高級社
chuzhuyi 出主意
cubaozuofa 粗暴做法
cun laoren xiehui/ cun laoxie 村老人協會/村老協
da yisheng 大醫生
dadao hui 大刀會
Dadianxia (Township) 大典下
Dai (family) 戴
Daluo (Mountain) 大羅山
dangquanpai 當權派
daogaohui 禱告會
Datong (Brigade) 大同
dayang miao 大垟廟
dayangshan jiao 大垟山教
dazhai 大齋
di fu fan huai 地富反壞
dian 點
dian fodeng 點佛燈
dianwu 玷污
difang 地方
Dingtian (Township) 汀田
dishang 地上
dixia 地下
dixia shili 地下勢力
Dong Renzhang 董仁漲
Dongkeng (Village) 東坑
Donglian (Brigade) 東聯

dongtang dian 東堂殿
Dongtian (Township) 董田
Dongtou (County) 洞頭
dongyue guan 東岳觀
dongyue miao 東岳廟
Du Chongchang 杜崇昌
Du Shaofu 杜紹甫
Du Zhixin 杜知信
Du Zhulai 杜祝來
Du Zhuxiong 杜祝雄
duanwu 端午
Duikeng (Village) 對坑
erfuye dian 二府爺殿
fahui 法會
fandao 反道
fandong huidaomen 反動會道門
Fang Jiesheng 范介生
fangrenziliu 放任自流
Fangzhuang (Township) 芳莊
feiwu 廢物
Feiyun (River) 飛雲江
Feng Zongde 馮宗德
Fenghuang (Mountain) 鳳凰山
fengjian fubi 封建復辟
fengjian mixin fubi 封建迷信復辟
Fengtagang (Brigade) 鳳塔崗
Fengxiang (Township) 鳳翔
fentan 分壇
fenxinhui 奮興會
fo 佛
Fu Shaodai 富紹戴
Fuding (County) 福鼎
Fuyang (Prefecture) 阜陽
fuyincun 福音村
fuzhong bing 浮腫病
Gaolou (District) 高樓
Gaoyao (County) 高要
geming qunzhong 革命群眾
geming yizhi 革命遺址
gongdi 公地
gongshangye dizhu 工商業地主

gongtong gangling 共同綱領
gongxiaoshe 供銷社
gongyou 公有
gongyou 共有
guanxunban 管訓班
guanyin hui 觀音會
guo 國
guochande 國產的
Hai'an (Township) 海安
Haicheng (Street) 海城
Haiyu (Township) 海嶼
He Chengxiang 何成湘
Hekoutang (Brigade) 河口塘
hexin xintu 核心信徒
heyi 合一
Hongqiao (District) 虹橋
hongse taifeng 紅色颱風
hongyan dian 洪巖殿
Hu Fulin 胡福林
Hu Yuming 胡玉明
Hu Zhilong 胡志龍
Hu Zhiping 胡志平
hua longchuan 划龍船
huaguang miao 華光廟
Huaguangye 華光爺
Huang Longbiao 黃龍彪
Huang Longcong 黃龍聰
Huang Xinrong 黃新榮
Huang Yaopan 黃姚判
Huang'ao (Village) 黃坳
Huangliao (Township) 黃寮
Huangtan (District) 黃坦
huangyang jiao 黃陽教
Huhan pai 呼喊派
Huli (Brigade) 湖里
Hushang'ao (Village) 湖上呇
huzhuzu 互助組
jiandu laodong 監督勞動
Jiang Lianghui 蔣良繪
Jiang Songling 蔣松齡
Jiang Xinghua 蔣醒華

Jianglong (Township) 江隆
Jiangshan (Village) 蔣山
jianshan tang 尖山堂
jiantangre 建堂熱
Jiaopu (Village) 焦浦
Jiaoshi (Village) 礁石
jiaotang 教堂
jiaotu 教徒
jiaoyu 教育
jiaozhu 教主
Jidujiao huodong changsuo 基督教活動場所
jieyong 借用
Jin Chengzhou 金成周
Jin Daoxing 金道興
Jin'ao (Mountain) 金鰲山
Jinbao (Mountain) 金堡山
Jinchuan (Township) 金川
jingchan gaige 經懺改革
jingchan lianying 經懺聯營
jingdu 淨度
Jinggu (Township) 荊谷
Jingning (County) 景寧
Jingzhou (mythical land) 荊州
jinnang 錦囊
jinqian hui 金錢會
jintian chaimiao, mingtian jianmiao 今天拆廟, 明天建廟
Jinyan (Township) 金巖
Jinyun (County) 縉雲
jiu'en 救恩
Jiuli (Township) 九里
Juhuichu 聚會處
juhuidian 聚會點
Kengkouyang (Village) 坑口垟
Kexianjin 刻仙巾
Kuangye jiaohui 曠野教會
Kutou (Village) 庫頭
Lanxi (County) 蘭溪
laodong gaizao 勞動改造
laoling shiye 老齡事業
laolingwei 老齡委
laonian huodong zhongxin 老年活動中心

laoniangong 老年宮
laopai 老派
laoren huodongshi 老人活動室
laorenting 老人亭
laoren xiehui 老人協會
Lei Gaosheng 雷高升
lenglengqingqing 冷冷清清
Li Binwen 李彬文
Li Rongyin 李榮銀
Li Xiuzhuo 李修灼
Li'ao (Town) 麗岙
lianchan chengbao zerenzhi 聯產承包責任制
Lianguang (cooperative) 聯光
lianhe libai 聯合禮拜
lianzhan 聯站
Lianzhong (Brigade) 聯中
lianzong 聯總
Liao Zhensheng 廖振生
Liaoxing 了性
Lin Fuzhen 林福臻
Lin Hongbing 林洪兵
Lin Mingzhu 林明鬶
Lin Naimei 林乃姆
Lin Youdi 林友弟
Lingxi (Town) 靈溪
Lingxia (Birgade) 嶺下
Lingya (Township) 嶺雅
Linjiayuan (Village) 林家院
lishi wenwu 歷史文物
Lishui (Prefecture) 麗水
Liu Bowen/Liu Ji 劉伯溫/劉基
Liu Ying 劉英
liujia gong 六甲宮
Long (Mountain) 隆山
Long Yue 龍躍
longtan si 龍潭寺
Longwan (District) 龍灣
Lubian (Village) 路邊
Lucheng (District) 鹿城
Lumu (Commune) 鹿木
Luofeng (Town) 羅鳳

Luonan (Township) 羅南
luoshi zongjiao zhengce 落實宗教政策
Meishukeng (Brigade) 梅樹坑
Meitou (Town) 梅頭
mengtou 蒙頭
miao 廟
Miao Zhitong 繆志同
miaozhong 廟眾
miejiao 滅教
min 民
mingjiao si 明教寺
mixinpin 迷信品
mixin touzi 迷信頭子
mixin zhiye fenzi 迷信職業分子
Mocheng (Township) 墨城
mofan gongguan 模範宮觀
moshou 沒收
mudaoyou 慕道友
Nanchen (Village) 南鎮
Nangang (District) 南港
Nanping (Township) 南坪
Nantian (District) 南田
Nanyang (Prefecture) 南陽
neidihui 內地會
Ni Guangdao 倪光道
niangnianggong 娘娘宮
Ningde (Prefecture) 寧德
niu gui she shen 牛鬼蛇神
nongye liushi tiao 農業六十條
nongyeshui 農業稅
nu lian she 女蓮社
Nu'ao (Brigade) 女岙
Oubei (Town) 甌北
Ouhai (District) 甌海
paidan 派單
Pan Bofeng 潘伯豐
Pan Jinyou 潘進友
Pan Shixing 潘時興
Peng Chongcai 彭崇彩
Peng Kexing 彭克興
Peng Yang 彭陽

pianqu 片區
Pichaitan (Brigade) 劈柴坦
pilao baogao 疲勞報告
Pingyang (County) 平陽
Pingyangkeng (Town) 平陽坑
pishi 批示
Puqian (Township) 浦前
pusa 菩薩
Puzhou (Township) 蒲州
Qianbu (Village) 前埠
Qiancang (Town) 錢倉
Qianku (Town) 錢庫
Qianzhuang (Village) 前莊
Qiaodun (Town) 橋墩
Qingtian (County) 青田
qitian dasheng 齊天大聖
qixing hui 七星會
Qu Zhenhan 瞿振漢
quancun 全村
renao 熱鬧
Rui'an 瑞安
Rui'an Fojiao xuexihui 瑞安佛教協會
Rui'an Jidujiao Sanzi Aiguo Weiyuanhui 瑞安基督教三自愛國委員會
Rui'an Jidujiao Xiehui 瑞安基督教協會
sanbaodian 三寶殿
sangai yichai 三改一拆
Sanjiang 三江
sanyu 三育
Shacheng (Village) 沙城
Shamen (Mountain) 沙門山
shan'gen dian 山根殿
Shang cun (Village) 上村
Shang'anchi (Village) 上岸池
Shangjin (Village) 上金
Shangma (Village) 上馬
shangong miao 山公廟
Shangwang (Commune) 上望
Shangyang (Village) 上垟
Shangdu (Village) 上都
Shankeng (Brigade) 山坑
Shantouxia (Village) 山頭下

Shao (family) 邵
Shao Yanliu 邵岩柳
Shao Yongsheng 邵永生
shaobingge 燒餅歌
Shaozhai (Village) 邵宅
Shayang (Village) 沙垟
Shen Liangshi 沈良式
sheng san 聖三
sheng wu 聖五
shengjing dian 聖井殿
shengshou si 圣壽寺
shijie zongtan 世界總壇
shi'erbu jiao 十二步教
Shibu (Village) 石埠
Shilong (Commune) 石龍
shoushi 首事
Shu Chengqian 舒成虔
Shu Xiaorong 舒小榮
Shuntai (Township) 順泰
sishitongtang 四世同堂
sizhong 寺眾
Su Yu 粟裕
taifo 抬佛
taiping long 太平龍
Taishun (County) 泰順
taiyin gong 太陰宮
Taizhou (Prefecture) 台州
Tang (River) 塘河
tang 堂
Tangkou (Village) 塘口
tangwu guanli xiaozu 堂務管理小組
Tangxia (District) 塘下
Tangxia li tui xiu ganbu zhigong xiehui 塘下離退休幹部職工協會
Taofeng (Commune) 陶峰
Taoshan (District) 陶山
tianfu miao 天福寺
Tianhe (Village) 天河
tianji 天機
tianxia 天下
tianzhu 天主
tiao lingwu 跳靈舞

tiaoji zhi yong 調劑之用
tonggong 同工
tonggou tongxiao 統購統銷
tongji gong 通濟宮
tongshan she 同善社
Tongxi (Village) 桐溪
touji daoba fenzi 投機倒把分子
toukao diguozhuyi 投靠帝國主義
tudi gaige fa 土地改革法
tudi miao 土地廟
Wang Hengqing 王橫清
Wang Muyong 王慕勇
wannian gong 晚年宮
weijiao 圍剿
Wencheng 文成
wenhua huodongshi 文化活動室
wenhuaguan 文化館
Wenling (County) 溫嶺
Wenzhou (Prefecture) 溫州
Wenzhou diqu zonghui 溫州地區總會
Wenzhou Qu jiaotong zonghui 溫州區交通總會
Ximen (Street) 西門
Wu Buxun 吳步勛
Wu Huanwen 鄔煥文
Wu Qingyan 吳青巖
Wu Shoukui 吳守奎
Wu Zhenqian 吳振錢
wubaohu 五保戶
wugongjing 五公經
Wujia (Village) 五甲
wulong shengmu gong 烏龍聖母宮
wulun 五倫
wuwei jiao 無為教
wuxian miao 五顯廟
wuzhen si 悟真寺
xi'ao gong 西岙宮
Xia cun (Village) 下村
Xianfang (Township) 咸芳
xiangbutong 想不通
xianghuo 香火
xiangyan/huo lengluo 香煙/火冷落

Xianjiang (District) 仙降
xianjuan 仙卷
Xiantan (Township) 仙譚
xiantian dao 先天道
Xianyan (Town) 仙巖
xiaoshenmiao 小神廟
xiaotan 小壇
Xiasheng (Village) 霞嵊
xidian gong 西店宮
Xie Duyin 謝篤寅
Xie Qingxian 謝卿仙
Xihu (Brigade) 西湖
Xijie (Village) 西街
Xikeng (Village) 西坑
xin kao 信靠
Xincheng (District) 莘塍
xinfangzhi 新方志
xinfode 信佛的
Xinmin (Commune) 新民
xinpai 新派
xintu 信徒
xinxinpai 新新派
Xinyang (Prefecture) 信陽
Xinzhou (Town) 莘周
Xitu (Village) 西涂
xiwei gong 溪尾宮
Xiyi (Village) 西一
Xu'nan (Brigade) 許南
xuanchuandui 宣傳隊
Xubei (Brigade) 許北
xuexiban 學習班
xundao gonghui 循道公會
Yandang (Mountain) 雁蕩山
Yang Chisheng 楊池生
Yang Duojia 楊多加
yangfuye 楊府爺
yantou gong 巖頭宮
Yaozhuang (Commune) 瑤莊
Ye Entu 葉恩土
Ye Jilang 葉紀郎
Ye Tingchao 葉挺超

Ye Zhiqing 葉志卿
ye pan tang 葉潘堂
Yesu 耶穌
yi gong yi miao 一宮一廟
yiguan dao 一貫道
ying luoshi 應落實
Ying Qiancheng 應錢誠
Yishan (Town) 宜山
yixiaocuo ren 一小撮人
yiyi renminbi 一億人民幣
yizhenfeng 一陣風
Yongjia (County) 永嘉
Yongqiang (Commune) 永強
You Daoshu 尤道樞
You Shuxun 尤樹勛
Yu Dubing 余督兵
Yu Naibao 余萘寶
Yuan Fanglie 袁芳烈
yuehan pai 約翰派
Yueqing (County) 樂清
Yuhuan (County) 玉環
yuhuan dian 玉皇殿
Zaoxi (Town) 藻溪
Zhang Busong 張步松
Zhang Buwang 張步旺
Zhang Dasheng 張達生
Zhang dechang 張德昌
Zhang Liquan 張禮全
Zhang Shidan 張士旬
Zhang Zhengcha 張正茶
Zhangdan (Brigade) 章旦
zhanglao 長老
Zhangzhai (Village) 張宅
Zhao Dianhua 趙典華
Zhao Dianren 趙典仁
Zhao Hongtian 趙洪田
Zhao Hongxu 趙洪緒
Zhao Hongzhu 趙洪柱
Zhaozhai (Village) 趙宅
Zheng Qingzan 鄭慶贊
zhengcexingde 政策性的

zhengfu pizhun 政府批准
zhengshou 征收
zhenshen taigu 真身太姑
zhishi 執事
Zhitong pai 志同派
Zhong cun (Village) 中村
zhongdian diqu 重點地區
zhongdian zongjiao 重點宗教
Zhongguo Yesujiao zilihui 中國耶穌教自立會
Zhongxing (Village) 中星村
Zhou Shouzhen 周壽真
Zhu Qimei 朱七姆
Zhu Shunli 朱舜理
Zhu Weifang 朱維芳
Zhuangquan (Village) 莊泉
Zhupaitou (Neighbourhood) 竹排頭
Zhushan (Village) 朱山
zhutan 主壇
zhutang 駐堂
Zhuyuan (Village) 朱元
Zi'ao (Commune) 梓岙
zongfuze 總負責
zongjiao 宗教
zongjiao gongzuo 宗教工作
zongjiao gongzuo dayuejin 宗教工作大躍進
zongjiao mixin 宗教迷信
zongjiao mixin zhiyezhe 宗教迷信職業者
zongtan 總壇
zongzu shili 宗族勢力
zuo tianxia 坐天下

Bibliography

Archival Sources and Internal Documents

Longquan City Archives 龍泉市檔案館, Longquan City, Lishui, Zhejiang.
Neibu Cankao 內部參考 (Internal Reference), 1954–1965, the Xinhua Agency, Beijing.
   Pingyang County Archives 平陽縣檔案館, Pingyang County, Wenzhou, Zhejiang.
Rui'an City Archives 瑞安市檔案館, Rui'an City, Wenzhou, Zhejiang.
 Taishun County Archives 泰順縣檔案館, Taishun County, Wenzhou, Zhejiang.
Wencheng County Archives 文成縣檔案館, Wencheng County, Wenzhou, Zhejiang.
   Wenling City Archives 溫嶺市檔案館, Wenling City, Taizhou, Zhejiang.
Wenzhou Prefectural Archives 溫州市檔案館, Wenzhou, Zhejiang.
Yueqing City Archives 樂清市檔案館, Yueqing City, Wenzhou, Zhejiang.

Local Gazetteers and Records of Local Religious Institutions

"Chengong jinduo sanshi zhounian shiji jianjie" 陳公晉鐸三十週年事跡簡介 (A brief introduction to deeds of priest Chen at the thirtieth anniversary of his ordination). http://www.tianren.org/life/show.asp?id=15836 (accessed on May 4, 2018).

"Wenzhou jiaohui shixing hebing" 溫州教會實行合併 (Wenzhou church to carry out a merger), *Tianfeng* 9 (1958): 20–21.

"Wenzhou jiaoqu de chuanjiao sishi" 溫州教區的傳教司事 (Catechists of Wenzhou diocese). http://www.tzjwzjq.com/Look_History.aspx?MID=22 (accessed on May 4, 2018).

"Work in the Wenchow Prefecture (Chekiang Province)." *China's Millions* (North American edition). Toronto: China Inland Mission, 1921, 86–87.

Aroud, Cyprien. "Catechist Work in Wenchow." *Catholic Missions* (1917), 152–153.

Chen Shangsheng 陳上聲. "Xiantan Xiang xiangzhang quanjia guizhu" 仙潭鄉鄉長全家歸主 (The whole family of Xiantan Township head converted). *Xiaduo yuekan* 1, no. 6 (1937): 36–37.

Chen Guiqiu 陳桂秋, ed. *Xiapu Xian Jidujiao zhi* 霞浦縣基督教志 (History of the Protestant Church in Xiapu County). Xiapu Xian: Xiapu Xian zongjiaozhi bianxiezu, 1992.

Chen Murong 陳慕榕 et al., eds. *Qingtian Xian zhi* 青田縣志 (Qingtian County gazetteer). Hangzhou: Zhejiang renmin chubanshe, 1990.

Cheng Shicen 程世岑, ed. *Pingyang Xian gong'an zhi* 平陽縣公安志 (Pingyang County public security gazetteer). Tianjin: Nankai daxue chubanshe, 1997.

Gao Shuibiao 高水標, ed. *Xinchang Xian gong'an zhi* 新昌縣公安志 (Xinchang County public security gazetteer). Beijing: Dangdai Zhongguo chubanshe, 1994.

Gao Yideng 高益登 and Nan Xian 南憲, eds. *Yuecheng Zhen zhi* 樂成鎮志 (Yuecheng Town gazetteer). Beijing: Dangdai Zhongguo chubanshe, 1990.

Lin Hongbin 林洪兵. "Wenzhou Aojiang Rui'an budao zhi jieguo" 溫州鰲江瑞安佈道之 結果 (The fruits of sermons in Aojiang and Rui'an of Wenzhou). *Tongwenbao: Yesujiao jiating xinwen* 1550 (1933): 7.

Longwan Qu shizhi bianzuan weiyuanhui and *Longwan Qu zhi* bianjibu 龍灣區史志編纂委員會, "龍灣區志"編輯部. *Longwan Qu zhi* 龍灣區志, (Longwan District gazetteer). Beijing: Zhonghua shuju, 2013.

Lü Shanxin 呂善信. "Taiping Xiang qiuyu mixin shijian huigu" 太平鄉求雨迷信事件回顧 (Memoir of the incident of rainmaking superstition at Taiping Township). In *Wushi niandai de Yongkang* (*Yongkang wenshi ziliao di shisan ji*) (Yongkang in the 1950s [Yongkang historical materials, volume 13]), Yongkang Shi zhengxie wenshi weiyuanhui, 2001.

Miao Zhitong 繆志同. *Wenzhou qu jiaohui shi* 溫州區教會史 (Church history in Wenzhou). Internal document, 2005–2006(?).

Nanyang Diqu difang shizhi bianzuan weiyuanhui 南陽地區地方史志編纂委員會, ed. *Nanyang Diqu zhi* 南陽地區志 (Nanyang Region gazetteer). Zhengzhou Shi: Henan renmin chubanshe, 1994.

Ni Guangdao 倪光道. "1978 nian qianhou de jiaohui shenghuo" 1978 年前後的教會生活 (Church life before and after 1978). *Tianfeng* 11 (2008): 8–9.

Pan Yiheng 潘貽衡. *Zhe'nan Rui'an Fojiao zhi* 浙南瑞安佛教志 (History of Buddhism in Rui'an of southern Zhejiang). Internal document, ca. 1992.

Rui'an jiaohui 瑞安教會. *Rui'an jiaohui shi* 瑞安教會史 (A history of Rui'an church). Internal document, 1998.

Rui'an Shi jiaoyu weiyuanhui jiaoyu zhi bianzhuanzu 瑞安市教育委員會教育志編撰組, ed. *Rui'an jiaoyu zhi* 瑞安教育志 (Rui'an education history). Nanchang: Jiangxi renmin chubanshe, 1992.

Rui'an Xian xiuzhiju 瑞安縣修志局. *Rui'an Xian zhi gao* 瑞安縣志稿 (Draft gazetteer of Rui'an County). Daziben (big character version). Rui'an: Rui'an Xian xiuzhiju, 1946–1948.

Rui'an Xian xiuzhiju 瑞安縣修志局. *Rui'an Xian zhi gao* 瑞安縣志稿 (Draft gazetteer of Rui'an County). Xiaoziben (small character version). Rui'an: Rui'an Xian xiuzhiju, 1946–1948.

Sharman, A. H. "Rural Evangelism in the Wenchow District." In *China Mission Year Book* (1917). Shanghai: The Christian Literature Society for China, 1917.

Shi Shihu 施世琥. *Ying Weixian zhuan* 應維賢傳 (Biography of Ying Weixian). Xianggang chubanshe, 2009.

Shu Chengqian 舒成虔. *Wushi nian jiaohui shenghuo huiyi* 五十年教會生活回憶 (Memoirs of fifty years' life in the church). Internal reference materials ("neibu cankao ziliao"), 2002.

Tang Yijun 湯一鈞, ed. *Xincheng Zhen zhi* 莘塍鎮志 (Xincheng Town gazetteer), Huangshan shushe, 1998.

Tang Jinhua 湯金華 et al., eds. *Ningde Diqu zhi* 寧德地區志 (Ningde Region gazetteer). Beijing: Fangzhi chubanshe, 1998.

Tao Dagong 陶大恭, ed. *Dadaohui shimo (Cangnan Xian wenshi ziliao di qi ji)* 大刀會始末 (蒼南縣文史資料第七輯) (A concise history of the Big Sword Association [Cangnan historical materials, volume 7]). Cangnan: Cangnan Xian zhengxie wenshi ziliao weiyuanhui, 1992.

Wang Dingsen 王鼎森 and Zeng Dahai 曾大海, eds. *Fangcheng Xian zhi* 方城縣志 (Fangcheng County gazetteer). Zhengzhou Shi: Zhongzhou guji chubanshe, 1992.

Wencheng Xian zhengxie wenshi weiyuanhui 文成縣政協文史委員會, ed. *Wencheng wenshi ziliao di san ji* 文成文史資料第三輯 (Wencheng historical materials, volume 3). Wencheng Xian zhengxie wenshi weiyuanhui, 1987.

Wenling Xian zhi bianzuan weiyuanhui 溫嶺縣志編纂委員會, ed. *Wenling Xian zhi* 溫嶺縣志 (Wenling County gazetteer). Hangzhou: Zhejiang renmin chubanshe, 1992.

Xinyang Diqu difang shizhi bianzuan weiyuanhui 信陽地區地方史志編纂委員會, ed. *Xinyang Diqu zhi* 信陽地區志 (Xinyang Region gazetteer). Beijing: Sanlian shudian, 1992.

Yang Dianzhong 楊典忠 et al., eds. *Yueqing Xian gong'anzhi* 樂清縣公安志 (A history of public security in Yueqing County). Beijing: Haiyan chubanshe, 1993.

Yang Duojia 楊多加. "Benzou rongyao de tianlu" 奔走榮耀的天路 (Running the glorifying heavenly path), ca. 2000. http://blog.sina.com.cn/s/blog_52dfd841010152ng.html (accessed on May 4, 2018).

Ying Weixian 應維賢, ed. *Rui'an Shi Daojiao zhi* 瑞安市道教志 (History of Daoism in Rui'an). Rui'an Daojiao xiehui, 2011.

Zhan Rujian 詹汝健 et al., eds. *Qingtian Xian gong'an zhi* 青田縣公安志 (History of public security in Qingtian County). Hangzhou: Zhejiang renmin chubanshe, 2006.

Zhang Chaoyin 張朝銀, ed. *Rui'an Shi longzhou huodong jianshi* 瑞安市龍舟活動簡史 (A concise history of dragon boat racing in Rui'an). Rui'an shi shiwei dangshi yanjiushi, difangzhi bangongshi. Internal document, 2004.

Zhang Gang 張棡. *Zhang Gang riji* 張棡日記 (Zhang Gang's diaries). Shanghai: Shanghai shehuikexueyuan chubanshe, 2003.

Zhang Zhebin 張哲彬, ed. *Ninghai Xian gong'anzhi* 寧海縣公安志 (Ninghai County public security gazetteer). Beijing: Zhonghua shuju, 2001.

Zhang Zhicheng 章志誠, ed. *Wenzhou huaqiao shi* 溫州華僑史 (History of overseas Wenzhounese). Beijing: Jinri Zhongguo chubanshe, 2009.

Zhejiang Sheng zongjiaozhi bianjizu 浙江省宗教志編輯組, ed. *Zhejiang Sheng zongjiaozhi ziliao huibian yi: Tianzhujiao* 浙江省宗教志資料彙編一: 天主教 (Documents on history of religion in Zhejiang, volume one: Catholicism). Internal document, 1993.

Zheng Datong 鄭大同. *Mengfu zhi lu—Jidu li shiyi de rensheng* 蒙福之路—基督里詩意的人生 (The path of blessing—poetic life in Christ). Hong Kong: Xundao weili zhongxin, 2010.

Zhi Huaxin 支華欣, ed. *Wenzhou Jidujiao* 溫州基督教 (Wenzhou Christianity). Hangzhou: Zhejiang Sheng Jidujiao xiehui, 2000.

Zhonggong Rui'an shiwei dangwei yanjiushi 中共瑞安市委黨史研究室, ed. *Zhongguo Gongchandang Rui'an lishi dashiji 1949–1999* 中國共產黨瑞安歷史大事記1949–1999 (A chronicle of the Chinese Communist Party in Rui'an 1949–1999). Beijing: Zhonggong dangshi chubanshe, 2001.

Zhou Konghua 周孔華 and Ruan Zhensheng 阮珍生, eds. *Wenzhou Daojiao tonglan* 溫州道教通覽 (A general survey of Daoism in Wenzhou). Hong Kong: Tianma Books, 1999.

Zhu Li 朱禮 et al., eds. *Wencheng Xian zhi* 文成縣志 (Wencheng gazetteer). Beijing: Zhonghua shuju, 1996.

Secondary Works and Other Materials

Aikman, David. *Jesus in Beijing: How Christianity Is Transforming China and Changing the Global Balance of Power*. Washington, DC: Regnery, 2006.

Benton, Gregor. *Mountain Fires: The Red Army's Three-Year War in South China, 1934–1938*. Berkeley: University of California Press, 1994.

Brown, Jeremy, and Matthew Johnson eds. *Maoism at the Grassroots: Everyday Life in China's Era of High Socialism*. Cambridge, MA: Harvard University Press, 2015.

Bush, Richard C. *Religion in Communist China*. Nashville, TN: Abingdon Press, 1970.

Cao, Nanlai. "Christian Entrepreneurs and the Post-Mao State: An Ethnographic Account of Church-State Relations in China's Economic Transition." *Sociology of Religion* 68, no. 1 (2007): 45–66.

Cao, Nanlai. *Constructing China's Jerusalem: Christians, Power, and Place in Contemporary Wenzhou*. Stanford, CA: Stanford University Press, 2010.

Cao, Nanlai 曹南來. *Wenzhou Jidutu yu Zhongguo caogen quanqiuhua* 溫州基督徒與中國草根全球化 (Wenzhou Christians and grassroots globalization). Hong Kong: The Chinese University Press, 2017.

Cao Shuji 曹樹基. *Dajihuang—1959 nian—1961 nian de Zhongguo renkou* 大饑荒—1959 年–1961 年的中國人口 (The great famine—Chinese population between 1959 and 1961). Hong Kong: Shidai guoji chubangongsi, 2005.

Chan, Wing-tsit. *Religious Trends in Modern China*. New York: Columbia University Press, 1953.

Chau, Adam Yuet. "Popular Religion in Shannbei, North-Central China." *Journal of Chinese Religions* 31 (2003): 39–79.

Chau, Adam Yuet. *Miraculous Response: Doing Popular Religion in Contemporary China*. Stanford: Stanford University Press, 2008.

Chau, Adam Yuet. "Chinese Socialism and the Household Idiom of Religious Engagement." In *Atheist Secularism and Its Discontents: A Comparative Study of Religion and Communism in Eurasia*, eds. Tam T. T. Ngo and Justine B. Quijada, 225–243. New York: Palgrave Macmillan, 2015.

Chau, Adam Yuet, ed. *Religion in Contemporary China: Revitalization and Innovation*. New York: Routledge, 2011.

Chen Cunfu 陳村富. "Zhejiang diqu Tianzhujiao he Xinjiao diaocha yanjiu" 浙江地區天主教 和新教調查研究 (An investigative research of Catholicism and Protestantism in Zhejiang). *Ding/Tripod* 131 (2004): 13–20.

Chen Fengsheng 陳豐盛. "Wenzhou Jidujiao shengshi fazhan licheng" 溫州基督教圣詩發展歷程 (The making of hymns in Wenzhou Christianity). *Jinling shengxue zhi* 1 (2009): 61–72.

Chen Fengsheng 陳豐盛. "Wenzhou jiaohui yigong fazhan licheng" 溫州教會義工發展歷程 (The development course of workers in Wenzhou church). *Jinling shengxue zhi* 3 (2010): 24–44.

Chen Xiaoyi 陳曉毅. *Zhongguoshi zongjiao shengtai: Qinyan zongjiao duoyangxing ge'an yanjiu* 中國式宗教生態: 青岩宗教多樣性個案研究 (Chinese religious ecology: a case study on religious diversity at Qingyan). Beijing: Shehui kexue wenxian chubanshe, 2008.

Chen Xun 陳勛. "Xiangcun shehui liliang heyi keneng? Jiyu Wenzhou laoren xiehui de yanjiu" 鄉村社會力量何以可能? 基於溫州老人協會的研究 (How is rural social power possible? Research on elderly people associations in Wenzhou). *Zhongguo Nongcun Guancha* 1 (2012): 80–88.

Cheng, Yuk-shing and Tsang Shu-ki. "The Changing Grain Marketing System in China." *The China Quarterly* 140 (1994): 1080–1104.

Clart, Philip. "'Religious Ecology' as a New Model for the Study of Religious Diversity in China." In *Religious Diversity in Chinese Thought*, eds. Perry Schmidt-Leukel and Joachim Gentz, 187–199. New York: Palgrave Macmillan, 2013.

DeMare, Brian James. *Mao's Cultural Army Drama Troupes in China's Rural Revolution*. Cambridge, UK: Cambridge University Press, 2015.

Deng Yanhua and Kevin J. O'Brien. "The Society of Senior Citizens and Popular Protest in Rural Zhejiang." *China Journal* 71 (2014): 172–188.

Deng Yanhua 鄧燕華 and Ruan Hengfu 阮橫俯. "Nongcun yinse liliang heyi keneng? Yi Zhejiang laonian xiehui weili" (How is gray power in rural China possible? A case study of elderly people associations in Zhejiang) 農村銀色力量何以可能？—以浙江老年協會為例. *Shehuixue yanjiu* 8 (2008): 131–54.

Ding Yuan 丁元, Han Feng 韓鋒, Du Jiangxian 杜江先, and Jia Ping 賈萍. "Yizhong xingshi diji de Jidujiao—Linyi Shi Jidujiao xianzhuang diaocha" 一種形式低級的基督教—臨沂市基督教現狀調查 (A lower form of Protestantism—investigation of Protestantism in Linyi City). *Minsu yanjiu* 2 (1986): 12–16.

Dong Chuanling 董傳嶺. "Jianguo liushinian huabei nongcun shehui shenghuo bianqian—Yi Shandong Sheng Liangshan Xian wei ge'an" 建國六十年華北農村社會生活變遷—以山東省梁山縣為個案 (The evolution of rural social life in the six decades after 1949—The case of Liangshan County, Shangdong Province). PhD dissertation. Nankai University, 2010.

Duan Qi 段琦. "Cangnan fuyin dahui yougan" 蒼南福音大會有感 (Comments on the Cangnan evangelical meeting). *Maitian*, Autumn issue, 2010. http://www.mtfy.org/magazine.php?mod=view&id=212 (accessed on May 4, 2018).

Duara, Prasenjit. *Culture, Power and the State: Rural Society in North China, 1900–1942*. Stanford, CA: Stanford University Press, 1988.

Duara, Prasenjit. "Knowledge and Power in the Discourse of Modernity: The Campaigns against Popular Religion in Early 20th Century China." *Journal of Asian Studies* 50, no. 1 (1991): 67–83.

Duara, Prasenjit. *Rescuing History from the Nation: Questioning Narratives of Modern China*. Chicago: University of Chicago Press, 1995.

Duara, Prasenjit. "The Discourse of Civilization and Pan-Asianism." *Journal of World History* 12, no. 1 (2000): 99–130.

Dubois, Thomas David. *The Sacred Village: Social Change and Religious Life in Rural North China*. Honolulu: University of Hawai'i Press, 2005.

Esherick, Joseph W. *The Origins of the Boxer Uprising*. Berkeley: University of California Press, 1998.

Feuchtwang, Stephan. *Popular Religion in China: The Imperial Metaphor*. Richmond, Surrey: Curzon Press, 2001.

Forster, Keith. *Rebellion and Factionalism in a Chinese Province: Zhejiang, 1966–1976*. Armonk, NY: M. E. Sharpe, 1990.

Friedman, Edward, Paul G. Pickowicz, Mark Selden, and Kay Ann Johnson. *Chinese Village, Socialist State*. New Haven, CT: Yale University Press, 1991.

Gan Mantang 甘滿堂. "Cunmin zizhi, zuzhi fazhan yu cunji zhili—yi Fujian Sheng xiangcun diaocha weili" 村民自治、組織發展與村級治理—以福建省鄉村調查為例

(Village autonomy, organizational development and village governance—a case study based on the investigation in rural Fujian). *Fuzhou daxue xuebao* 3 (2007): 98–106.

Gan Mantang 甘滿堂. "Xiangcun caogen zuzhi yu shequ gonggong shenghuo: Yi Fujian xiangcun laonian xiehui wei kaocha zhongxin" 鄉村草根組織與社區公共生活：以福建鄉村老年協會為考察中心 (Rural grassroots organizations and communal life: a case study of old age associations in rural Fujian). *Fujian xingzheng xueyuan xuebao* 107 (2008): 17–21.

Gan Mantang 甘滿堂 and Zhang Xiaoting張孝廷. "Chuantong shequ ziyuan dongyuan yu nongmin de you zuzhi kangzheng" 傳統社區資源動員與農民的有組織抗爭 (Mobilization of traditional community resources and organized peasant resistance). *Liaodong xueyuan xuebao* 12, no. 5 (2010): 58–65.

Goldstein, Melvyn C., Ben Jiao, and Tanzen Lhundrup. *On the Cultural Revolution in Tibet: The Nyemo Incident of 1969*. Berkeley: University of California Press, 2009.

Gong Xuezeng 龔學增. "Zhongguo Gongchandang de zongjiao—guojia guan" 中國共產黨的宗教—國家觀 (The conception of religion and state of the Chinese Communist Party). *Xibei minzu daxue xuebao* 3 (2011): 13–24.

Goossaert, Vincent. "1898: The Beginning of the End for Chinese Religion?" *Journal of Asian Studies* 65, no. 2 (2006): 307–335.

Goossaert, Vincent. "State and Religion in Modern China: Religious Policies and Scholarly Paradigms." *Bulletin of the Institute of Modern History Academia Sinica* 54 (2006): 169–201.

Goossaert, Vincent, and David A. Palmer. *The Religious Question in Modern China*. Chicago: University of Chicago Press, 2011.

Handler, Richard, and Jocelyn Linnekin. "Tradition, Genuine or Spurious." *The Journal of American Folklore* 97, no. 385 (1984): 273–290.

Hansen, Mette Halskov. "Organising the Old: Senior Authority and the Political Significance of a Rural Chinese 'Non-governmental Organisation.'" *Modern Asian Studies* 42, no. 5 (2007): 1057–1078.

Harrison, Henrietta. *The Missionary's Curse and Other Tales from a Chinese Catholic Village*. Berkeley: University of California Press, 2013.

Hershatter, Gail. *The Gender of Memory: Rural Women and China's Collective Past*. Berkeley: University of California Press, 2011.

Hu Qiting 胡啟聽. "Zhuanxing shiqi cunzhuang quanli jiegou bianhua de shizheng fenxi—Wenzhou Shi Dingtian Zhen X Cun ge'an yanjiu" 轉型時期村莊權力結構變化 的實證分析—溫州市汀田鎮 X 村個案研究 (Empirical analysis of village power structure in transitional period, a case study of X village in Dingtian Town, Wenzhou). *Liaoning xinzheng xueyuan xuebao* 4 (2006): 9–12.

Huang, Philip C. C. "Rural Class Struggle in the Chinese Revolution." *Modern China* 21, no. 1 (January 1995): 105–143.

Hunter, Alan, and Chan Kim-Kwong. *Protestantism in Contemporary China*. Cambridge: Cambridge University Press, 1993.

Inouye, Melissa Wei-Tsing. *China and the True Jesus: Charisma and Organization in a Chinese Christian Church*. Oxford: Oxford University Press, 2019.

Jones, Stephen. "Chinese Ritual Music under Mao and Deng." *British Journal of Ethnomusicology* 8 (1999): 27–66.

Jones, Stephen. *Plucking the Winds: Lives of Village Musicians in Old and New China*. Leiden: CHIME Foundation, 2004.

Jones, Stephen. "Revival in Crisis: Amateur Ritual Association in Hebei." In *Religion in Contemporary China: Revitalization and Innovation*, ed. Adam Chau, 154–181. New York: Routledge, 2011.

Kao, Chen-yang. "The Cultural Revolution and the Emergence of Pentecostal-Style Protestantism in China." *Journal of Contemporary Religion* 24, no. 2 (2009): 171–188.

Katz, Paul R. *Demon Hordes and Burning Boats: The Cult of Marshal Wen in Late Imperial Chekiang.* Albany: State University of New York Press, 1995.

Katz, Paul R. *Religion in China and Its Modern Fate.* Waltham, MA: Brandeis University Press, 2014.

Kuhn, Philip. *Chinese among Others: Emigration in Modern Times.* Lanham, MD: Rowman & Littlefield, 2009.

Kung, James Kai-sing and Shouying Liu. "Farmers' Preferences Regarding Ownership and Land Tenure in Post-Mao China: Unexpected Evidence from Eight Counties." *The China Journal* 38 (July 1997): 33–63.

Lee, Joseph Tse-Hei. "Politics of Faith: Patterns of Church-State Relations in Maoist China (1949–1976)." *Historia Actual Online* 17 (2008): 129–138.

Lee, Joseph Tse-Hei. "Politics of Faith: Christian Activism and the Maoist State in Chaozhou, Guangdong Province." *The China Review* 9, no. 2 (2009): 17–39.

Li Bingjun 李秉鈞 et al., eds. *Qiannian gucha—Benji si* 千年古刹本寂寺 (A historical temple of a thousand years: Ultimate Tranquility Temple). Rui'an Shi yuhai wenhua yanjiuhui Benji si zhi bianxiezu, 2009.

Li Shizhong 李世眾. "Wanqing jiaohui shili de xieru yu difang quanli geju de yanhua" 晚清教會勢力的楔入與地方權力格局的演化 (The intrusion of Christian churches and the evolution of local power dynamics in the late Qing). *Shilin* 5 (2005): 39–47.

Lian, Xi. *Redeemed by Fire: The Rise of Popular Christianity in Modern China.* New Haven, CT: Yale University Press, 2010.

Lippit, Victor. *Land Reform and Economic Development in China.* White Plains, NY: International Arts and Sciences Press, 1974.

Liu Shuhe 劉書鶴. "Lun biange zhong de nongcun yanglao shiye" 論變革中的農村養老事業 (On transforming old-age support enterprise in rural areas). *Renkou yu jingji* 4 (1988): 23–28.

Liu Shuhe 劉書鶴. "Yingjie nongcun renkou laolinghua de yixiang zhongda juece—lun fazhan nongcun laonian xiehui" 迎接農村人口老齡化的一項重大決策—論發展農村老年協會 (A major measure for the aging problem in rural areas—on developing old-age associations). *Renkou xuekan* 5 (1993): 61–64.

Lo, Shih-Chieh. "The Order of Local Things: Popular Politics and Religion in Modern Wenzhou, 1840–1940." PhD dissertation, Brown University, 2010.

Madsen, Richard. *China's Catholics: Tragedy and Hope in an Emerging Civil Society.* Berkeley: University of California Press, 1998.

Mao Zedong 毛澤東. "Hunan nongmin yundong de kaocha baogao" 湖南農民運動的考察報告 (Report on the peasant movement in Hunan). In *Mao Zedong xuanji di yi juan* (Anthology of Mao Zedong, volume 1). Beijing: Renmin chubanshe, 1991.

Mariani, Paul P. *Church Militant: Bishop Kung and Catholic Resistance in Communist Shanghai.* Cambridge, MA: Harvard University Press, 2011.

Mo Fayou 莫法有. *Wenzhou Jidujiao shi* 溫州基督教史 (History of Christianity in Wenzhou). Hong Kong: Alliance Bible Seminary Press, 1998.

Nedostup, Rebecca. *Superstitious Regimes: Religion and the Politics of Chinese Modernity.* Cambridge, MA: Harvard University Asian Center, 2010.

Ngo, Tam T. T., and Justine B. Quijada, eds. *Atheist Secularism and Its Discontents: A Comparative Study of Religion and Communism in Eurasia*. New York: Palgrave Macmillan, 2015.

Oi, Jean, and Andrew Walder, eds. *Property Rights and Economic Reform in China*. Stanford, CA: Stanford University Press, 1999.

Ownby, David. *Falun Gong and the Future of China*. Oxford: Oxford University Press, 2008.

Palmer, David A. *Qigong Fever: Body, Science, and Utopia in China*. New York: Columbia University Press, 2007.

Palmer, David A. "Religiosity and Social Movements in China: Divisions and Multiplications." In *Social Movements in China and Hong Kong: The Expansion of Protest Space*, eds. Gilles Guiheux and Khun Eng Kuah-Pearce, 257–282. Amsterdam: Amsterdam University Press, 2009.

Palmer, David A. "Chinese Redemptive Societies and Salvationist Religion: Historical Phenomenon or Sociological Category?" *Journal of Chinese Ritual, Theatre and Folklore* 172 (2011): 21–72.

Palmer, David A. "Dao and Nation: Li Yujie—May Fourth Activist, Daoist Cultivator, and Redemptive Society Patriarch in Mainland China and Taiwan." In *Daoism in the Twentieth Century: Between Eternity and Modernity*, eds. David A. Palmer and Xun Liu, 173–195. Berkeley: University of California Press, 2012.

Perry, Elizabeth J. *Challenging the Mandate of Heaven: Social Protest and State Power in China*. Armonk, NY: M. E. Sharpe, 2002.

Peterson, Glen. "The Struggle for Literacy in Post-Revolutionary Rural Guangdong." *The China Quarterly* 140 (1994): 926–943.

Poon, Shuk-wah. *Negotiating Religion in Modern China: State and Common People in Guangzhou, 1900–1937*. Hong Kong: The Chinese University Press, 2011.

Qing Heping 秦和平. "20 shiji wu liushi niandai Wazu diqu Jidujiao de tiaoshi ji fazhan zhi renshi" 20 世紀五六十年代佤族地區基督教的調適及發展之認識 (A probe into adaptation and development of Protestantism in Wa regions in the fifties and sixties of the twentieth century). In *Zhongguo bianjiang minzu yanjiu (di san ji)* (Studies of China's frontier regions and nationalities, volume 3), ed. Dalizhabu, 197–222. Beijing: Zhongyang minzu daxue chubanshe, 2010.

Qingquan 清泉. "Huishou yiwang de Wenzhou jiaohui tese xiaozu—daogaohui" 回首以往的溫州教會特色小組—禱告會 (A retrospect of prayer meetings—groups with Wenzhou church characteristics). *Maizhong*, September issue, 2007. http://www.wheatseeds.org/wheatseeds/2007-07.09/wz/25.html (accessed on May 4, 2018).

Qingquan 清泉. "Wenzhou jiaohui dashi niandaibiao xia" 溫州教會大事年代表 (下) (Chronicle of events in Wenzhou church: part 2). *Maizhong*, April issue, 2007. http://www.wheatseeds.org/wheatseeds/2007-04.08/wz/08.html (accessed on May 4, 2018).

Ruf, Gregory A. *Cadres and Kin: Making a Socialist Village in West China, 1921–1991*. Stanford, CA: Stanford University Press, 1998.

Scott, James C. *Seeing like a State: How Certain Schemes to Improve the Human Condition Have Failed*. New Haven, CT: Yale University Press, 1998.

Shehe 舍禾. "Wenzhou jiaohui guanli moshi qiantan" 溫州教會管理模式淺探 (A preliminary research of management patterns in Wenzhou church). *Shengming jikan*, June issue, 2011. http://www.cclife.org/View/Article/2566 (accessed on May 4, 2018).

Shue, Vivienne. *Peasant China in Transition: The Dynamics of Development Toward Socialism, 1949–1956*. Berkeley: University of California Press, 1980.

Shue, Vivienne. *The Reach of the State: Sketches of the Chinese Body Politic.* Stanford, CA: Stanford University Press, 1988.

Siu, Helen F. *Agents and Victims in South China: Accomplices in Rural Revolution.* New Haven, CT: Yale University Press, 1992.

Siu, Helen F. "Recycling Rituals: Politics and Popular Culture in Contemporary Rural China." In *Unofficial China: Popular Culture and Thought in the People's Republic,* eds. Perry Link, Richard Madsen and Paul Pickowicz, 121–137. Boulder: Westview Press, 1989.

Siu, Helen F. "Recycling Tradition: Culture, History, and Political Economy in the Chrysanthemum Festivals of South China." *Comparative Studies in Society and History* 32, no. 4 (1990): 765–794.

Smith, Steve A. "Local Cadres Confront the Supernatural: The Politics of Holy Water (Shenshui) in the PRC, 1949–1966." *The China Quarterly* 188 (2006): 999–1022.

Smith, Steve A. "Talking Toads and Chinless Ghosts: The Politics of 'Superstitious' Rumors in the People's Republic of China, 1961–1965." *American Historical Review* 111, no. 2 (2006): 405–427.

Smith, Steve A. "Redemptive Religious Societies and the Communist State, 1949 to the 1980s." In *Maoism at the Grassroots: Everyday Life in China's Era of High Socialism,* eds. Jeremy Brown and Matthew Johnson, 340–364. Cambridge, MA: Harvard University Press, 2015.

Strauss, Julia C. "Paternalist Terror: The Campaign to Suppress Counterrevolutionaries and Regime Consolidation in the People's Republic of China, 1950–1953." *Comparative Studies in Society and History* 44 (2002): 80–105.

Su Cuiwei 蘇翠薇 and Xiong Guocai 熊國才, eds. "Yunnan Jidujiao fazhan kuai, huodong luan wenti fenxi ji duice" 雲南基督教發展快, 活動亂問題分析暨對策 (Analysis and resolution for rapid growth and chaotic activities of Christianity in Yunnan). In *Yunnan zongjiao qingshi baogao 2003–2004* (A report on religious conditions in Yunnan, 2003–2004), eds. Xiong Shengxiang and Yang Guozheng, 73–90. Kunming: Yunnan daxue chubanshe, 2004.

Swidler, Ann. "Culture in Action: Symbols and Strategies." *American Sociological Review* 51, no. 2 (1986): 273–286.

Tao Feiya. "Christianity and the Communist Revolution," In *Handbook of Christianity in China,* Volume 2: *1800–Present,* eds. R. G. Tiedemann, 708–716. Leiden: Brill.

Ter Haar, Barend J. *The White Lotus Teachings in Chinese Religious History.* Honolulu: University of Hawai'i Press, 1992.

Unger, Jonathan. "The Decollectivization of the Chinese Countryside: A Survey of Twenty-eight Villages." *Pacific Affairs* 58, no. 4 (Winter, 1985–1986): 585–606.

Wang Lei 王磊. Shangdi yu zuzong: Yongjia Xian Fenglinzhuang de Jidujiao, zongzu yu shequ zhengzhi (1860–1896) 上帝與祖宗：永嘉縣楓林莊的基督教、宗族與社區政治 (1860–1896) (God and ancestors: Protestant churches, lineages, and communal politics in Fenglinzhuang, Yongjia County, 1860–1896), MA thesis, East China Normal University, 2013.

Wang Meng 王猛, "20 shiji san sishi niandai Jizhong genjudi miaohui yanjiu" 20 世紀三四十年代冀中根據地廟會研究 (A study of temple fairs in the central Hebei revolutionary base in the 1930s and 1940s). MA thesis, Hebei Normal University, 2011.

Wang, Xian. "Islamic Religiosity, Revolution, and State Violence in Southwest China: The 1975 Shadian Massacre." MA thesis, University of British Columbia, 2013.

Wang Xiaoxuan 汪小烜. "Yixiang, guxiang, qiaoxiang: liudong de Wenzhou shehui—yige lishi de kaocha" 異鄉, 故鄉, 僑鄉: 流動的溫州社會——一個歷史的考察(Foreign land, native land, adoptive land—a fluid Wenzhou society from historical perspective). In *Jiangyi ji* 講藝集 (Collected writings in pursuit of learning), eds. Chen Ruihuan and Wu Tianye, 1–20. Shanghai: Fudan daxue chubanshe, 2016.

Wang Ximing 王習明. "Zuzhi wangluo, jingji shiti yu laoren fuli—Zhejiang Rui'an Zhaozhai laonian xiehui diaocha" 組織網絡, 經濟實體與老人福利—浙江瑞安趙宅老年協會調查 (Organizational networks, economic entities and old people welfare—an investigation of senior resident association in Zhaozhai Village, Rui'an, Zhejiang). *Wenzhou Luntan* 3 (2009): 48–55.

Welch, Holmes. "Buddhism under the Communists." *The China Quarterly* 6 (1961): 1–14.

Welch, Holmes. *Buddhism under Mao.* Cambridge, MA: Harvard University Press, 1972.

Xu Hongtu 徐宏圖 and Kang Bao 康豹 (Paul Katz), eds. *Pingyang Xian, Cangnan Xian chuantong minsu wenhua yanjiu* 平陽縣, 蒼南縣傳統民俗文化研究 (Studies of traditional folk culture in Pingyang and Cangnan Counties). Beijing: Minzu chubanshe, 2005.

Yang, C. K. *Religion in Chinese Society: A Study of Contemporary Functions of Religion and Some of Their Historical Factors.* Berkeley: University of California Press, 1961.

Yang, Fenggang. *Religion in China: Survival and Revival under Communist Rule.* Oxford; New York: Oxford University Press, 2012.

Yang Jisheng 楊繼繩. *Mubei—Zhongguo liushi niandai dajihuang jishi* 墓碑—中國六十年代 大饑荒紀實 (Tombstone—a historical record of the great Chinese famine in the 1960s). Hong Kong: Tiandi tushu chuban gongsi, 2008.

Yang, Mayfair Mei-hui, ed. *Chinese Religiosities: Afflictions of Modernity and State Formation.* Berkeley: University of California Press, 2008.

Yang, Mayfair Mei-hui. "Postcolonial Complex, State Disenchantment, and Popular Reappropriation of Space in Rural Southeast China." *Journal of Asian Studies* 63, no. 3 (2004): 719–755.

Ying Fuk-Tsang 邢福增. *Fandi, aiguo, shulingren: Ni Tuosheng yu jidutu juhuichu yanjiu* 反帝, 愛國, 屬靈人: 倪柝聲與基督徒聚會處研究 (Anti-imperialism, patriotism and the spiritual man: A study on Watchman Nee and the "Little Flock"). Hong Kong: The Christian Study Centre on Chinese Religion and Culture, 2005.

Ying Fuk-Tsang 邢福增. "Zhongguo Jidujiao de quyu fazhan: 1918, 1949, 2004 中國基督教的區域發展: 1918, 1949, 2004 (The regional development of Protestant Christianity in China: 1918, 1949 and 2004)." *Hanyu Jidujiao xueshu lunping* 3 (2007): 153–197.

Ying Fuk-Tsang. "The CPC's Policy on Protestant Christianity, 1949–1957: An Overview and Assessment." *Journal of Contemporary China* 23, no. 89 (2014): 884–901.

Ying Weixian 應維賢 and Shi Shihu 施世琥, eds. *Liangchu guan yu Zhaoming taizi* 梁儲觀與昭明太子 (Pavilion of Liang [dynasty] crown prince and crown prince Zhaoming). Shenzhen: Haitian chubanshe, 2008.

Yu Binghui 余炳輝. "Zhengzhi, jingji, shehui: dui Wenzhou moshi de zai kaocha" 政治, 經濟, 社會: 對溫州模式的再考察 (Politics, economy, society: a revisit to the Wenzhou model). *Zhongguo nongcun guancha* 2 (1988): 9–18.

Yu, Dan Smyer. "Apologetics of Religion and Science: Conversion Projects in Contemporary China," In *Atheist Secularism and Its Discontents: A Comparative Study of Religion and Communism in Eurasia*, eds. Tam T. T. Ngo and Justine B. Quijada, 155–172. New York: Palgrave Macmillan, 2015.

Zhang Fen 張奮. "Pingyang Qiancang chenghuang miaohui" 平陽錢倉城隍廟會 (City god temple fair in Qianchang, Pingyang). In *Pingyang Xiang, Cangnan Xiang chuantong minsu wenhua yanjiu* 平陽縣, 蒼南縣傳統民俗文化研究 (Studies of traditional folk culture in Pingyang and Cangnan), eds. Xu Hongtu and Kang Bao (Paul Katz), 104–139. Beijing: Minzu chubanshe, 2005.

Zhang Xiaomin 張孝民. "Ta zaishi de rizi—jinian zhupu Miao Zhitong" 他在世的日子—紀念主僕繆志同 (When he was in the world—in memory of god's servant Miao Zhitong). https://wzbxcc.blogspot.de/2013/08/blog-post.html (accessed on May 4, 2018).

Zhang Zhiyi 張執一. *Zhang Zhiyi wenji* 張執一文集 (The works of Zhang Zhiyi). Beijing: Huawen chubanshe, 2006.

Zhang Zhongcheng 張忠成. "Cong Wenzhou jiaohui de muqu xianxiang kan jiaohui de muyang guanli" 從溫州教會的牧區現象看教會的牧養管理 (Pastoring and administration of church through the phenomenon of pastoral district in Wenzhou church). *Jingling shengxue zhi* 1 (2011): 53–85.

Zhao Jiazhu 趙嘉朱, ed. *Zhongguo huidaomen siliao jicheng* 中國會道門史料集成 (A comprehensive compilation of historical materials on redemptive societies in China). Beijing: Zhongguo shehui kexue chubanshe, 2004.

Zhao Shaozhong 趙紹忠. "Yizhi tebie 'xuanchuandui'" 一隻特別 "宣傳隊" (A special propaganda team). In *Wencheng wenshi ziliao di san ji*, 54–60. Wencheng: Wencheng Xian zhengxie wenshi weiyuanhui, 1987.

Zhejiang Sheng renkou pucha bangongshi 浙江省人口普查辦公室, ed. *Zhejiang Sheng renkou tongji ziliao huibian 1949–1985* 浙江省人口統計資料彙編 1949–1985 (Census data collection in Zhejiang Province, 1949–1985). Hangzhou: Zhejiang Sheng renkou pucha bangongshi, 1986.

Zhonggong zhongyang tongyi zhanxian gongzuozu 中共中央統一戰線工作組, ed. *Tongzhan zhengce wenjian huibian (di si juan)* 統戰政策文件彙編 (第四卷) (Collections of the united front policies, volume 4). Beijing: Zhonggong zhongyang tongyi zhanxian gongzuozu, 1958.

Zhongguo shehuizhuyi yanjiuyuan malie yanjiusuo diaochazu 中國社會主義研究院馬列研究 所調查組. "Yitiao juyou Zhongguo tese de fazhan shehuizhuyi nongye de xinluzi—Zhejiang Wenzhou nongcun diqu diaocha baogao" 一條具有中國特色的發展社會主義農業的新路子—浙江溫州農村地區調查報告 (A Chinese-character new way of socialist agricultural development—an investigation report of rural areas in the Wenzhou region of Zhejiang). *Makesizhuyi yanjiu* 2 (1984): 287–298.

Zhu Xinming 朱心明. "Kangri genjudi zhili huidaomen yanjiu" 抗日根據地治理會道門研究 (A study of control of reactionary societies, teachings and sects in revolutionary bases). MA thesis, Shanghai Normal University, 2006.

Zhu Yujing 朱宇晶. *Guojia tongzhi, difang zhengzhi yu Wenzhou de Jidujiao* 國家統治, 地方政治與溫州的基督教 (State rule, local politics and Christianity in Wenzhou). PhD dissertation, Chinese University of Hong Kong, 2011.

Index

For the benefit of digital users, indexed terms that span two pages (e.g., 52–53) may, on occasion, appear on only one of those pages.